Bishop Thirlwall's
HISTORY OF GREECE

This judiciously compiled selection opens up to the modern reader the fascinating work of an almost forgotten historian of ancient Greece.

Connop Thirlwall's *A History of Greece* appeared in eight volumes between 1835 and 1844 and ran to a second edition (1846–52). This single volume provides a representative selection of excerpts from the original – each one edited to suit the conventions of modern scholarship. Peter Liddel's introduction places Thirlwall's history in the context of nineteenth-century historiography of ancient Greece. He also examines Thirlwall's freethinking intellectual background and analyses his disavowal of certainty, his use of material evidence and analogy, and his sophisticated understanding of the relations between ancient and modern.

Unlike his successor George Grote, Thirlwall had no particular axe to grind: scholarship, narrative clarity and frank acknowledgment of ambiguity were more important to him than any political message. He was both objective and innovative.

Connop Thirlwall (1797–1875) was a fellow of Trinity College, Cambridge from 1818 to 1834, prior to a career in the Church. Much influenced by contemporary German scholarship, he translated Niebuhr's *History of Rome* and Schleiermacher's work on St Luke before producing *A History of Greece*.

Peter P. Liddel is Lecturer in Ancient History at the University of Manchester. He is author of articles on Greek history and historiography and of *Liberty and Obligation in Classical Athens* (OUP, 2007).

CONNOP THIRLWALL, D.D.
c. 1840
from the portrait by Samuel Lawrence

Connop Thirlwall (from J. Thirlwall, *Connop Thirlwall, Historian and Theologian*, London and New York: Macmillan, 1936).

Bishop Thirlwall's
HISTORY OF GREECE

A Selection

edited and introduced by
Peter P. Liddel

BRISTOL
PHOENIX
PRESS

Cover illustration: 'Pericles bursting into tears as he places the funeral garland on his dead son' from one of the original title pages of The Rev. Connop Thirlwall's eight-volume *A History of Greece*; all eight are used as illustrations in this volume.

First published in 2007 by
Bristol Phoenix Press
an imprint of The Exeter Press
Reed Hall, Streatham Drive
Exeter, Devon, EX4 4QR
UK

www.exeterpress.co.uk

© editorial material Peter P. Liddel 2007

British Library Cataloguing in Publication Data
A catalogue record for this book is available from the British Library.

ISBN 978 1 904675 29 7

Typeset by Carnegie Book Production, Lancaster, in Adobe Garamond 10¾ and Myriad Pro 9½.

Printed in Great Britain
by Athenaeum Press Ltd, Gateshead, Tyne & Wear

Table of Contents

Preface

This is not the first time that Thirlwall's *History of Greece* has been revisited. In the mid-nineteenth century, Leonhard Schmitz wrote *A History of Greece, from the earliest times to the destruction of Corinth, B.C. 146 mainly based upon that of Connop Thirlwall* (London, 1856), and the third and fourth volumes of Henry Smith Williams' 25-volume *Historians' History of the World* (London, 1907) reprinted parts of Thirlwall's work on Heroic and Hellenistic Greece. In the first decade of the twenty-first century, Google Book Search (http://books.google.com/) has made the entire text of Thirlwall's *History* searchable on-line.

For this new abridged edition I have selected excerpts specifically to highlight what is best about Thirlwall's *History*, in the hope of making a contribution to the understanding of the development of modern historiography. I have chosen to include those parts of Thirlwall's *History* that best illustrate his virtues and the principles of his version of Liberal Anglican Historiography. Chapter 1 of this abridgement illustrates his principle that history requires geographical contextualisation, and reflects growing contemporary awareness of the Greek landscape and seascape. Chapter 2 shows Thirlwall's encounter with the debate about the origins of the earliest Greeks, a subject which was brought to the attention of modern scholarship by Martin Bernal's *Black Athena*. Chapter 3 illustrates both Thirlwall's introduction of Niebuhrian principles for historiographical readings of mythological literature and his attempt at a pioneering social history of the Heroic Age.

The idea that freedom, combined with trans-cultural connectivity, gives rise to invention and imagination looms large in chapters 4 and 5 of this abridgement. Thirlwall's enthusiasm for Federalism was disappointed by the history of Greece, but surfaces here in chapters 4, 7, 8 and 9: Philip, Alexander and the Hellenistic Greeks succeeded where the early Greeks failed.

Chapter 6, a narrative of the decline of Athens, shows clearly Thirlwall's observance of the principle that history is a cycle of birth, decay and rebirth. For Thirlwall, the rebirth of Greece took place owing to the efforts of Philip and Alexander (chapters 7 and 8), and his account provides a balanced account of the response of Greek politics to the rise of Macedon.

Chapters 9 and 10 are Thirlwall's unique solution to the problem of where to end a narrative history of Greece: as the Hellenistic period goes on, he concentrates more closely on the military-political sphere; after Roman intervention, the account becomes gradually more concise before returning to a meditation on the landscape of Greece, albeit in its desolate, post-classical, form. Finally, in an Appendix, I have included the substance of Thirlwall's critique of Hegel on Socrates, Thirlwall's most daring foray into the realms of philosophy.

With the exception of the Appendix, I have drawn exclusively from the first edition (1835–44). The etchings are scans from the first edition owned by the library of Trinity College Dublin Classical Society; I thank Jo Day for her help in digitally enhancing their appearance.

Thirlwall's *History* is long, and this abridgement amounts to around one-sixteenth of his eight-volume first edition: this means I have been unable to include much of the narrative on the development of Sparta, the Persian wars or the Peloponnesian war. A notable omission is his chapter entitled 'National Institutions and Forms of Government' (vol. I, chapter 10). My hope is that the taster provided here will inspire the reader to turn to the unabridged edition.

Peter P. Liddel, April 2007

Introduction[1]

Peter P. Liddel

Thirlwall and his predecessors

This abridgement of Bishop Connop Thirlwall's *A History of Greece* (1st edn 1835–44; 2nd edn 1845–52) aims to contribute to the understanding of narrative history-writing in the nineteenth century by raising awareness of a largely forgotten history of ancient Greece. There are several justifications for the study of the modern historiography on ancient Greece: the re-reading of apparently obsolete histories of Greece reminds modern scholars of forgotten interpretations of the ancient world; it reveals the origins of conceptions and misconceptions about ancient history; it helps trace the reception of ancient ideas by the modern world. And yet it exists also for its own sake, as a barometer of the state of ancient history at any given moment in time.

Thirlwall's history was one of the many multi-volume 'national histories' published in English in the eighteenth and nineteenth centuries.[2] Single-author works within that genre were particularly revealing about both their creators and the state of their discipline. In the attempt to even out the varying textures and voices of ancient sources, authors reconfigured history into a narrative using methods and interpretations which would distinguish them from their predecessors. In the case of the narrative history of ancient Greece, the market was particularly crowded and competitive.[3] At the start of the nineteenth century the combination of the Romantic attachment to Hellenism and the French revolutionary enthusiasm for ancient models of politics meant that the emerging historiography of Greece was highly politically charged.[4]

Of Thirlwall's predecessors[5] the most famously maligned was William Mitford, who took to writing a history of Greece on the suggestion of his friend Edward Gibbon.[6] Mitford's work (*History of Greece*, 4 vols, London, 1784–1808) performed an important service, creating a history of Greece that was closely based on the ancient sources. But Mitford aimed also to offset what he saw as the misinterpretation of ancient political forms by American and French Revolutionaries, to refute revolutionary doctrines in general and to correct the unwarranted eulogising of Greek political life. It is no surprise then that his party prejudices are often more striking than his scholarship.

Mitford's history reflects the heavy politicisation of the narrative history of Greece at the start of the nineteenth century. John Gillies, for instance, prefaced his *History of Greece* (1st edn 1792–3) with the statement that he intended to expose 'the dangerous turbulence of Democracy and arraign the despotism of the tyrants while showing at the same time the incurable evils of Republicanism, and the positive advantages of Monarchy'.[7] Edward Bulwer Lytton, a supporter of electoral reform in 1835, began a revisionist history in the shape of *Athens: its Rise and Fall*, the first two volumes of which appeared in 1837.[8] However, the third volume, containing the promised re-assessment of Athenian democracy, remained unpublished until 2004.[9] It was therefore left to George Grote's *History of Greece* to publicise a favourable response to Athenian democracy.[10] However, Grote went further in reaction to his Tory predecessor, stating that: 'My purpose in writing it was to rectify the erroneous statements as to matter of fact which [Mitford's] history contained, as well as to consider the general phenomena of the Grecian world under what I thought a juster and more comprehensive point of view'.[11] This 'juster point of view' was the interpretation of Periclean Athens as an enlightened democracy, guaranteeing equal opportunity for citizens to participate in political processes and to be free to rule in their own interests.

Thirlwall's position on Athenian democracy has been recognized by modern scholarship as a halfway house between Mitford and Grote (see below, chapter 3).[12] And the treatment of Athenian democracy was not as central to his history as it was to that of Mitford, Grote or Bulwer Lytton. Thirlwall professed to do his best to steer clear of the controversies of his predecessors, stating early on that he intended to:

> [D]efine the notion of democracy, as the word was commonly under-
> stood by the Greeks, so as to separate the essence of the thing from

the various accidents which have sometimes been confounded with it by writers who have treated Greek history as a vehicle for conveying their views on the questions of modern politics, which never arose in the Greek republics (vol. i p. 408).[13]

This statement detached him from the controversy about whether or not democratic Athens was a model of government worthy of emulation. It could be interpreted as an assertion of an elusively ideal state of objectivity but, in the case of Thirlwall, we may read it as an expression of his recognition of the complexity of the relationship between the modern and the ancient worlds. Similarly, his enthusiasm for Federalism, which emerges at several points, was expressed always apropos the ancient world, and never with explicit reference to contemporary experiments in federal government.

Thirlwall's history was published in its first edition in Dionysius Lardner's popular Cabinet Cyclopaedia series between 1835 and 1844, aiming at audiences with different degrees of access to original sources:

> One consisting of persons who wish to acquire something more than a superficial acquaintance with Greek history, but who have neither leisure nor means to study it for themselves in its original sources; the other of such as have access to the ancient authors, but often feel the need of a guide and an interpreter (vol. i p. v).

Thirlwall clearly envisaged his readership would consist not only of scholars but readers from all walks of life: readers in subscription and private libraries, libraries of associations and town and country houses and the new free libraries and reading rooms opening in Britain in the 1840s.[14] In the chain of works reacting to Mitford, Thirlwall preceded by two years Bulwer Lytton's publication, which was more closely directed to the interests of the general reader alone:

> These volumes were not only written, but actually in the hands of the publisher, before the appearance, and even, I believe, before the announcement of the first volume of Mr Thirlwall's History of Greece, or I might have declined going over any portion of the ground cultivated by that distinguished scholar. As it is, however, the plan I have pursued differs materially from that of Mr Thirlwall,

and I trust that the soil is sufficiently fertile to yield a harvest to either labourer.[15]

Bulwer Lytton published his first two volumes, but laid aside his history before completing the second instalment, probably because of the success and superiority, in scholarly terms, of Thirlwall.[16] Thus Thirlwall's work surpassed its first competitor.

John Herman Merivale, writer for the *Edinburgh Review*, dedicated his review to examining Thirlwall's views on the origins of the Pelasgians, the national identity of the Greeks, and the composition of the Iliad. But he expressed reservations about Thirlwall's reluctance to take sides in scholarly debates:

> There are few subjects on which it is safer to doubt, and more preposterous to dogmatize, than those connected with the primitive history of the Greeks. But in a work evincing no common ability and research, we naturally look for something more, when we reach points on which there exists a 'lis mota' between learned combatants, than a mere exposition of conflicting hypotheses and of the difficulties which beset each.[17]

But the reviewer ended on a positive note, describing the work as 'an able and philosophical performance,'[18] the latter term a reference to his ability to seek the deeper causes of phenomena. Thirlwall's publication continued: originally he intended the work to extend only to 5 volumes,[19] but it ended up filling 8. The initial success of the work inspired translations into French and German.[20] The second edition in English suggests that Thirlwall aspired to a more scholarly audience: the engravings that had appeared at the frontispiece of each volume of the first edition were replaced by a selection of maps; the use of footnotes was extended to make mention of scholarly debates that had arisen since publication of the first edition.

Thirlwall's first real competitor was Grote. The two overlapped in their time at Charterhouse, but may not have known each other.[21] Grote began his history in the early 1820s, but publication did not begin until 1846.[22] Grote claimed that he had not intended to compete with Thirlwall:

> If my early friend Dr Thirlwall's History of Greece had appeared a few years sooner, I should probably never have conceived the

design of the present work at all; I should certainly have not been prompted to the task by any deficiencies, such as those which I felt and regretted in Mitford.[23]

Grote continued his work in spite of Thirlwall's history, and indeed Grote's history was perceived to have eclipsed the work of his predecessor. When Grote's first volume appeared in 1846, Thirlwall was publishing his second edition. Thirlwall made revisions in his work down as far as volume vi chapter 47, with his publisher announcing in a notice at the start of volume vi dated August 1851 that he had no time to carry on with the revision.[24] The date is significant. March 1850 saw the publication of volume viii of Grote's history.[25] This was the famous volume in which Grote revived the reputation of the Sophists, guaranteeing his place as a revolutionary in the writing of Greek history. Importantly he discredited Thirlwall's apportionment of right reason to Socrates and wrong reason to the Sophists.[26] Henceforth Thirlwall laid aside his Greek history and instead concentrated on his duties as Bishop of St David's.[27] Thirlwall himself contributed to the oblivion of his own work. His depreciation of his history is typified in his letter to a friend dated 10th April, 1867:

> I cannot approve of your making yourself a martyr by reading or attempting to read the history, which is generally admitted to be excessively dry and hard—worse, if possible, than a charge … God knows I have little reason to be proud of it.[28]

John Stuart Mill wrote in a review of Grote's history that Thirlwall's work was remedial but lacked passion or political sentiment:

> [T]he character of Dr Thirlwall's mind has not led him to speculate much, or with any clear and positive result, on the phaenomenon of political society. Even his impartiality seems rather that of a person who has no opinion, than of one who has an unbiased opinion … But we do say that the mere facts, even of the most interesting history, are of little value without some attempt to show how and why they came to pass; that a mere narrative of events, without the causes and agencies which gave them birth—a history of Greece, which does not put in evidence the influences of Grecian institutions and of Grecian opinions and feelings—may be a useful

work, but is not the history which we look for, and are entitled to demand.[29]

John Stuart Mill was the wrong person to have as a detractor. Grote's work soon became the standard narrative history of Greece. There were some Thirlwall partisans: Edward Freeman, Regius Professor of Modern History at Oxford from 1884–92,[30] argued that Thirlwall's history was preferable, at least for the purposes of students, and that the publication of Grote's history:

> [i]n no way sets aside the sterling work of Bishop Thirlwall ... its comparative shortness, the greater clearness and terseness of the narrative, the freedom from discussions and digressions, all join to make it far better fitted for such a purpose. But for the political thinker, who looks to Grecian history chiefly in its practical bearing, Mr Grote's work is far better fitted.[31]

Freeman thought that Thirlwall's work was also commendable for its sections on Alexander and the Hellenistic Greece;[32] and, though he had a vested interest, sharing Thirlwall's enthusiasm for Federal government,[33] he was right. The Bishop of St David's was a coherent historian, and one who embodied many of the ideals of post-enlightenment history writing. This can be shown by reference both to his intellectual background and to some of the most important passages in his history.

Thirlwall's background

Connop Thirlwall was born in London in February 1797, son of Rev. Thomas Thirlwall and Susannah Connop of Mile End. His grandfather, Thomas Thirlwall, claimed descent from the barons of Thirlwall Castle in Northumberland. He was a day scholar at Charterhouse from 1810 to 1813; and in 1818 graduated from Trinity College, Cambridge, in the same year being elected fellow of Trinity. Between 1827 and 1832 he held the college offices of junior bursar, junior dean and head lecturer; he lectured in classics, examined four times for the recently-established classical tripos between 1828 and 1834.[34] Already trained as a lawyer, Thirlwall was ordained priest in 1828. Of the details recorded in various biographical accounts,[35] his efforts in public life are most worth mentioning. They appear to be related to liberalism and a concern for institutional de-dogmatisation. As a fellow at Trinity he represented the views of those who thought that dissenters should be allowed to take degrees and that compulsory chapel should be abolished. His liberalism was manifested later in his support for the disestablishment of the Irish Church in 1868, and in his support for a bill in April 1845 enlarging the annual grant and making a donation for repairs to the seminary at Maynooth.[36] He supported the admittance of Jews to the House of Commons; as Bishop of St David's he preached in Welsh, championed the Eisteddfod and encouraged the study of Celtic remains.[37]

In 1834 his open letter 'On the Admission of Dissenters to Academical Degrees' condemned compulsory chapel at college: 'our colleges are not Theological seminaries. We have no theological colleges, no theological tutors and no theological students' and he condemned compulsory chapel as a 'heartless mechanical device'.[38] His views got the better of him. Five days later the master Christopher Wordsworth called on him to resign his appointment as assistant tutor. In November 1834 Lord Brougham offered him a living at Kirby Underdale, 16 miles east of York; there he must have made substantial progress in his history; in 1840 he was offered the Bishopric of St David's, in which capacity he appears for some time at least to have continued his research into Greece.

As Christopher Stray has noted, the tendency to offer clerical promotion to Greek scholars, common at the time, deprived the universities of the men who might have formed the core of an academic community.[39] It is worth noting that the churchman's voice frequently appears in A History of Greece: Thirlwall enthused about the connection between religion and morality in early Greece (vol.i p.195); he saw Philip as an instrument of Providence (vol.v p.170). His concern for religious de-dogmatisation in the modern world, however, did not affect his recognition that a divine force—or at least man's belief in a divine force—was sometimes the motor behind historical change even in the third century BC (vol. viii p.51).

Thirlwall adhered to the view that personal experiences influenced the historian's interpretation of history. In a letter to a friend dated July 1815 he expressed admiration for the writers of antiquity 'who spent their lives in active employment, and who were as well known by their actions in their own day as they are by their writings in ours'. They were compared to modern scholars 'whose talents are either entirely buried in obscurity or known to the world only through the medium of the press'.[40] However, beyond his youth Thirlwall became absorbed in clerical duties and participation in the theological and political debates of the time and he was consequently unable to dedicate time to historical research.

The most important aspects of Thirlwall's intellectual background relate to Liberal Anglicanism and German scholarship. Duncan Forbes placed Thirlwall's history within the Liberal Anglican school of histori-ography.[41] This group of historians conceived of history as governed by laws of Providence, which directed that civilisations followed a pattern of rise and fall. The cycle of individual civilisations worked in isolation from each other but all followed general laws of development. Accordingly, the study of history, as an investigation of the rise and fall of civilisa-tions, contributed to man's understanding of the laws governing this pattern and led in turn to a more enlightened understanding of God, man and nature. Classical history was a particularly promising field of study, as it offered two complete cycles of civilisation: the Greek and the Roman.

In the field of classics and ancient history, the clearest exponent of this line of thought was Headmaster of Rugby School and prominent liberal churchman Thomas Arnold (1795–1842), who published an edition of Thucydides particularly noted for its appendices on geographical points. In the preface to the first edition of the third volume of his *Thucydides*, dated January 1835, he pointed out that no one had subjected early Greek history to the kind of analysis that Niebuhr had carried out on the mythology of early Rome, showing the mixture of history and fable. This notice tacitly flagged Thirlwall's forthcoming history. Indeed, Arnold's statements in the first appendix of his first volume are highly illumi-nating about the Liberal Anglican view of history, and appear to be a more idealistic, more theoretical formulation of the approach to history that surfaces in Thirlwall's *History of Greece*:

> States, like individuals, go through certain changes in a certain order, and are subject at different stages of their course to certain peculiar disorders. But they differ from individuals in this, that though the order of the periods is regular, their duration is not so; and their features are more liable to be mistaken, as they can only be distin-guished by the presence of their characteristic phenomena. One state may have existed a thousand years, and its history may be full

of striking events, and yet it may be still in its childhood: another may not be a century old, and its history may contain nothing remarkable to a careless reader, and yet it may be verging to old age. The knowledge of these periods furnishes us with a clue to the study of history, which the continuous succession of events related in chronological order seems particularly to require.[42]

For Arnold states at corresponding stages in their civilisation could exhibit comparable degrees of cultivation and behaviour, even if they were divided by a thousand years of history. Both Arnold and Thirlwall made extensive use of organic parallel. Thirlwall clearly perceives that the legends of 'Heroic' Greece give an impression of the infancy of Greek society (see below, chapter 3). It is also clear that Greece under Roman rule was the senescence of Greece, the result of a decline that had commenced, at least in Athens, at the time of the Peloponnesian War. Working along the same lines, Arnold made it clear that the history of the fifth century BC represented the state of maturity of the ancient Greek world, which itself afforded modern parallels:

Where Thucydides, in his reflections on the bloody dissensions at Corcyra, notices the decay and extinction of the simplicity of old times, he marks the great transition from ancient history to modern, the transition from an age of feeling to one of reflection, from a period of ignorance and credulity to one of inquiry and scepticism. How such a transition took place in part in the sixteenth century; the period of the Reformation, when compared with the ages preceding it, was undoubtedly one of inquiry and reflection. But still it was an age of strong feeling and of intense belief; the human mind cleared a space for itself vigorously within a certain circle; but except in individual cases, and even those scarcely avowed, there were still acknowledged limits of authority, which inquiry had not yet ventured to question.[43]

Thirlwall, like Grote, never travelled to Greece; the English traveller Col. Leake commented that this was a cause of certain deficiencies in his history.[44] This failure also meant that he was betraying one of the principles of the liberal Anglican school of history—the notion that 'experience' of a location was essential to the writing of its history. Indeed,

Arnold felt that the progress of technology would in future contribute towards historical understanding by facilitating wider travel:

> It will be strange if the establishment of steam vessels on the Mediterranean does not within the next ten years do more for the geography of Thucydides than has ever been done yet; for it will enable those who are at once scholars and geographers to visit the places of which he speaks personally; and I cannot but think that most of the difficulties of his descriptions will then vanish. To a practiced eye the shortest view of a country will explain more than any maps or descriptions can do without it; if a man be also really familiar with the ancient writers, and has the state of the ancient world vividly present to his mind, so as to know what their warfare was, what their ships were, &c.; and not to be deriving all his notions from modern experience.[45]

By way of compensation, Thirlwall showed a concern for using travellers' reports in his history; he made extended use of material evidence and in particular inscriptions, the use of which had been pioneered in Boeckh's *Die Staatshaushaltung der Athener* of 1817.

The work of Thirlwall was vital in the transmission of German methods of scholarship to English theologians, classicists and ancient historians. Thirlwall's anonymous translation of Schleiermacher's *Ueber die Schriften des Lukas: Ein kritischer Versuch* illustrated his own approval of the rationalisation of theology.[46] In this work Schleiermacher denied the divinity of Christ and rejected the idea that divine revelation was behind the composition of the gospels. As part of their attempt to broaden the focus of Cambridge classical scholarship beyond concern for linguistic minutiae, in 1831 Thirlwall and Julius Hare, a fellow of Trinity College, founded the journal *Philological Museum*.[47] This aimed to serve as a platform for the broader application of the methods of German scholarship. The preface to the first volume announced that the field of interest would include ancient history, classical philology, Oriental literature, biblical criticism and modern philology. The journal produced some sterling essays on classical subjects and published Walter Savage Landon's *Imaginary Conversations* between ancient historical characters.[48] However, the intention to reach out to other subjects was never fulfilled. Not all the print-run of 1015 was sold, and the journal appeared only in 1832 and 1833: the experiment proved unmarketable.[49]

Nevertheless, the venture provided Thirlwall with a firm grounding in the methods of German philology. Thirlwall's translation of Niebuhr's *Römische Geschichte*[50] and his reading of the work of Karl Otfried Müller and others instructed him that mythology could be understood as a natural expression of a people's consciousness at an early stage of their development, which meant that within mythology there was likely to be a kernel of historical truth waiting to be discovered by scientific analysis. This was a position of some sophistication compared to the extreme credulity or incredulity of his predecessors. Thirlwall's understanding opened the way for Grote's position that mythology must be seen as an expression not of historical truth but as indicative rather of the consciousness of those civilisations which developed the myths.

A History of Greece

Thirlwall's *History of Greece* combines narrative with descriptive analysis; the author shows concern for historical events but also for the daily life of individuals,[51] the development of political institutions, the historical evolution of culture and the relationship between political structures and political events. Such a formula is familiar to the modern student of Greek history. The work is divided into 8 volumes and 66 chapters. Appendices iron out conflicts between the sources on *minutiae* such as 'The number of Spartan tribes' and 'The date of the Battle of Marathon'. The history begins with a chapter on the topographical features of Greece; thereafter the narrative is ordered chronologically. The first volume explores the origins of—and degree of—civilisation of the earliest inhabitants of Greece, as well as the characteristics of the 'Hellenic nation'. Thirlwall attempts a Niebuhrian analysis of the mythology of the 'Heroic Age', the nature of its civilisation, the early history of Sparta and the national institutions and forms of government in early Greece. The second volume starts with a history of Attica from the earliest times down to the expulsion of the Pisistratids; it explores the connection between colonisation, Greek intercourse with the whole Mediterranean and the progress of art and literature. Next come the Ionian revolt and the Persian wars. The third volume is an Athenocentric history of the fifth century, showing a concern for the emergence of democracy and the progress of art and culture in Athens. From the fourth volume onwards, examinations of culture and the state of civilisation are more closely intertwined; the fourth volume covers the period from the end of the Sicilian expedition to the Peace of Antalcidas; the fifth Greek and Macedonian history to the end of the (Third) Sacred war; the sixth and seventh volumes form a connected history of the period from 346 to the Battle of Ipsus (301); the final volume was a pioneering synthesis of Greek history in the Hellenistic period.

As Merivale pointed out, one of Thirlwall's most striking habits is, after a careful examination of scholarship, the disavowal of certainty. This tendency is one aspect of his cautious employment of literary sources in the composition of historical narrative. Nowhere is this clearer than in his investigation of the 'foreign settlers' in chapter 3 of his history. According to the traditional interpretation of Greek mythology, which endured from late Antiquity until the eighteenth century, Phoenician and Egyptian settlers colonised Greece and were central to the development of early Greek culture. This belief was deconstructed by the German scholar Müller, who had cast doubt on the extent to which such a mythology formed the basis of a historical reality.[52] Müller suggested instead that Greek civilisation was partly autochthonous and partly shaped by invasions from the North. Ultimately, Thirlwall does not give the old or new models his unqualified consent. Indeed, Thirlwall's main interest in the debate was the effect that such settlers or visitors might have had on the arts, culture and religion of early Greece. Thirlwall did not rule out non-Greek influences on Greek culture: later in his history he allowed for Egyptian influence in Greek art (vol.ii pp.109–15) and also attributed part of the genius of Pythagoras to his experience of foreign cultures (vol.ii pp.140–2). Yet importantly, too, he is sceptical of the idea that invasion or migration is the major catalyst in historical change.

Thirlwall saw himself as a pioneer of the 'building block' method of constructing a balanced narrative history. It relied both on sceptical interpretation of mythology and also on local and minute research performed by others.[53] This understanding was particularly marked in his discussion of scholarship on Pythagoras:

At least one half of it is a mass of the dullest and most unpoetical fictions, expanded into the empty form of a political history; and

in the remainder we should seek in vain for any of the facts which
alone render the subject interesting. No view of any social relations
enlivens the dry investigation of dates, events, and persons. This
however is not to be considered as a defect, but as a limit which the
author prescribed to himself. But it is to be hoped that some one
will be found to undertake something more and better. Perhaps
a greater number of particular histories—*monographies* as the
Germans call them—is wanted to prepare a foundation (vol. ii
p. 156 n.).

Closely related was Thirlwall's attempt to employ material evidence in
his history. He was the first narrative historian of Greece to exploit the
potential contribution of epigraphical research, published from 1828
in Boeckh's *Corpus Inscriptionum Graeacarum*.[54] Inscriptional evidence
contributed to political narrative, as is particularly obvious in his analysis
of the diplomacy of the Aetolian League (vol. viii pp. 206–12). Thirlwall's
description of the Parthenon, drawing on the work of the Danish traveller
Brønsted, provided the kind of vivid description that would convey an
impression of the achievements of Periclean Athens (vol. iii pp. 62–5).[55]
The consideration of material evidence was essential also for gauging
the level of cultivation of an ancient society and, accordingly, the place
that it occupied on the scale of civilisations. Thus the development of
Pelasgian civilisation could be most clearly revealed by the examination
of other Cyclopean or Pelasgian remains (vol. i pp. 61–2).

The idea that climate and geography were important categories of
causal explanation was an aspect of historical understanding that was
enunciated by Montesquieu and passed into German scholarship of
the eighteenth century.[56] The consideration of both the environment
of Greece and archaeological evidence contributed to the historian's experience of a civilisation, particularly important for an author
and for readers who never visited Greece. The History opened with a
geographical description of Greece which was reliant on the accounts
of travellers—and with a very definite assertion of the importance of
geographical forms in history: 'the character of every people is more or
less closely connected with that of its land' (vol. i p. 1).

But it was through the use of analogy that the development of Greek
society could be accurately plotted on the scale of civilisations. Thirlwall
was not the first historian of Greece to use comparisons in his account of

Greek history or to reason from parallel cases. The tendency was innate to his predecessors' political interpretations of history: Gillies had written a comparison between Philip II of Macedon and Frederick of Prussia, in which Frederick is praised and Philip severely judged.[57] But, whereas Gillies' goal was the composition of an encomium for Frederick, Thirlwall aimed to contribute to historical understanding. The use of comparison illustrated the differences between the ancient and modern world, helping to locate ancient Greece on the scale of civilisations. For Thirlwall the ancient world did not equate simply with the modern world; but careful selection of comparanda could lead to a better understanding and clearer evaluation of ancient society. The systematic nature of his approach is indicated by the breadth of comparisons drawn and by the fact that the stage of civilisation of subject and comparandum were held to correspond revealingly. His estimation of Greece in what he termed the Heroic Age establishes that it was a civilisation prodigious from an early stage, comparing favourably with:

> [The] gross intemperance which prevails in the banquets of the northern Europeans at a corresponding stage in their development. Viewed merely as a spectacle designed for public amusement, and indicating the taste of the people, the Olympic games might justly claim to be ranked far above all similar exhibitions of other nations. It could only be for the sake of a contrast, by which their general purity, innocence, and humanity would be placed on the strongest light, that they could be compared with the bloody sports of a Roman or a Spanish amphitheatre. And the tournaments of our chivalrous ancestors, examined by their side, would appear little better than barbarous shows, widely removed from the simplicity of nature, and yet immeasurably inferior to the Greek spectacle in the genuine refinement of art—if this comparison did not remind us of the law by which women were forbidden, under pain of death, to be seen at Olympia during the games, and did not thus present the most unfavourable aspect in which they can be viewed (vol. i p. 393).

However, Greece did not develop evenly. Thirlwall thought that the Spartans lagged behind the other Greeks in their habits and culti-vation. By comparing the marriage ceremony of the Spartans and that 'which prevails today among the Circassian tribes', he communicated the notion that Spartan customs were secretive and considerably less civilised than those of the other Greeks (vol. i p. 327). Indeed, even in the fourth century, Spartan behaviour was backward: the Spartan de-synoicism of Mantinea was comparable with the distribution of the population of Milan by Frederic I in 1162 (vol. v p. 7 n. 1). His comparisons are often more complicated than they at first appear and are sometimes tinged with irony:[58]

> The conduct of the Athenians in the conquest of Melos is far less extraordinary than the openness with which they avow their principles. But, unjust as it was, it will not to a discerning eye appear the more revolting, because it wanted that varnish of sanctity, by which acts of much fouler iniquity have been covered in ages which have professed to revere a moral law. Their treatment of the vanquished—whatever may have been its motive—was unworthy of a civilised nation. Yet some allowance may fairly be claimed for the general rigour of the ancient usages of war. The milder spirit of modern manners would not have punished men who had been guilty of no offence but the assertion of their rightful independence, more severely than by tearing them from their families, and locking them up in a fortress, or transporting them to the wilds of Scythia. But our exultation at the progress of humanity may be consistent with a charitable indulgence for the imperfections of a lower stage of civilisation (vol. iii p. 361–2).

In this case, Thirlwall used analogy also to highlight the mistakes and flaws of the ancient world, which can be excused by reference to their 'lower stage of civilisation'. He stressed, however, that neither had the moderns achieved that spirit of mildness which they claimed. Thirlwall approached the Athenian hysteria after the mutilation of the Herms and the profanation of the Eleusinian Mysteries in a similar way:

> When we review the whole course of these proceedings at a distance which secures us from the passions that agitated the actors, we may be apt to exclaim: 'In all history it would be difficult to find such another instance of popular frenzy.' But the recollection that these are the very words in which Hume spoke of our own Popish

Plot, may serve to moderate our surprise, and our censure of the Athenians. Their credulity was in one respect at least less absurd than that of our forefathers, inasmuch as there was an evident, strange and mysterious fact, on which it reposed. We indeed see so little connection between acts of daring impiety and designs against the state, that we can hardly understand how they could have been associated together as they were in the minds of the Athenians. But perhaps the difficulty may not without reason have appeared much less to the contemporaries of Alcibiades, who were rather disposed by their views of religion to regard them as inseparable (vol. iii p. 397).

In 1678, Titus Oates, an anti-Catholic protester, swore in court that he knew of a Franco-Catholic plot to murder King Charles and his Protestant supporters and replace them with a Catholic government. The report was blown out of all proportion and many Catholics were arrested and tried. The plot was little more than an invention but, at the height of the furore, legislation was passed which required all members of the Houses of Commons and Lords to swear an anti-Catholic declaration. Thirlwall noted that the Athenians experienced a comparable hysteria but that this was excusable because they lacked the ability to separate impiety and acts against the state.

On the other hand the artistic and literary production of the age of Pericles, which illustrated the progress of the Athenians, compared favourably with Renaissance Florence (vol.iii p.70); the Athenians were more fastidious in their taste than the audience of Shakespearean drama (vol.iii p.74). To the credit of the Athenians their enlightenment was supported by public funds that were the result of popular exertion rather than wealthy benefactors. However, just as in the 1530s expenses on the arts (such as the tomb of the Medici in Florence or the frescoes in the Sistine chapel) exhausted the financial power of the Medici company and so undermined the bases of their power, so in Periclean Athens expenditure on the Athenian Akropolis was bound to provoke jealousy from the Athenian allies. In both Periclean Athens and in sixteenth-century Florence expenditure in support of the arts contributed to the disintegration of the powers that had allowed that very investment.

The cycle of civilisation was not an upward spiral but a wheel; and it was through analogy that Thirlwall was able to illustrate that at the time of the Peloponnesian War, Athenian society was in decline. Popular morality was one of the first aspects of life to disintegrate in late fifth-century Athens: thus, when the plague came, the Athenians behaved with more barbarity to each other than did the populations of Milan in 1630 or Marseilles in 1346, thus providing 'a striking contrast to the sublime charity, which has made the plagues of Milan and of Marseilles bright spots in the history of religion and humanity' (vol.iii p.139).

Moving on in time, the mid-fourth century BC brought Greek society up to the eighteenth century AD, at least in terms of the rhetoric of inter-national diplomacy. The fear that the Athenians felt towards Philip II as he loomed on the fringes of central Greece was compared to the English reaction to the development and expansion of Russia under Peter the Great:

> If in the reign of Peter the Great the power of Russia had been known to threaten the liberty of Europe, would a English orator have been guilty of falsehood or exaggeration, who should have spoken of the Czar, as a Muscovite, the Barbarian? Or would the ascendancy of such a power cease to be accounted a terrible calamity, if it were wielded by a prince of Teutonic blood, and conversant with all the refinements of European culture? (vol. v p. 322 n. 1).

The 'prince of Teutonic blood, conversant with all the refinements of European culture' was possibly Tsarina Catherine II, the Great (1762–96); Thirlwall is implying that the ascendancy of Russia under Peter the Great would have been no less terrifying had it taken place under the leadership of a Europeanised monarch. In this case, analogy contributed to the understanding of ancient rhetoric, illustrating that Demosthenes' branding of Philip as a barbarian could be explained by reference not to his cultural alterity but to his threat to Athenian liberty. While the advance of Philip was comparable with the struggles of the great powers of the eighteenth century, Alexander the Great fell outside the sphere of Greek history, instead being a part of universal history (vol. vi p. 120). The age of Alexander therefore brought the analogy up to the present-day situation:

> The change which had taken place in the relations between Greece and Persia after the battle of Salamis was as great as that which

Europe has experienced in its relation to the Turks since the battle
of Lepanto. The power of Persia had become one of the chief
securities of Greek liberty (vol. vii p. 131).

Ending the History

Of Thirlwall's predecessors, Mitford closed his history at the death of
Alexander, as did Goldsmith;[59] Gillies wrote a separate work on the
Hellenistic period.[60] Thirlwall continued his history to 146 BC; he ends
his brief examination of Roman Greece with a discussion of the causes of
Greek decline. At this point it is clear that he had completed a description
of the whole cycle of Greek civilisation. The Hellenistic period from the
death of Alexander to the Roman invasion clearly represents the 'old age'
of Greece, to which modern history offered no parallel. What modern
analogy could be drawn to the Roman invasion of the already divided
Greek world in the second century BC? The reader can only come to
the worrying conclusion that the modern world faces a similar fate if it
fails to learn from the mistakes of the ancient Greeks. Thirlwall was also
sceptical about the kind of lessons that the ancient world held out for
moderns. However, at the end of the work, the reader is distracted by
the new hope represented, at least in the Balkans, by the independence
of Greece, where a new cycle of history appears to have begun.

> The better the free Greeks become acquainted with the people
> from which they believe themselves sprung, the more unwilling
> they must be to part with the persuasion of such an illustrious
> origin. But still it is well that they should remember that their title
> to the sympathy of civilised Europe and to the rich inheritance of
> their land and their language, does not rest on their descent but has
> been earned by struggles and sacrifices of their own equal to any
> recorded in history: struggles and sacrifices however, in which their
> Albanian brethen who make no pretensions to such a descent, bore
> their full share. And it might perhaps be a less burdensome and
> yet equally animating consciousness of their relation to their great
> predecessors, if they were content to regard them, not as ancestors,
> whom they represent and whom they may therefore be expected
> to resemble and emulate, but simply as departed benefactors,
> whose memory they are bound to cherish, while they enjoy their

bequests, but not so as either to overlook their errors and faults, or to strain after the excellence of a mould, which the power that formed it appears to have broken (vol. viii p. 473).

While Thirlwall considered it possible to discern cyclical patterns of civilisation, he considered the operation of transferring ideas from the ancient to the modern age to be problematic, perceiving the context of the ancient past to be irrevocable. It is perhaps only at this point, at the end of the eighth volume, that Thirlwall appears to reveal what might be the point of history—the demonstration of a series of virtues which, though they cannot be emulated, can be appreciated by the modern age; and also the demonstration of ancient errors which the modern age threatens to repeat.

The value of Thirlwall's *History of Greece* lies in its powers of synthesis, his readiness to admit uncertainty about the resolution of historical problems, his inclusion of material evidence and the reports of travellers, his ability to arrange the history of Greek civilisation as a cycle of rise and fall and his sophisticated understanding of the relationship between the ancient and modern worlds. His history appears to have coincided with the wider project of Liberal Anglican historiography—to uncover the laws of civilisations with the aim of remedying the current situation of the world. Thirlwall's history, however, was only tacitly a contribution to this project. Scholarship, narrative clarity and the recognition of ambiguity were more important to Thirlwall than the communication of any political message. It was this recognition of uncertainty that guaranteed his obscurity, because it opened the field for someone else to answer the questions that he posed and to introduce a more explicit meaning to Greek history. All of this was carried out, as is widely recognised, in Grote's *History of Greece*. Grote's history appeared more coherent because he was committed to a cause; it was fashionable and entertaining to the political mind. Thirlwall's effort at modernist objectivity was ultimately too balanced to be a hit.

The collective amnesia about Thirlwall's history was a nineteenth-century solution to the dispute about the correct way to write history. But one achievement of historiography is to recognize that a multitude of historical narratives, carried out with different methods and upon different premises, deserve simultaneous appreciation.[61] Today the study of ancient Greek history is driven not only by new discoveries but also by new interpretations and ideas; a plurality of interpretations of narrative is desirable—even necessary—for an understanding of the past.

'Let then no student of history scorn the guidance of the great Bishop of St David's any more than he will scorn the guidance of the living Bishop of Chester!'[62]

Notes

1. Parts of this introduction were aired in a paper at the Hibernian Hellenists' 40th Anniversary meeting, National University of Ireland, Maynooth, October 2003. I am grateful for the comments made by the audience, in particular those of Judith Mossman and Prof. G. L. Huxley. I am grateful also to Oswyn Murray, Christopher Stray and Kyriakos Demetriou for their comments on earlier and later drafts.

2. For instance, James Mill, *A History of British India*, 3 vols, London, 1818; 4th edn, 9 vols, London, 1840–8; Robert Southey, *History of Brazil*, 3 vols, London, 1810–19. Thomas Moore, *History of Ireland*, 4 vols, London, 1837–46, was published in Dionysius Lardner's *Cabinet Cyclopaedia*. See in general, T. P. Peardon, *The Transition in English Historical Writing, 1760–1830*, PhD. Colombia, 1933.

3. The single-author, multi-volume history of Greece was in fashion before the First World War, reaching its peak in the mid-nineteenth century, with the histories of Mitford, Goldsmith, Gillies, Bulwer Lytton, Thirlwall, Grote, ending with those of Meyer, Busolt and Beloch, the final volume of whose work was not published until 1927. A collective history, the *Cambridge Ancient History*, was planned at the start of the twentieth century by J. B. Bury and was based on the *Cambridge Modern History*, founded 1902. On the *Cambridge Ancient History*, see P. J. Rhodes 'The Cambridge Ancient History', *HISTOS* 3, 1999 (electronic publication).

4. See F. Hartog, 'La Révolution française et l'Antiquité. Avenir d'un illusion ou cheminement d'un quiproquo?' 7–46 in C. Avlami (ed.), *L'Antiquité Grecque au XIXe Siècle: Un* exemplum *contesté?*, Paris, 2000.

5. See now K. N. Demetriou, *George Grote on Plato and Athenian Democracy*, Koinon 2, Frankfurt-am-Main, 1999, especially chapter 2, 'British Historians of Ancient Greece, 1739–1847'.

6. Mitford's brother, Lord Redesdale, wrote a short account of the historian and the intentions of the history. This was published as a preface to the first volume of the edition of 1838 (pp. ix–xliv); cf. G. P. Gooch, *History and Historians in the Nineteenth Century*, London, 1913, p. 308.

7. John Gillies, *The History of Ancient Greece, its Colonies and Conquests*, 6th edn, London, 1820, vol. i p. iii.

8. Edward Bulwer Lytton, *Athens: Its Rise and Fall. With views of the literature, philosophy, and social life of the Athenian People*, 2 vols, Paris, 1837.

9. O. Murray (ed.), *Athens: Its Rise and Fall* by Edward Bulwer Lytton, London, 2004.

10. George Grote, *History of Greece*, 12 vols., London, 1846–56.

11. Grote, *History of Greece*, 10th edn, Everyman's Library, London and New York, 1906, vol. i p. xv.

12. Demetriou, (above, note 5), 51–7; F. Turner, *The Greek Heritage in Victorian Britain*, London, 1981, pp. 211–12; J. T. Roberts, *Athens on Trial: The Antidemocratic Tradition in Western Thought*, Princeton, 1994, p. 238.

13. All references to Thirlwall unless stated are to Lardner's edition, London, 1835–44.

14. Thirlwall was interested in the advancement of learning among all social classes: see 'The advantages of literary and scientific institutions for all classes: a lecture delivered at the Town Hall, Carmarthen, on December 11th, 1849', published by the Carmarthen Literary and Scientific Institution; cf. his pamphlet *English Education for the Middle Classes, A Sermon*, London, 1853. Suggestions on the form of free libraries were made in the *Manchester Guardian*, January 19th, 1842.

15. Bulwer Lytton (n. 8 above), 1837, vol. i p. viii.= Murray (ed.) (n. 9 above), p. 38.

16. Bulwer Lytton did, however, correct or disagree with Thirlwall at points in his history: Murray's edn (n. 9 above), pp. 217 n. 8 and 371 n. 13.

17. [John Herman Merivale], 83–108, *Edinburgh Review* 62, Oct. 1835–June 1836, p. 84. There were few serious reviews of the history: see K. Demetriou, 'Bishop Connop Thirlwall: Historian of Ancient Greece', *Quaderni di Storia* 56, 2002, p. 52 n. 6. By contrast Grote's work produced a great deal of response: see now Kyriakos Demetriou (ed.), with notes and introductions, *Classics in the Nineteenth Century: Responses to George Grote*, 4 vols, Bristol, 2003.

18. [Merivale], (n. 17 above), p. 108.

19. [Merivale], p. 108.

20. Translations of Thirlwall's *History of Greece*: French: A. Joanne (tr.) *Histoire des origines de la Grèce ancienne*, Paris, 1847 and 1852 (vols 1 and 2); German: L. Haymann and L. Schmitz (trr.), *Geschichte von Griechenland*, Bonn, 1839–40 (vols 1 and 2), with introduction by F. G. Welcker. L. Schmitz later wrote *A History of Greece, from the earliest times to the destruction of Corinth, based on that of C. Thirlwall*, published by Longman's, London, 1851, and translated into German in 1859.

21. O. Murray in *The History of the University of Oxford*, vol. vi, part 1, 1997, p. 528 n. 66 proposes that they did not meet until after both had published; M. L. Clarke, *George Grote: a biography*, London, 1962, p. 7 that they in all likelihood knew each other at Charterhouse.

22. Demetriou, (n. 5 above).

23. In the second edition of 1849, containing a preface dated March 1846, p. vi.

24. Notice, vol. vi.

25. Implied by H. Grote, *Personal Life of George Grote, compiled from family*

documents, private memoranda, and original letters to and from various friends, London, 1873, 195.

26. F. Turner, *The Greek Heritage in Victorian Britain,* London, 1981, pp. 274–83.

27. He would write only one more piece on the ancient world, in 1857, 'Greece and Assyria', given to the *Royal Society of Literature* in 1857, essentially a review of Kruger's *Geschichte der Assyrier und Iraner vom 13ten bis zum 5ten Jrhdt. v. Christos,* reprinted in Rev. J. J. S. Perowne (ed.) *Thirlwall's Remains, Literary and Theological,* vol. iii, *Essays, Speeches and Sermons,* London, 1878, pp. 154–187.

28. D. Stanley (ed.), *Letters to a Friend,* 1882, p. 128; in a letter dated 18th April, 1867, he selectively praised Grote's work, 'Grote's great work is not less distinguished by extensive and accurate *learning,* than by depth and originality of thought, and it is very *popular* with readers who are able to appreciate these qualities', *ibid.,* p. 131. Thirlwall wrote to Grote on 21st June, 1847, congratulating him on the work, calling his own inferior and acknowledging that it would be superseded, H. Grote, *Personal Life of George Grote, compiled from family documents, private memoranda, and original letters to and from various friends,* London, 1873, 173.

29. A. Robson and J. Robson, *Collected Writings of John Stuart Mill, vol. xxiv: Newspaper Writings June 1835–June 1847,* p. 868.

30. See Momigliano, A. D., 'Liberal Historian and Supporter of the Holy Roman Empire: E. A. Freeman', 197–208 in G. Bowersock and T. J. Cornell (edd.) *A. D. Momigliano: Studies in Modern Scholarship,* California, 1994.

31. E. A. Freeman, 'The Athenian Democracy', (a review of Grote's *History,* originally published in the *North British Review,* May 1856) in *Historical Essays,* second series, London, 1873, p. 108.

32. E. A. Freeman, 'Alexander the Great', (a review of vol. xii of Grote's *History,* originally published in Edinburgh Review, April 1857) in *Historical Essays,* second series, London, 1873, p. 163.

33. E. A. Freeman, *History of Federal Government, from the foundation of the Achaian league to the disruption of the United States,* London, 1863. Thirlwall's enthusiasm for Federal government is clear not only in his description of the Aetolian and Achaean confederacies of the Hellenistic era, but also in his description of the Amphictyonies of Greece, vol. i p. 373.

34. On the establishment of the Classical tripos by Christopher Wordsworth in 1822 and its subsequent history, see C. Stray, *Classics in 19th and 20th Century Cambridge: curriculum, culture and community,* Cambridge Philological Society, Supplementary Volume 24, 1999.

35. K. Demetriou, 'Bishop Connop Thirlwall: Historian of Ancient Greece', *Quaderni di Storia* 56, 2002, pp. 49–90; B. Gibson, 'The Papers of Bishop Connop Thirlwall of St David's', *Journal of Welsh Ecclesiastical History* 9, 1992, pp. 64–7; R. Brinkley, 'Connop Thirlwall, Bishop of St David's', *Ceredigion* 7, 1973, pp. 131–49; G. Rees, 'Connop Thirlwall: Liberal Anglican', *Journal of the Historical Society of the Church in Wales* 14. 1964, 66–76; J. C. Thirlwall, *Connop Thirlwall. Historian and Theologian,* London, 1936; J. W. Clark,

Dictionary of National Biography, vol. xix, London, 1898/9, pp. 618–21.

36. On the Irish question: J. C. Thirlwall, *Bishop Connop Thirlwall. Historian and Theologian*, London, 1936, pp. 245–57.

37. Forbes, 1952, p. 117; J. Thirlwall (n. 35 above) p. 151.

38. Cited by Demetriou (n. 17 above), p. 57.

39. C. Stray, *Classics Transformed: Schools, Universities, and Society in England, 1830–1960*, Oxford, 1998, p. 61.

40. In *Letters, Literary and Theological*, ed. J. Perowne, London, 1881, p. 25.

41. D. Forbes, *The Liberal Anglican Idea of History*, Cambridge, 1951.

42. Reprinted in: T. Arnold, *Thucydides: The History of the Peloponnesian War*, 8th edition, Oxford, 1874, app. I to vol. i, p. 503.

43. Arnold (n. 42 above), Preface to vol. i, p. xiv.

44. In a letter to George Finlay: see J. M. Hussey (ed.), *The Journals and Letters of G. Finlay*, Camberley, Surrey, 1995, vol. ii p. 622. Thirlwall had, however, taken the Grand Tour: J. Thirlwall (n. 35), p. 100.

45. Arnold, Preface to second edition dated October 1839, reprinted in 8th edn, vol. i, pp. iii–iv.

46. Translation of Schleiermacher's *Ueber die Schriften des Lukas: Ein kritischer Versuch*, 1825: 'A Critical Essay on the Gospel of St. Luke, by Dr. F. Schleiermacher; with an Introduction by the Translator, containing an Account of the Controversy respecting the Origin of the first three Gospels since Bishop Marsh's Dissertation', London, 1825. Reprinted by T. N. Tice, *Luke: a critical study*, Schleiermacher Studies and Translations no. 13, Lewiston, NY, 1993.

47. See C. Stray, (ed.), *Philological Museum*, Bristol, 2004.

48. Thirlwall's contributions to the *Philological Museum* were reprinted in Rev. J. J. S. Perowne (ed.), *Thirlwall's Remains, Literary and Theological*, vol. iii, *Essays, Speeches and Sermons*, London, 1878.

49. See C. Stray, 'Scholars and Gentlemen', in H. D. Jocelyn (ed.), *Studies in Classical Scholarship in 19th-Century Great Britain*, Liverpool, 1996, pp. 19–20.

50. B. G. Niebuhr, *The History of Rome*, 3 vols., trr. J. C. Hare and C. Thirlwall, and (vol. iii) W. Smith (Cambridge, 1828–32; London, 1842). See N. Vance, 'Niebuhr in England: history, faith, order', 83–98 in B. Stuchtey and P. Wende (edd.), *British and German Historiography, 1750–1950*, Oxford, 2000.

51. On the emergence of interest in the private life in eighteenth century narrative histories, see Mark Salber Philips, 'Reconsiderations on History and Antiquarianism: Arnaldo Momigliano and the Historiography of Eighteenth-Century Britain', *Journal of the History of Ideas* 57, 1996, pp. 297–316.

52. In works such as *Orchomenos und die Minyer* of 1820, *Die Dorier* of 1824 and *Prolegomena zu einer wissenschaftlichen Mythologie* of 1825.

53. As Momigliano pointed out, the marriage of the antiquarian investigation and narrative history writing was an essential stage in the development of the late-eighteenth century historiography, first witnessed in the work of Edward Gibbon. See A. Momigliano, *The Classical Foundations*

of Modern Historiography, Berkeley, 1990; *ibid.*, *Essays in Ancient and Modern Historiography*, Middletown, Oxford, 1977; ibid., *Studies in Modern Scholarship*, G. W. Bowersock and T. J. Cornell (edd.), Berkeley, 1994.

54. Boeckh's *Die Staatshaushaltung der Athener* of 1817 was the first book on Greek history to make extensive use of epigraphical evidence. It was cited by Thirlwall in both its original and in G. C. Lewis' translation of it as *The Public Economy of Athens*, London, 1828.

55. The first volume of Brønsted's *Reisen* consisted of a detailed report from the island of Kea, the second volume was a study of the Parthenon in its historical context. It was published simultaneously in French and German as *Voyages dans la Grèce accompagnés de recherches archéologiques, et suivis d'un apercu sur toutes les enterprises scientifiques qui ont en lieu en Grèce depuis Pausanias jusq'à nos jours*. I–II, Paris, 1826–30, and *Reisen und Untersuchungen in Griechenland nebst Darstellung und Erklärung vieler neuentdeckten Denkmälern griechischen Styls, und einer kritischen Übersicht aller Unternehmungen dieser Art von Pausanias bis auf unsere Zeiten*, I–II, Paris, 1826–30. On Brønsted, see J. Isager (ed.), *Interviews with Ali Pacha of Joanina in the autumn of 1812: with some particulars of Epirus, and the Albanians of the present day by Peter Oluf Brøndsted*, Athens, 1999; J. Christiansen, *The Rediscovery of Greece: Denmark and Greece in the 19th Century*, Ny Carlsberg Glyptothek, 2000, 18–40. Gillies' report of the Parthenon is more cursory: Gillies, 1820, vol. ii, p. 171.

56. P. H. Reill, *The German Enlightenment and the Rise of Historicism*, Berkeley, 1975, pp. 127–60.

57. J. Gillies, *A View of the Reign of Frederick II of Prussia; with a parallel between that Prince and Philip II of Macedon*, Dublin, 1789.

58. For Thirlwall's interest in irony, see his essay 'On the Irony of Sophocles', *Philological Museum* ii, 1833, 483–537.

59. O. Goldsmith, *The Grecian History, from the Earliest State to the Death of Alexander the Great*, 2 vols, London, 1774.

60. J. Gillies, *History of the World from the Reign of Alexander to that of Augustus*, 2 vols, London, 1807. However, Gillies' 1820 *History* amalgamated his works to produce a study of history of Greece and beyond from the Trojan War to Augustus. Another early history of the Hellenistic period was John Gast's *History of Greece from the Accession of Alexander of Macedon till its Final Subjection to the Roman Power*, London, 1782.

61. E. A. Freeman recognised that the histories of Thirlwall, Grote and Curtius each have their separate values, and should not be regarded as 'superseding' one another, in 'Historical Writers', in *The Methods of Historical Study: eight lectures read in the University of Oxford in 1884, with the inaugural lecture on The office of the historical professor*, London, 1886, 286–8.

62. *The Methods of Historical Study: eight lectures read in the University of Oxford in ... 1884, with the inaugural lecture on The office of the historical professor*, London, 1886, 288. The Bishop of Chester was the historian William Stubbs (1825–1901).

Selections from
A HISTORY OF GREECE
by
The Rev. Connop Thirlwall

Publisher's Note

The chapter numbers relate only to this selection from Thirlwall's *A History of Greece*.
A bold font has been used to distinguish editorial comment from Thirlwall's own text.

A
HISTORY OF GREECE.
By
THE REV: CONNOP THIRLWALL.

Fellow of Trinity College, Cambridge.

VOL. I.

Lycurgus placed the infant Charilaus in the Royal seat and in the presence of the company proclaimed it King of Sparta.

p. 296

London:
PRINTED FOR LONGMAN, ORME, BROWN, GREEN, & LONGMANS, PATERNOSTER ROW;
AND JOHN TAYLOR, UPPER GOWER STREET.

Introduction

Advertisement

Thirlwall's most explicit discussion of methodology was in the 'Advertisement', bound into the first volume.

The plan of the little work begun in this volume has been considerably enlarged since it was first undertaken, and the Author fears that a critical eye may be able to detect some traces of this variation from the original design, in the manner of treating one or two subjects. He would be glad if he might believe that this was its chief defect. But he is most serious that the object which he has had in view should be understood.

He thought it probable that his work might fall into the hands of two different classes of readers, whose wants might not always exactly coincide, but were equally worthy of attention; one consisting of persons who wish to acquire something more than a superficial acquaintance with Greek history, but who have neither leisure nor means to study it for themselves in its original sources; the other of such as have access to the ancient authors, but often feel the need of a guide and an interpreter. The first of these classes is undoubtedly by far the largest: and it is for its satisfaction that the work is principally designed. But the Author did not think that this ought to prevent him from entering into the discussion of subjects which he is aware must be chiefly, if not solely, interesting to readers of the other description, and he has therefore dwelt on the earlier part of the history at greater length than would have been proper in a merely popular narrative. Perhaps he may venture to add, that it is the part which seemed to him to have been most neglected by preceding English writers, and to deserve more attention than it had commonly received among us. It was written before the first (the last published) volume of Mr. Clinton's Fasti had appeared.

Another consequence resulting from the nature of his plan, is, that he has found it necessary to subjoin a greater number of notes and references than may seem to accord with the unpretending form of the work. He regrets the room which they occupy, and would have been glad to have thought himself at liberty to omit them. But he believes he may safely appeal to the experience of every one conversant with these matters, to attest, that they have not been needlessly multiplied. Wherever it could be done without presuming too much on the reader's knowledge, he has contented himself with generally pointing out the sources from which they were drawn, and has only introduced a particular reference, where either his conclusions might be thought questionable, or the precise passage which he had in his mind was likely to escape notice, or was particularly interesting and instructive. If however he should be thought not to have observed the right mean in this respect, or sometimes to have addressed himself to too narrow a circle, or even to have amused himself instead of his readers he consoles himself by the prospect, that in the progress of his work, as its subject becomes more generally familiar and attractive, he shall have less and less need of indulgence on this head.

Trinity College, 12th June 1835.

Geographical Outlines of Greece

Liberal Anglican historians were concerned that narrative history should be based on 'experience' of its settings. Thirlwall never travelled to Greece, but he rated highly the reports of modern travellers for creating a setting for his work in the shape of a geographical description. The description gives notice of both ancient and modern evidence, relying on the testimony of modern British travellers, principally Leake, Dodwell and Gell.[1] The decision to rely heavily on British travellers was partly patriotic, as he revealed in a review in *Philological Museum*:

> Wherever else an Englishman may sometimes feel ashamed of his birth, in Greece he must thank God that he is a countryman of Gell, and Leake and Dodwell, and not of Fourmont and Pouqeville.[2]

This statement owed something to the negative reputation of French explorers: it was well known that the French traveller Fourmont was guilty of epigraphical forgery,[3] and it has been suggested that he destroyed genuine inscriptions in order to remain their sole authority.[4]

The character of every people is more or less closely connected with that of its land. The station which the Greeks filled among nations, the part which they acted, and the works which they accomplished, depended in a great measure on the position which they occupied on the face of the globe. The manner and degree in which the nature of the country affected the bodily and mental frame, and the social institutions of its inhabitants, may not be so easily determined; but its physical aspect is certainly not less important in a historical point of view, than it is striking and interesting in itself. An attentive survey of the geographical site of Greece, of its general divisions, and of the most prominent points on its surface, is an indispensable preparation for the study of history. In the following sketch nothing more will be attempted, than to guide the reader's eye over an accurate map of the country, and to direct his attention to some of those indelible features, which have survived all the revolutions by which it has been desolated.

The land which its sons called *Hellas*, and for which we have adopted the Roman name *Greece*, lies on the south-east verge of Europe, and in length extends no further than from the thirty-sixth to the fortieth degree of latitude. It is distinguished among European countries by the same character which distinguishes Europe itself from the other continents,—the great range of its coast compared with the extent of its surface; so that while in the latter respect it is considerably less than Portugal, in the former it exceeds the whole Pyrenean peninsula. The great eastern limb which projects from the main trunk of the continent of Europe grows more and more finely articulated as it advances towards the south, and terminates in the peninsula of the *Peloponnesus*, the smaller half of Greece, which bears some resemblance to an outspread palm. Its southern extremity is at a nearly equal distance from the two neighbouring continents: it fronts one of the most beautiful and fertile regions of Africa, and is separated from the nearest point of Asia by the southern outlet of the *Aegean* Sea,—the sea, by the Greeks familiarly called their own, which, after being contracted into a narrow stream by the approach of the opposite shores at the *Hellespont*, suddenly finds its liberty in an ample basin as they recede toward the east and west, and at length, escaping between Cape Malea and Crete, confounds its waters with the broader main of the Mediterranean. Over that part of this sea which washes the coast of Greece a chain of islands, beginning from the southern headland of Attica, Cape Sunium, first girds Delos with an irregular belt, the *Cyclades*, and then, in a waving line, links itself to a scattered group (the *Sporades*) which borders the Asiatic coast. Southward of these the interval between the two continents is broken by the larger islands *Crete* and *Rhodes*. From the isle of Cythera, which is parted by a narrow channel from Laconia, the snowy summits of Cretan Ida are clearly visible, and from them the eye can probably reach the Rhodian Atabyrus,* and the mountains of Asia Minor; smaller islands occupy a part of the boundary which this line of view may be conceived to fix to the Aegean. The sea which divides Greece from Italy is contracted, between the Iapygian peninsula and the coast of Epirus, into a channel only thirty geographical miles in breadth; and the Italian

---

* Diodorus, v 59; Apollod. iii 21. On the distance at which objects may be distinguished in the atmosphere of the Archipelago, see Dodwell, *Travels in Greece*, vol. 1, p. 194.

coast may be seen not only from the mountains of Corcyra, but from the low headland of the Ceraunian hills.

Thus on two sides Greece is bounded by a narrow sea; but toward the north its limits were never precisely defined. The word Hellas did not convey to the Greeks the notion of a certain geographical surface, determined by natural or conventional boundaries: it denoted the country of the *Hellenes*, and was variously applied according to the different views entertained of the people which was entitled to that name. The original Hellas was included in the territory of a little tribe in the south of Thessaly. When these Hellenes had imparted their name to other tribes, with which they were allied by a community of language and manners, Hellas might properly be said to extend as far as these national features prevailed. Ephorus regarded Acarnania, including probably the southern coast of the Ambracian gulf up to Ambracia, as the first Grecian territory on the west (Strabo viii 334). Northward of the gulf the irruption of barbarous hordes had stifled the germs of the Greek character in the ancient inhabitants of Epirus, and had transformed it into a foreign land; and it must have been rather the collection of its ancient fame, as the primitive abode of the Hellenes, than the condition of its tribes after the Persian war, that induced Herodotus to speak of *Thesprotia* as part of Hellas (ii 56). On the east, Greece was commonly held to terminate with Mount *Homole* at the mouth of the Peneus; the more scrupulous, however, excluded even Thessaly from the honour of the Hellenic name, while Strabo, with consistent laxity, admitted Macedonia. But from Ambracia to the mouth of the Peneus, when these were taken as the extreme northern points, it was still impossible to draw a precise line of demarcation; for the same reason which justified the exclusion of Epirus applied, perhaps much more forcibly, to the mountaineers in the interior of Aetolia, whose barbarous origin, or utter degeneracy, was proved by their savage manners, and a language which Thucydides describes as unintelligible. When the Aetolians bade the last Philip withdraw from Hellas, the Macedonian king could justly retort, by asking where would they fix its boundaries, and by reminding them that of their own body a very small part was within the pale from which they wished to exclude him. 'The tribe of the

Agraeans, of the Apodotians, and the Amphilochians,' he emphatically observed, 'is not Hellas' (Polybius xvii 5).

There follows a description of Thessaly and Central Greece based on travellers' accounts and passages from the ancient sources.

The peculiar conformation of the principal Boeotian valleys, the barriers opposed to the escape of the streams, and the consequent accumulation of the rich deposits brought down from the surrounding mountains, may be considered as a main cause of the extraordinary fertility of the land. The vale of the Cephisus especially, with its periodical inundations, exhibits a resemblance on a small scale, to the banks of the Nile,—a resemblance which some of the ancients observed in the peculiar character of its vegetation. The profusion in which the ordinary gifts of nature were spread over the face of Boeotia, the abundant returns of its grain, the richness of its pastures, the materials of luxury furnished by its woods and waters, are chiefly remarkable, in a historical point of view, from the unfavourable effect they produced on the character of the race, which finally established itself in this envied territory. It was this cause, more than the dampness and thickness of their atmosphere, that depressed the intellectual and moral energies of the Boeotians, and justified the ridicule which their temperate and witty neighbours so freely poured on their proverbial failing (Athenaeus x 11). The Attic satire might have been suspected, and large abatement might have been thought necessary for national prejudice, as well as for poetical exaggeration, had it not been confirmed by the grave evidence of Polybius, who records that, after a short effort of vigorous ambition, the Boeotians sank into a depth of grovelling sensuality, which has no parallel in the history of any Grecian people (Polybius in Athenaeus x 418). Yet they were warm lovers of poetry and music, and carried some branches of both arts to eminent perfection.

A wild and rugged, though not a lofty, range of mountains, bearing the name of Cithaeron on the west, and Parnes toward the east, divides Boeotia from *Attica*. Lower ridges, branching off to the south, and sending out arms toward the east, mark the limits of the principal districts which compose this little country, the least proportioned in extent of any on the face of the earth to its fame and importance in the history of mankind. The most extensive of the Attic plains, though it is by no means a uniform level, but is broken by a number of low hills, is that in which Athens itself lies at the foot of a precipitous rock, and in which, according to the Attic legend, the olive, still its most valuable production, first sprang up. It is bounded on the east by *Pentelicus*, and by the range which, under the names of the greater and lesser *Hymettus*,* advances till it meets the sea at Cape *Zoster*. The upper part of Pentelicus, which rises to a greater height than Hymettus,† was distinguished, under the name of *Epacria*, or *Diacria*, as the Attic Highlands. This range, which, after trending eastward, terminates at Cape *Cynossema*, forms with Parnes and the sea the boundary of the plain of *Marathon*. On the eastern side of Hymettus a comparatively level tract, separated from the coast by a lower range of hills, seems to have been that which was called *Mesogaea*, or the Midland. The hills which enclose it meet in the mountainous mine district of *Laurium*, and end with Cape *Sunium*, the southernmost foreland of Attica. The Attic mariner, as he sailed round Sunium, could discern the spear and the crest of his tutelary goddess in front of her temple on the Athenian rock. The tract on the coast between Sunium and Cape *Zoster*, a tract of low hills and undulating plains, was designated by the name of *Paralia*, as the maritime region of Attica, though the whole land was entitled to the appellation *Acte*, whence perhaps it derived the name of Attica, from the form in which it advanced into the sea. On the western side, the plain of Athens is bounded by a chain of hills, issuing from Parnes, and successively bearing the names of *Icarius*, *Corydallus*, and *Aegaleus*, as it stretches toward the sea, which at Cape *Amphiale* separates it by a channel, a quarter of a mile in width, from the island of *Salamis*. It parts the plain of Athens from that of *Eleusis*, which contained the *Thriasian* and the *Rharian* fields, celebrated in the Attic mythology as the soil which had been first enriched by the gifts of Demeter, or Ceres, the goddess of harvests.

---

* Called also *Anudros*, the waterless.

† Gell, *It. Of Greece*, p. 95.

Attica is, on the whole, a meagre land, wanting the fatness of the Boeotian plains, and the freshness of the Boeotian streams. The waters of its principal river, the *Cephisus*, are expended in irrigating a part of the plain of Athens,* and the *Ilissus*, though no less renowned, is a mere brook, which is sometimes swollen into a torrent. It could scarcely boast of two or three fertile tracts, and its principal riches lay in the heart of its mountains, in the silver of Laurium, and the marble of Pentilicus (Xenophon, *de Vectig.* i 4). It might also reckon among its peculiar advantages the purity of its air,† the fragrance of its shrubs, and the fineness of its fruits. But in its most flourishing period its produce was never sufficient to supply the wants of its inhabitants, and their industry was constantly urged to improve their ground to the utmost. Traces are still visible of the laborious cultivation which was carried by means of artificial terraces, up the sides of their barest mountains.‡ After all, they were compelled to look to the sea even for subsistence. Attica would have been little but for the position which it occupied, as the south-east foreland of Greece, with valleys opening on the coast, and ports inviting the commerce of Asia. From the tops of its hills the eye surveys the whole circle of the islands, which form its maritime suburbs, and seem to point out its historical destination.

There follows a description of Megarid, Western Greece and the Peloponnese, based on modern travellers' accounts and excerpts from ancient authors.

When the necessary deduction has been made for the inequalities of its surface, Greece may perhaps be properly considered as a land, on the whole, not less rich than beautiful. And it probably had a better claim to this character in the days of its youthful freshness and vigour. Its productions were various as its aspect: and if other regions were more fertile in grain, and more favourable to the cultivation of the vine, few surpassed it in the growth of the olive,

---

* As in the time of Sophocles. See the interesting illustration of an obscure passage, *Oed. C.* 717, given by F. Thiersch in his *Etat actuel de la Gréce* vol. ii, p. 26.
† Celebrated by Eurip. *Medea*, 829; and in Plutarch *de Exil.* 13.
‡ Parnes and Aegaleus, Dodwell, vol. i, pp. 505, 509.

and of other valuable fruits. Its hills afforded abundant pastures: its waters and forests teemed with life. In the precious metals it was perhaps fortunately poor; the silver mines of Laurium were a singular exception; but the Peloponnesian mountains, especially in Laconia and Argolis, as well as those of Euboea, contained rich veins of iron and copper, as well as precious quarries. The marble of Pentelicus was nearly equalled in fineness by that of the isle of Paros, and that of Carystus in Euboea. The Grecian woods still excite the admiration of travellers, as they did in the days of Pausanias, by trees of extraordinary size. Even the hills of Attica are said to have been once clothed in forests (Plato, *Critias*, 111c); and the present scantiness of its streams may be owed in a great measure to the loss of the shades which once sheltered them. Herodotus observes, that, of all the countries of the world, Greece enjoyed the most happily tempered seasons. But it seems difficult to speak generally of the climate of a country, in which each district has its own, determined by an infinite variety of local circumstances. Both in Northern Greece and in Peloponnesus the snow remains long on the higher ridges; and even in Attica the winters are often severe. On the other hand, the heat of the summer is tempered, in exposed situations, by the strong breezes from the north-west (the *Etesian* winds), which prevail during that season in the Grecian seas; and it is possible that Herodotus may have had their refreshing influence chiefly in view.

Greece lies in a volcanic zone, which extends from the Caspian— if it does not extend still further east—to the Azores, and from the 45th to the 35th degree of latitude,* the greater part of the world known to the Greeks. Though no traces of volcanic eruptions appear to have been discovered in Greece, history is full of the effects produced there by volcanic agency; and permanent indications of its physical character were scattered over its surface, in the hot springs of Thermopylae, Troezen, Aedepsus, and other places. The sea between Peloponnesus and Crete has been, down to modern times, the scene of surprising changes wrought by the same forces; and not long before the Christian era, a new hill was thrown up

---

* Hoff, *Geschichte der Veraenderungen der Erdoberflaeche*, vol. ii, p. 99.

on the coast near Troezen, no less suddenly than the islands near Thera were raised out of the sea.* Earthquakes, accompanied by the rending of mountains, the sinking of land into the sea, by temporary inundations, and other disasters, have in all ages been familiar to Greece, more especially to Peloponnesus. And hence some attention seems to be due to the numerous legends and traditions which describe convulsions of the same kind as occurring still more frequently, and with still more important consequences, in a period preceding connected history; and which may be thought to point to a state of elemental warfare, which must have subsided before the region which was its theatre could have been fitted for the habitation of man. Such an origin we might be inclined to assign to that class of legends which related to struggles between Poseidon and other deities for the possession of several districts: as his contests with Athene (Minerva) for Athens and Troezen (Paus. ii 30.6); with the same goddess, or with Hera (Juno) for Argos—where he was said, according to one account, to have dried up the springs, and according to another, to have laid the plain under water;† with Apollo for the isthmus of Corinth (Paus. ii 1.6). We might be led to put a like interpretation on the poetical traditions, which spoke of a period when several of the islands between Greece and Asia—as Delos and Anaphe,‡ and even Rhodes (Pindar *Ol.* vii), and Cyprus (Eustath. *Ad Dion. P.* v 508), were yet covered by the sea, out of which they rose at the bidding of some God. And still greater weight may seem to belong to a tradition preserved by the priests of Samothrace, an island famous for its ancient mystic worship, who told of a great convulsion, which had burst the barriers that once separated the Euxine from the Aegean, and had opened the channels of the Bosphorus and the Hellespont (Diod. v 47). It would not be difficult to connect this tradition with a poetical legend, in which Poseidon was said to have struck the land called Lycaonia, or Lyctonia, with his trident, and to have scattered its fragments, as islands, over the sea (Orph. Arg. 1287). But the vast magnitude of the changes described by these legends, may reasonably awaken

---

*   Ovid, *Metaph*, xv 296; Strabo i 158.
†   Apollod. ii 1.4.9; Paus. ii 22.4.
‡   Conon 49; Apollon. R. iv 1718.

a suspicion that they were mere fictions, which did not even spring out of any popular belief, but were founded on an opinion which prevailed in the Alexandrian period of Greek literature among the learned, and which was adopted in its full extent by the elder Pliny. Thus we find Callimachus speaking generally of islands, as formed of the fragments which Poseidon had severed with his trident from the mountains (*H. in Del.* 30–6). Pliny is more explicit: he does not hesitate to deliver, as a notorious fact, that nature had torn Sicily from Italy; Cyprus from Syria; Euboea from Boeotia (*NH* ii 90); and again, Atalante, Macris, and Ceos (*NH* iv 20), from Euboea; and that the sea had not only burst through the straits of the Bosporus, the Hellespont, Rhium, and Leucas—though in this last instance the channel was notoriously artificial; but that it had taken the place of the land in the Propontis, and in the gulfs of Corinth and Ambracia. We may perhaps most safely conclude not that these late writers had access to any better information than we now possess on this subject, but that they were less afraid of raising a great pile of conjecture on a very slender basis of facts.

CHAPTER TWO

The Inhabitants of Early Greece

The Earliest Inhabitants of Greece

Thirlwall's discussions of early Greek history are characterised by a sceptical approach to the sources and a pragmatic approach to the limits of human knowledge. In his discussion of ancient accounts of the Pelasgians, Thirlwall adheres to the principle used by Müller and Niebuhr, that mythology contains a kernel of truth about the early stages of human existence. He is interested not only in the origins of the Pelasgians, but in the degree of civilization which they achieved. This is measured by, amongst other things, their archaeological remains, in which he includes 'The Treasury—or Tomb of Atreus', now recognized as a Mycenean burial chamber. Scholarly interest in the Pelasgians now concentrates on the Greek perception of them.[1]

All we know about the earliest inhabitants of Greece, is derived from the accounts of the Greeks themselves. These accounts relate to a period preceding the introduction of letters, and to races more or less foreign to that which finally gave its name to the country. On such subjects tradition must be either vague and general, or filled with legendary and poetic details. And therefore we cannot wonder that, in the present case, our curiosity is in many respects entirely disappointed, and that the information transmitted to us is in part scanty and imperfect, in part obscure and confused. If we only listen to the unanimous testimony of the ancients, we find that the whole amount of our knowledge shrinks into a very narrow compass: if we venture beyond this limit, we pass into a boundless field of conjecture, where every step must be made on disputable ground, and all the light we can obtain, serves less to guide than to perplex us. There are however several questions relating to the original population of Greece, which it may be fit to ask, though we cannot hope for a completely satisfactory answer—if for no other purpose, at least to ascertain the extent of our knowledge. This is the main end we propose in the following enquiry; but we shall not scruple to pursue it, even where we are conscious that it cannot lead to any certain result, so far as we see any grounds to determine our opinion on the most interesting points of a dark and intricate subject.

The people whom we call Greeks—the Hellenes—were not, at least under this name, the first inhabitants of Greece. Many names have been recorded of races that preceded them there, which they, in later times, considered as barbarous, or foreign in language and manners to themselves. Among these names, that of the Pelasgians claims our first and chief attention, both because it appears to have been by far the most widely spread, and because it continued longer than the others—so late as the fourth century before our era—to be applied to existing races. So that on the notions we connect with it, our view of the ancient state of Greece must mainly depend, and to it we may most reasonably look for the fullest and clearest information the case admits of. Homer, as well as Herodotus and Thucydides, speaks of the Pelasgians only as occupying some insulated points, and those not in the continent of Greece, but in Crete, and Asia Minor, where in the Trojan war they side with the Trojans against the Greeks. But that in earlier times they were widely diffused in Greece itself, is established by unquestionable evidence, and is confirmed by allusions which occur in the Homeric poems to their ancient seats. We even meet with expressions in ancient writers, which, at first sight, seem to justify the supposition that the whole of Greece was once peopled by Pelasgians. 'All,' says Strabo, 'are pretty well agreed, that the Pelasgians were an ancient race, which prevailed throughout all Greece, and especially by the side of the Aeolians in Thessaly:' and since the Aeolians were commonly supposed to have sprung from Deucalion, who first reigned in countries westward of Thessaly, while the higher antiquity of the Pelasgians was universally admitted, this statement appears

in substance to coincide with that of Herodotus, who speaks of the
Pelasgians as inhabiting the country afterward called Greece. But
in another passage, where he observes that what Hecataeus had said
of Peloponnesus—that barbarians inhabited it before the Greeks—
might be applied to nearly the whole of Greece, Strabo illustrates
his meaning by a long list of other races, which he seems to consider
as equally ancient and equally foreign; so that the prevalence he
ascribes to the Pelasgians can only be understood as subject to the
same restrictions with which it is spoken of by Thucydides, who
mentions them as the tribe which, before the rise of the Hellenes,
had spread its name more widely than any other over the country.
And this view must also have been that of Herodotus; since, when
he is describing the growth of the Hellenic nation as the effect of
its union with the Pelasgians, he adds, that it received an accession
from many other barbarous tribes. There can therefore be no doubt
that the Greeks regarded the Pelasgians as only one, though the
most powerful, among the races anciently settled in Greece.

We arrive at the same conclusion, if we inquire into the particular
regions occupied by the Pelasgians: for we then find that, according
to ancient tradition, they were not spread uniformly over the whole
of Greece; but that, while in some districts they are exclusively
mentioned, in others they appear among a crowd of other tribes,
and that in others again no trace of them seems to be found. If we
approach Greece from the north, we meet with the first distinct
evidence of their presence on the eastern side of the Pindus in
Thessaly. It is attested, not by the general voice of antiquity, but
by monuments which both prove the existence of the people, and
afford some insight into their character and condition. A district,
or town, in the south-east of Thessaly, is mentioned in the Iliad
as the Pelasgian Argos. The opinion entertained by some of the
ancients, that this Argos was a part of the great Thessalian plain, one
region of which bore the name of Pelasgiotis in the latest period of
Greek history, is confirmed by Strabo's remark, that the word *Argos*
signified a plain in the dialects of Thessaly and Macedonia. In the
richest portion of this tract, on the banks of the Peneus, stood one
of the many cities called *Larissa*,—a word which was perhaps no less
significant than Argos, and, according to one derivation, may have

meant a fortress, or a walled town. Most of the Larissas known to have been founded in the very ancient times, may be clearly traced to the Pelasgians;* and there is therefore good reason for believing that the word belonged to their language, and for considering it as an indication of their presence. Beside the celebrated city on the Peneus, there were two other towns of the same name, one on the northern, the other not far from the southern border of Thessaly; from which it seems fair to infer that the Pelasgians once possessed the whole country. Yet they were not exclusively known there under that name; for we find the people who continued in after ages to be called Perrhaebians occupying the same seats in the earliest times; and we learn that Simonides spoke of them as the Pelasgian part of the new population formed by the irruption of the Lapiths in Thessaly. The same, therefore, may have been the case with other tribes, of which it is not expressly recorded,—as it probably was with the Dolopes, who, as well as the Pelasgians, are mentioned as ancient inhabitants of the island of Scyros; and the Athamanes, who were neighbours of the Perrhaebians, and like them were expelled by the Lapiths (Strabo ix 442). Beside the names of Argos and Larissa, another occurs in Thessaly, which carries us back into the most remote antiquity, and is no less intimately connected with the Pelasgian race. Achilles, in the Iliad, invokes Jupiter as the Dodonaean, Pelasgian, king; and it was a disputed point among the ancients, whether the Dodona from which the god derived this epithet lay in Thessaly or Epirus. The Iliad testifies the existence of a Thessalian Dodona in the land of the Perrhaebians; and, by describing a river which flowed through the adjacent region as a branch of the infernal Styx, seems plainly to mark this Dodona as the seat of a worship similar to that which prevailed in Epirus, the mythical realm of Aidoneus; and some ancient writers maintained that the oracle of the Pelasgian Jupiter had been transplanted from Thessaly to the Thesprotian Dodona.†

If, according to the more common opinion, which was supported

---

*   A list of them is given by Strabo, ix 440; Steph. Byz. s.v. Raoul Rochette, *Col. Gr.* i 178.

†   Either from Dodona (or Bodona), Fr. Steph. Byz. *Dodone* or from Scotoussa (Strabo vii).

by the authority of Aristotle (*Meteor.* i 14), Homer spoke of the western Dodona as sacred to the Pelasgian god, the Iliad would contain the earliest allusion to the abode of the Pelasgians in Epirus. That this country was one of their most ancient seats, and that the Thesprotian Dodona belonged to them, is universally admitted. Yet the race described in the Iliad as dwelling round the sanctuary, was called by a different name; they were the *Helli*, or *Selli*: and they appear to have been not merely the ministers of the temple, but a considerable tribe; for they occupied a region named, no doubt from them, Hellopia (Strabo vii 328). Another people, whom Aristotle places along with the Helli, 'in the parts about Dodona and the Achelous,' were the *Graeci*; and it cannot be doubted that this race, from which the Italian name of the Hellenes has been transmitted through the Roman into the modern European languages, must have been extensively spread. We find the Pelasgians however distinctly connected with a third people, who are said to have ruled over all Epirus before it fell under the dominion of the Molossians—the *Chaones*: they are described, like the Selli, as interpreters of the oracle of Jupiter, and Chaonia is called Pelasgian (Strabo vii; Steph. Byz. *Chaonia*). But if we pursue our inquiry along the coast of the Adriatic into Greece, we immediately lose sight of the Pelasgians: in Aetolia and Acarnania, the earliest known inhabitants bear different names, as *Leleges, Taphians, Teleboans, Curetes*. So too after leaving Thessaly, as we proceed southward, we meet with no Pelasgians before we come into Boeotia. Here their name occurs, indeed, but only as one among a great number of barbarous tribes, the ancient possessors of the country; and the way in which they are mentioned, seems to imply that they gained a footing here after the rest. 'Boeotia, it is said, was first inhabited by the barbarians, *Aones*, and *Temmices*, and *Leleges*, and *Hyantes*. Afterward the Phoenicians, the followers of Cadmus, took possession of it; and his descendants continued masters of nearly all Boeotia, till they were dislodged, first by the expedition of the Epigoni from Argos, and afterwards again by the Thracians and Pelasgians.' These Pelasgians, according to Ephorus, were driven out of Boeotia into Attica by a revolution, which Thucydides places sixty years after the Trojan war (Strabo ix 401).

But Attica, as we learn from Herodotus, had long before this event been peopled by the Pelasgians. According to his view, the Athenians of his own day were a Pelasgian race, which had settled in Attica from the earliest times, and had undergone no change, except by successively receiving new names, and by adopting a new language. 'The Athenians,' he says, 'when the Pelasgians were in possession of the country now called Hellas, were Pelasgians, named *Cranai*; but under the reign of Cecrops they were called *Cecropidae*; when Erechtheus succeeded to the kingdom, they changed this name for that of Athenians; and when Ion, son of Xuthus, became their general, they took the name of Ionians.' This is indeed, strictly speaking, a history only of Athens; but it evidently includes that of Attica; and we perceive in it the same distinction, which we have already so frequently met with, between the name and the blood of the people. As in Thessaly there were Pelasgians who were called Perrhaebians, and perhaps likewise Dolopes, and Athamanes, as in Epirus they were called Selli, Chaones, and apparently also Graeci; so, in Attica, no period is mentioned during which the name of the Pelasgians prevailed, though Herodotus holds it unquestionable that the Athenians always belonged to that nation. There was indeed a people which dwelt for a time in Attica, and was known there by the name of Pelasgians, or Pelargians. A monument of their presence was preserved to the latest times, in the Pelasgian wall with which the citadel of Athens was fortified. But they were strangers who, as Herodotus says, became neighbours to the Athenians and received a portion of land as the price of their services in building the wall (ii 51). According to Ephorus, they were the same Pelasgians who were driven out of Boeotia after the Trojan war; and Pausanias found some reasons for believing that they had migrated from Acarnania, and that they were originally Sicels (ii 23.3); whether he meant by this, that their more ancient seats lay in Sicily, or Italy or Epirus, is doubtful: but it looks as if this tribe were only called Pelasgians because it was not known to what race they belonged.

There follows a notice of the Pelasgians of the Peloponnese.

[T]he name Pelasgians was a general one, like that of Saxons, Franks or Alemanni; but each of the Pelasgian tribes had also one peculiar to itself. We shall find ground for believing that the nation was once spread much more widely than the name: but at all events, we cannot be sure that, in every instance, both the general and the particular name of each tribe have been preserved: it is much more probable that, in the numberless migrations and revolutions which took place in the period we are now considering, either one or the other has often been lost: and therefore, if we inquire into the relations between the Pelasgians and the other barbarous tribes by which Greece is said to have been anciently peopled, their names alone cannot guide us to any safe conclusion; and whenever we decide the question without any other grounds, we shall be as much in danger of separating kindred races, as of confounding those which were most foreign to each other.

There follows a notice of other non-Greek tribes connected with the Pelasgians.

As to the quarter from which the Pelasgians came into Greece, we cannot expect to learn any thing from the Greeks, since they themselves were content with their ignorance on this subject, and were not even tempted to inquire into it. The ancient writers, who recorded their historical knowledge or opinions in the form of poetical genealogies, when they had ascended to the person whom they considered as the common ancestor of the nation, thought it enough to describe him as the son of a god, or as the natural fruit of the earth itself, or uniting both these views in a third, as framed by the divine will out of some brute matter. Thus many of these genealogies terminate, as we have seen, in children of the soil; and though the Greek word that denoted this (*autochthones*) was some times vaguely used to express the antiquity of a race, there can be no doubt that it was generally received, not only by the vulgar but by the educated men, and without reference to any peculiar philo-sophical system, like that of Empedocles, in its most literal sense. Hence Plato, in the funeral oration, in which he embraced all the topics that could flatter the vanity of the Athenians, dwells upon this popular notion, which was certainly not his own. 'The second praise,' he says, 'due to our country is, that at the time when the whole earth was sending forth animals of all kinds, wild and tame, this our land proved barren and pure of wild beasts, and from among all animals chose and gave birth to man, the creature which excels the rest in understanding, and alone acknowledges justice and the gods.' With the same right that the Athenians claimed this glory for themselves, the Arcadians boasted of being older than the moon;* and, indeed, when the principle was once admitted, and the agency of an intelligent Creator excluded, since the mechanical difficulty costs no more to overcome in many instances than in one, there was no reason why every valet should not have produced its first man, or rather a whole human harvest. The antiquity of the Arcadians was asserted by the genealogical poet Asius of Samos, who is supposed to have flourished so early as the beginning of the Olympiads, who sang of the Arcadian Pelasgians, that 'the black earth sent him forth in the shady mountains, that the race of mortals might exist' (Paus. viii 1.4). According to the more commonly received opinion, the Argive Pelasgians were the eldest of the race (Dionys. *A. R.* i 17). But the only question among the antiquarians was, from what part of Greece had it issued: none thought of tracing it to any foreign nation as its earlier home. The presence of the Pelasgians in Greece, is not only the first unquestionable fact in Greek history, but the first of which any tradition has been preserved.

This fact however does not merely set bounds to our inquiries, beyond which they find no ground to rest on; it also warrants a conclusion, which it is useful to bear in mind. It seems reasonable to think that the Pelasgians would not have been, as they appeared to Ephorus, the most ancient people of whose dominion in Greece any rumour remained (Strabo vii 327), if they had not been really the first that left some permanent traces there. If they were not the original inhabitants of the country, at least no nation more powerful or more civilised can easily be imagined to have been there before them; and if any of the tribes whose names are coupled with theirs belonged to a different, and a more ancient race, it is probable that the obscurity which covers them is owing to their

---

* *Proselenoi.* Other explanations have been given of the word (as pre-Hellenic). Its true derivation does not concern us here.

utter feebleness and insignificance. On the other hand, though to the Greeks the history of the Pelasgians began in Greece, and we are therefore unable to pursue it further, it should be remembered that this is only an accidental termination of our researches, and that the road does not necessarily end, where the guide stops. If we believe that the Pelasgians really existed, we must also believe that they either sprang out of the ground, or dropped from the clouds, or that they migrated into Greece from some part of the earth nearer to that where mankind first came into being. But though we have the strongest grounds for adopting the last of these opinions, we must be cautious not to confound it with others which neither flow from it, nor are necessarily connected with it. Reason and authority may unite to convince us, that the Pelasgians were a wandering people, before they settled in Greece; but neither supplies an answer to any of the numberless questions which this fact suggests. Yet most of the views that have been formed of them in modern times, appear to have been, at least secretly, affected by a preference given to some single conjecture over a multitude of others equally probable. For the sake of guarding against such prepossessions, it is useful to remember the great diversity of ways by which such a country as Greece may have received its first population; and that we have no historical evidence to determine us in favour of one hypothesis, to the exclusion of the rest: but that the variety and apparent inconsistency of the local traditions relating to the Pelasgians would incline us to suppose, that they came into Greece, not from a single side, nor during a single period, nor under the same circumstances; but that many tribes were gradually comprehended under the common name, which, though connected together by a national affinity, had been previously severed from each other, and had passed through different conditions and turns of fortune. The Greek traditions about their migrations rest on no firmer ground than the opinion that they were somewhere or other in a literal sense natives of the Greek soil: if we reject it, there is no necessity to imagine that either their seats in the north, or those in the south of Greece, were the more ancient, or that the connection of parent and colony subsisted, immediately or remotely, between their most widely parted settlements.

There follows discussion of the course of Pelasgian migrations and relations between the Pelasgians and Greeks.

To know that a nation which has any fair claim to affinity with the Greeks was not, at any period to which probable tradition goes back, a horde of helpless savages, is in itself not unimportant. The same evidence which disposes us to believe that the Pelasgians spoke a language nearly akin to the Hellenic, must render us willing to admit that, before they came into contact with any foreign people in Greece, they may have tilled the ground, planted the vine, launched their boats on the sea, dwelt together in walled towns, and honoured the gods, as authors of their blessings, with festive rites and sacred songs. And it is satisfactory to find that all this, if not clearly ascertained, is at least consistent with the general tradition. But even this is far from giving us a notion of the precise point of civilisation to which the Pelasgians had advanced, before the Greeks overtook and outstripped them, and still less does it disclose any peculiar features in their national character. Fully to discuss the former of these subjects, it would be necessary to enter into a very wide and arduous field of enquiry, and to examine the pretensions set up on behalf of the Pelasgians to the art or writing, to religious mysteries, and to a theological literature. But as this would lead us away from our main object, it will be better to reserve these questions till we are called upon to notice them so far as they bear on the progress of society among the Greeks. For the present we shall only touch on one subject, which affords us surer ground for observation, and perhaps the best measure for judging of the condition and the character of the Pelasgians. The most ancient architectural monuments in Europe, which may perhaps outlast all that have been reared in later ages, clearly appear to have been works of their hands. Their huge structures, remains of which are visible in many parts of Greece, in Epirus, in Italy, and the western coast of Asia Minor, and which are commonly described by the epithet Cyclopean, because, according to the Greek legend, the Cyclopes built the walls of Tiryns and Mycenae, might more properly be called Pelasgian from their real authors. The legendary Cyclopes indeed are said to have been brought over from Lycia by Proetus,

king of Argos, the founder of Tiryns. But this tradition, whatever
may have been its foundation, is certainly not a sufficient clue for
tracing the style as well as the name, to Argolis, nor a safe ground
for ascribing its origin to a different race from the Pelasgians. The
epithet most probably expresses nothing more than the wonder
excited by these gigantic works in the Greeks of a more refined
age. It suggests however that the point of view from which they
may reflect some light on the people to which they belong. The
earliest of them are so rude, that they seem at first sight to indicate
nothing more than a capacity confined to undertakings which
demanded much toil and little skill, and a state of society settled
enough to encourage such exertions. In this respect it matters little
whether they were productions of free labour, or tasks imposed by a
foreign master. The gradual progress that may be traced, through a
series of easy transitions, from these shapeless masses to regular and
well-contrived buildings, seems to show, that in those of the rudest
workmanship, the sense of symmetry, the most distinguishing
feature in the Greek character, was only suppressed in the struggle
of an untaught people with the difficulties that beset the infancy
of art. The interval between the style, if it may be so called, of
the most unsightly Cyclopean wall, and that of edifices like the
treasury or tomb of Atreus, is perhaps not so wide as that which
separates works of the latter class from what may be conceived to
have been the simplest form of the Doric temple; though they were
much further removed from that stage, in which necessity is still
the parent of invention, utility is its only guide, beauty its unsought,
and seemingly accidental, result.

Foreign Settlers in Greece

This subject—and the related question of the extent of African or Asiatic influence
on Greek civilisation—is probably the only area which has drawn attention to the
work of Thirlwall in the twentieth century. Martin Bernal, in his controversial work
Black Athena, argued that ancient Greek civilisation was founded on the colonisation
of Greece by Phoenicians and Egyptians in the second millennium BC.[2] In so doing he
argued that whereas this 'Ancient Model' had survived in the pre-1820 scholarship, by
the 1820s it was replaced by the so called 'Aryan Model', which took the stance that

Greek civilisation was partly autochthonous and shaped partly by invasions from the north. Bernal focused on Thirlwall as one of the importers into anglophone scholarship of the fundamentally racist 'Ayrian tradition' developed by German antiquarians such as Karl Otfried Müller and Niebuhr. Bernal lets Thirlwall off the hook mildly: despite being guilty of 'systematical racism', Thirlwall is credited with the standard compromise—Egyptians no and Phoenicians maybe.[3] But Bernal fails to stress the state of principled uncertainty that Thirlwall expresses about the issue.[4]

In a comparatively late period,—that which followed the rise of a historical literature among the Greeks,—we find a belief generally prevalent, both in the people and among the learned, that in ages of very remote antiquity, before the name and dominion of the Pelasgians had given way to that of the Hellenic race, foreigners had been led by various causes from distant lands to the shores of Greece, and there had planted colonies, founded dynasties, built cities, and introduced useful arts and social institutions, before unknown to the ruder natives. The same belief has been almost universally adopted by the learned of modern times, many of whom, regarding the general fact as sufficiently established, have busied themselves in discovering fresh traces of such migrations, or in investigating the effects produced by them on the moral and intellectual character, the religious or political condition, of the Greeks. It required no little boldness to venture even to throw out a doubt as to the truth of an opinion sanctioned by such high authority, and by the prescription of such a long and undisputed possession of the public mind; and perhaps it might never have been questioned, if the inferences drawn from it had not provoked a jealous inquiry onto the grounds on which it rests. When however this split was once awakened, it was perceived that the current stories of these ancient settlements afforded great room for reasonable distrust, not merely in the marvellous features they exhibit, but in the still more suspicious fact, that with the lapse of time their number seems to increase and their details to be more accurately known, and that the further we go back the less we hear of them, till, on consulting the Homeric poems, we lose all traces of their existence. We can here neither affect to disregard the controversies that are still agitated on this subject, and repeat the common traditions without warning the reader of their questionable character, nor can we discuss the arguments of either side. But as it seems possible, and even necessary, to take a middle course between the old and new opinions, it will be proper to explain why we cannot embrace either with an unqualified assent.

A slight inspection of the Greek stories about the foreign settlers seems sufficient to show, that neither the authority on which they rest, nor the internal evidence, is such as to satisfy a cautious enquirer. We must here briefly notice their leading features. The principal colonies brought to Greece from the East are said to have been planted in Argolis, on the opposite side of the Saronic gulf, and in Boeotia. The Pelasgians were still masters of the plain of Argos, when Danaus, driven out of Egypt by domestic feuds, landed on the coast, was raised to the throne by the consent of the natives, and founded a town, afterwards the citadel of Argos, and known by the Pelasgian name Larissa. He is said to have given his name to the warlike Danai, once so celebrated, that Homer uses this as a general appellation for the Greeks, when that of the Hellenes was still confined to a narrow range. The later Argives showed his tomb in their market-place, and many other monuments of his presence. The popular belief is confirmed by the testimony of Herodotus, who mentions the migration of Danaus without any distrust, and even learnt in Egypt the name of the city from which he came: and the historian's evidence appears to be backed by an independent tradition, which he found existing at Rhodes, that Danaus had landed there on his passage, and founded a temple of Minerva at Lindus, to which, in the sixth century BC, Amasis king of Egypt sent offerings in honour of its Egyptian origin. This is the naked abstract of the tradition; and when so related, stripped of all its peculiar circumstances, it may seem perfectly credible, as well as amply attested. On the other hand, the popular legend exhibits other features, apparently original, and not to be separated from its substance, which are utterly incredible, and can scarcely be explained without transporting the whole narrative out of the sphere of history into that of religious fable. All authors agree that Danaus fled to Greece, accompanied by a numerous family of daughters (fifty is the received poetical number), to escape from the persecution of their suitors, the sons of his brother Aegyptus. This is an essential part of the story, which cannot be severed from the rest without the most arbitrary violence. The Danaids, according to Herodotus, founded the temple at Lindus, and instructed the Pelasgian women at Argos in the mystic rites of Demeter. To them too was ascribed the discovery of the springs, or the wells, which relieved the natural aridity of a part of the Argive soil. Before Herodotus, Aeschylus had exhibited on the Attic stage the tragical fate of the sons of Aegyptus, who had pursued the fugitives to Greece, and, after forcing them to the altar, were slain by their hands. A local legend related that Lerna, the lake or swamp near Argos, had been the scene of the murder, and that the heads of the suitors were there buried, while their bodies were deposited in a separate monument.* One of the main streams of Lerna derived its name from Amymone, one of the sisters, to whom Neptune, softened by her beauty, had revealed the springs which had before disappeared at his bidding. This intimate connection between the popular legend and the peculiar character of the Argive soil, which exhibited a striking contrast between the upper part of the plain and the low grounds of Lerna, must be allowed to give some colour to the conjecture of the bolder critics, who believe the whole story of Danaus to have been of purely Argive origin, and to have sprung up out of these local accidents, though all attempts hitherto made to explain its minuter features seem to have failed. The Argive colonies in the east of Asia Minor might be conceived to have contributed something toward the form which it finally assumed even before Egypt was thrown open to the Greeks. But the historian cannot decide between these contending views, and must resign himself to the uncertainty of the fact, unless it can be maintained by some stronger evidence, or more satisfactorily explained.

If we could consent to swell the list of the foreign settlers with the conjectures of modern critics, we should not consider the arrival of Danaus as an insulated fact. We might have spoken of Inachus, who is called the first king of Argos, and is said to have given his name to its principal river: hence, in the mythical genealogies, he

---

* Apollod. ii 1.5.11. Pausanias inverts the story (ii 24.2).

is described as a son of Oceanus, the common parent of all rivers. Yet on this ground it has sometimes been supposed that he too came to Greece across the sea. We as little venture to rely on such inferences, as to construe the fabled wanderings of Io, the daughter of Inachus, into a proof that, even before the time of Danaus, intercourse subsisted between Greece and Egypt. If however, we turn northward of the Isthmus, we find another Egyptian prince at Megara, where, according to the tradition which Pausanias heard there, Lelex, having crossed over from Egypt, founded the dynasty which succeeded that of Car, the son of Phoroneus, and gave his name to the Leleges. But this solitary and ill-attested legend, which was manifestly occasioned by the ancient rivalry of the Carian and the Lelegian races, cannot serve to prove the Egyptian origin of the latter people, which seems not to have been suspected by any other ancient authors. In Attica we meet with reports of more than one Egyptian colony. The first, led by Cecrops, is said to have found Attica without a king, desolated by the deluge which befell it, a century before, in the reign of Ogyges. If we may believe some writers of the latest period of Greek literature, Cecrops gave his own name to the land, and on the Cecropian rock founded a new city, which he had called Athens, after the Goddess Athene, whom, with the Romans, we name Minerva. To him is ascribed the introduction not only of a new religion, of pure and harmless rites, but even the first element of civil society, the institution of marriage; whence it may be reasonably inferred, that the savage natives learned from him all the arts necessary to civilized life. But, notwithstanding the coincidence with which this story has been repeated in modern times, the Egyptian origin of Cecrops is extremely doubtful. It is refuted by the silence of elder Greek poets and historians; and even in the period when it became current, is contradicted by several voices, which describe Cecrops as a native of the Attic soil: and the undisguised anxiety of the Egyptians to claim the founder of Athens for their countryman could excite the distrust of a writer so credulous and uncritical as Diodorus (i 29). Not content with Cecrops, they pretended to have sent out Erechtheus with a supply of corn for the relief of their Attic kinsmen, who rewarded his munificence with the crown; he in return completed his work of beneficence, by founding the mysteries of Eleusis on the model of those which were celebrated in Egypt in honour of Isis. A third Egyptian colony was said to have been led to Attica by Peteus, only one generation before the Trojan war. The arguments of the Egyptians seem to have been as weak as their assertions were bold. The least absurd was that they derived from the Oriental character of the primitive political institutions of Attica. But some more distinct marks of Egyptian origin would be necessary to countervail the tacit dissent of the Greek authors who might have been expected to be best informed on the subject. Nor is their silence to be explained by the vanity of the Athenians, who were accustomed indeed to consider themselves as children of the Attic soil, but were not on that account reluctant to believe that their land had been early visited by illustrious strangers. We purposely abstain from insisting on the result of mythological enquiries, which tend to show that both Cecrops and Erechtheus are fictitious personages, and that they belong entirely to a homesprung Attic fable. Such attacks would be wasted on tales which scarcely present the semblance of a historical foundation.*

---

* It may however be proper to remind the reader, that the question as to an Egyptian colony in Attica does not depend upon the opinion which may be formed on the existence or the origin of Cecrops. Whatever may be thought on that point, arguments such as those which are urged with great ability by F. Thiersch, in his *Epochen der bildenden Kunst*, p. 26f., from the Attic religion and art, particularly from the names, offices, and mutual relations of Athene (Neitha), Hephaestus (Phthath), and their son Apollo (Cicero *Nat. De.* iii 22), and from the Egyptian physiognomy of Athene on the ancient Attic coins— such arguments will still be equally entitled to attention.—On the other hand, it is difficult to acquit the ingenious and eloquent author of a too willing credulity, when he attempts to trace the expedition of Cecrops, or of the colonists whom he represents, over the sea to Thrace, and thence to the southern extremity of Greece, and, for this purpose, not only accepts such an authority as Isidore (*Or.* xv 1) to prove that Cecrops built the city of Rhodes (which has been commonly believed, on the authority of Diodorus, to have been first founded Ol. xciii 1), but even condescends to rake up out of Meursius (*De Regg. Athe.* i 7) the testimony of an Albert abbot of Stade, who, it seems, has recorded in his Chronicle that Cecrops built the temple at Delphi, and founded Lacedaemon. His two other citations (from Stephanus and Strabo) are certainly not so ludicrously weak, but they prove nothing. That there should have been a district in Thrace called Cecropis, as is asserted by Stephanus (Kekropia), may be believed, and

The opinion of a foreign settlement in Boeotia is undoubtedly supported by much better authority. That Cadmus led a Phoenician colony into the heart of the country, and founded a town named Cadmea, which afterwards became the citadel of Thebes, was a tradition which had certainly been current in Boeotia long before the time of Herodotus, who not only confirms it by the weight of his own judgment—which is not here biassed, as in the case of Danaus, by the Egyptian priesthood—but also by some collateral evidence. He had ascertained, that one of the most celebrated Athenian families traced its origin to the companions of Cadmus: that another division of them had been left behind in the isle of Thera; and that his kinsman Thasus had given his name to the island where the Phoenicians opened the gold mines which were still worked in the days of the historian. These may indeed, so far as Cadmus is concerned, be considered as mere ramifications of the Theban legend, not more conclusive than the tradition that followers of Cadmus settled in Euboea. But they at least prove that Phoenicians had very early gained a foothold on the islands and shores of Greece. Thebes boasted of having received the precious gift of letters from her Phoenician colonists; and Herodotus adopts this opinion after a diligent inquiry, which ought to be wholly disregarded, because he was deceived by some monuments which were either forged or misinterpreted. The Oriental derivation of the name of Cadmus is indeed as uncertain as the original import of that of Phoenix, which Hellanicus gives to his father, but which was used by the Greeks as one of the proper names of their native heroes. Thebes likewise showed what were thought to be traces of Phoenician worship;* and the story of the sphinx, whatever may have been its origin, may seem to point if not to Phoenicia, at least toward the East. On the

---

accounted for from the widespread power of Athens, without going back to the time of Cecrops; and Strabo's remark (ix 407), that Cecrops ruled over Boeotia, was a natural inference from the probably well-founded tradition, that it once contained two towns, named Eleusis and Athens.

* Cadmus was said to have dedicated a statue of Athene at Thebes, with the title of Onga; on which Pausanias (ix 12.2) observes, that this name, which is Phoenician (cf. Steph. Byz. *Ogkaiai* and *Chna*), contradicts the opinion of those who hold Cadmus to have been, not a Phoenician, but an Egyptian.

other hand, modern writers find, in the legends of Cadmus and his consort Harmonia, in their connection with Samothrace, and with the mysterious Cabiri, decisive marks of a Pelasgian origin; insist upon the inland position of Thebes as inconsistent with the ordinary character of a Pelasgian settlement; and consider the epithet of the *Tyrian* Cadmus as a chronological error, which betrays the late rise of the story, the authors of which substituted Tyre for the elder Sidon. As if to increase our perplexity, an ingenious attempt has been made to prove that the Cadmeans were a Cretan colony.*

There is still another celebrated name which we must add to this list, before we proceed to consider the subject in a different point of view. According to a tradition which appears to be sanctioned by the authority of Thucydides, Pelops passed over from Asia to Greece with treasures which, in a poor country, afforded him the means of founding a new dynasty. His descendants sat for three generations on the throne of Argos: their power was generally acknowledged throughout Greece and in the historian's opinion, united the Grecian states against Troy. The renown of their ancestor was transmitted to posterity by the name of the southern peninsula, called after him Peloponnesus, or the isle of Pelops. The region of Asia, from which Pelops came, is not uniformly described any more than the motives of his migration. Most authors, however, fix his native seat in the Lydian town of Sipylus, where his father was fabled to have reigned in more than moral prosperity, till he abused the favour of the gods, and provoked them to destroy him. The poetical legends varied as to the marvellous causes through which the abode of Pelops was transferred from Sipylus to Pisa, where he won the daughter and the crown of the bloodthirsty tyrant Oenomaus, as the prize of his victory in the chariot-race. The authors who, like Thucydides, saw nothing in the story but a political transaction, related that Pelops had been driven from his native land by an invasion of Ilus, king of Troy (Paus. ii 22.3); and hence it has very naturally been inferred that, in leading the Greeks against Troy, Agamemnon was merely avenging the wrongs of his ancestor.† On the other hand,

---

*   Welcker, *Ueber eine Kretische Colonie in Theben.*
†   By Kruse, *Hellas*, i p. 485.

it has been observed, that, far from giving any countenance to this hypothesis, Homer, though he records the genealogy by which the sceptre of Pelops was transmitted to Agamemnon, no where alludes to the Asiatic origin of the house. As little does he seem to have heard of the adventures of the Lydian stranger at Pisa. The zeal with which the Eleans maintained this part of the story, manifestly with a view to exalt the antiquity and the lustre of the Olympic games, over which they presided, raises a natural suspicion, that the hero's connection with the East may have been a fiction, occasioned by a like interest and propagated by like arts. This distrust is confirmed by the religious form which the legend was finally made to assume, when it was combined with an Asiatic superstition, which found its way into Greece after the time of Homer. The seeming sanction of Thucydides loses almost all weight, when we observe that he does not deliver his own judgment on the question, but merely adopts the opinion of the Peloponnesian antiquarians, which he found best adapted to his purpose of illustrating the progress of society in Greece.

There can scarcely be a more irksome or unprofitable labour, than that of balancing arguments of this nature and watching the fluctuation of the scales, as a new conjecture is thrown on either side. We turn with impatience from this ungrateful task, to make a few general remarks, which may perhaps assist the reader in appreciating the comparative value of these traditions. We must repeat, that none of these stories, considered by themselves, have any marks of truth sufficient to decide the conviction of a scrupulous inquirer; nor can their number be safely held to make up for their individual deficiency in weight. Yet there are other grounds which seem to justify the belief, that at least they cannot have been wholly destitute of historical foundation. Even if we had no such distinct accounts of particular persons and events, it would scarcely possible to doubt that, at a period long prior to that represented by the Homeric poems, migrations must have taken place from various parts of the East to the shores of Greece. We have sufficient evidence, that in the earliest times Greece was agitated by frequent irruptions and revolutions, arising out of the flux and reflux of the nations which fought and wandered in the countries adjacent to its north-eastern borders. We have ample reason to believe, that during the same period the western regions of Asia were not in a more settled state. Such movements appear to be indicated by the history of the Phrygians, who are said to have passed out of Europe into Asia Minor, which nevertheless was most probably their earlier seat; by the expedition of the Amazons, which left such deep traces in the legends of Attica, and the neighbouring countries; perhaps by that of the fabulous Memnon, which the Greek poets connected with the siege of Troy.* It cannot surprise us, that, while Macedonia and Thrace were a highway, or a theatre of war, for flying or conquering tribes, other wanderers should have bent their course to Greece across the Aegean. Its islands appear from time memorial to have been the steps by which Asia and Europe exchanged a part of their unsettled population. Thus, in the remotest antiquity, we find Carians occupying both sides of the Saronic Gulf; and Sicyon derived one of its most ancient names from a people, who are described as among the earliest inhabitants of Cyprus, Rhodes, and Crete.†

When, thus prepared to contemplate Greece as a land, not secluded from the rest of the world, but peculiarly open and inviting to foreign settlers, we again consider the stories of the various colonies said to have been planted there by strangers from the East, we are struck by some coincidences which cannot have been the result of design, and therefore bespeak a favourable hearing. It is on the *eastern* side of Greece, that with the solitary and doubtful exception of Pelops, we find these colonies planted—a restriction which the nature of the case indeed required, but which would not have been observed by religious fraud or patriotic vanity. While this appears an argument of some moment, when the question is viewed from the side of the West, it is met by another stronger and alike independent on the side of the East. The history of the countries from which these colonies or adventurers are said to have issued, tells of domestic revolutions, generally coinciding with the date of the supposed settlements in Greece, by which a portion of their inhabitants was

---

*   See an essay on this subject in the *Philological Museum*, iv.
†   In an essay in the *Philological Museum*, iv.

driven into foreign lands. Egypt, having been long oppressed by a hostile race, which founded a series of dynasties in a part at least of her territory, is said to have finally rid herself, by a convulsive effort, of these barbarous strangers who were dispersed over the adjacent regions of Asia and Africa. If we admit the truth of these traditions, which appear to rest on good grounds, it seems scarcely possible to doubt that the movement occasioned by this shock was propagated to Greece; and it seems highly probable that some of these outcasts, separating themselves from their brethen, found means of embarking on the coasts of Egypt or Palestine, and wandered over the Aegean until they reached the opposite shore, while others may have been led to the same quarter by a more circuitous road. Hence we are inclined not altogether to reject the testimony, or rather the opinion, of an author, who, though undoubtedly much later than Hecataeus, the predecessor of Herodotus, whose name he bears, may have been delivering more than a mere conjecture of his own, when he relates that the migrations of Danaus and Cadmus were occasioned by this Egyptian revolution (Diod. fr. xl). If, indeed, any weight could be attached to an obscure report of a Hellenic dynasty among those of the shepherd kings, we might suppose that an intercourse between the two countries had been opened at a still earlier period.* At all events, an objection which has often been urged against the common story,—that the Egyptians in the earliest times were strangers to maritime expeditions, and shrank with abhorrence from the sea,—loses all its force against this hypothesis. It is true that neither the Egyptians in the time of Herodotus, nor the Greeks before the Alexandrian period, viewed the migration of Danaus and Cadmus in this light. They considered Danaus as an Egyptian by birth, and Cadmus, in general as a native of Phoenicia. This however, if the fact was as here supposed, would be a very natural mistake; and with regard to Cadmus, we find that there was an ancient controversy on the question whether he came from Phoenicia or from Egypt (Paus. ix 12.2). An author who wrote a little before our era, and who professes to have examined the

---

* According to Goar's reading, a dynasty of Hellenic shepherds occurs in Syncellus, p. 114 (ed. Bonn).

subject with great attention, relates, that Cadmus was a powerful chief among those Phoenicians who conquered Egypt, and established the seat of their empire at Thebes, and that it was from Egypt he set out to found a dynasty in the West, where he named the Boeotian Thebes, after the city which he had left (Conon 37). If Cadmus was such a Phoenician, we need no longer be startled by the inland position of his new capital, and shall have no occasion for the fanciful conjecture, that he chose it with a view to form a commercial communication between distant parts of the coast,*—a destination, of which we find not the slightest hint in the ancient legends of Thebes.

It seems to be only in some such sense as that here explained, that it is possible to conceive Egyptian colonies to have been ever planted in Greece: for the expedition of Sesotiris, even if admitted to be a historical event, can scarcely serve as a foundation for a story. We would not decide indeed, whether, among the earliest inhabitants of Greece, some of totally different race from these Phoenician fugitives may not have taken nearly the same course; but settlers of purely Egyptian blood, crossing the Aegean, and founding maritime cities, appears to be inconsistent with everything we know of the national character. Here however a new question arises. It is in itself of very little importance, whether a handful of Egyptians or Phoenicians were or were not mingled with the ancient population of Greece. All that renders this inquiry interesting, is the effect which the arrival of these foreigners is supposed to have produced on the state of society in their new country. Herodotus represents the greater part of the religious notions and practices of the Greeks, the objects and forms of their worship, as derived from Egypt. When we consider that among the Greeks, as in most other nations, it was religion that called forth their arts, their poetry, perhaps even their philosophy, it will be evident how many interesting questions depended on this: and as it is the degree in which the religious and intellectual culture of the Greeks was derived from foreign sources that constituted the whole importance of the controversy, so it is the point on which the decision must finally hinge. But neither the study of Greek

---

* This is Kruse's mode of solving the difficulty, i p. 481.

mythology nor the history of Greek art, has yet arrived at such a stage of maturity, as to enable the historian to pronounce with confidence on the rival hypotheses, one of which fetches from the east what the other regards as the native growth of the Grecian soil. The difficulty is much increased, if we interpret the traditions about the Egyptian colonies in that which appears to be their most probable sense. We know something about the religion and the arts of the Egyptians, and of the Phoenicians on the coast of Syria. But as to the Phoencian conquerors of Egypt, we have no information to ascertain the relation in which they stood to the natives, and how far they were qualified to be the bearers of all that Herodotus believed Egypt to have imparted to Greece. The author from whom Diodorus drew his account of Danaus and Cadmus (fr. xl), ascribed their expulsion to the resentment and alarm excited in the Egyptians by the profaneness of the strangers, who neglected their rites, and threatened the total subversion of the national religion. If there is any truth in this statement, they must have been very ill fitted to instruct the Pelasgians in the Egyptian mysteries, and a boundless field is opened for conjecture as to the influence they exerted on the Greek mythology.

There follows an account of legends of Phoenician–Greek contact.

It may be questioned whether the policy of the Phoenicians ever led them to aim at planting independent colonies in the islands or on the continent of Greece; and whether they did not content themselves with establishing factories, which they abandoned when their attention was diverted to a different quarter. In their early expeditions, the objects of piracy and commerce appear to have been combined in the manner described by Homer and Herodotus. But it is highly probable that, wherever they came, they not only introduced the products of their own arts, but stimulated the industry and invention of the natives, explored the mineral and vegetable riches of the soil, and increased them by new plants and methods of cultivation. Undoubtedly also their sojourn, even where it was transient, was not barren of other fruits—some of which were perhaps rather noxious than useful. There are several parts of Greek mythology which bear strong marks of a Phoenician origin: and as we know that the character of their own superstition was peculiarly impure and atrocious, it seems by no means incredible, that many of the horrid rites which are described as prevailing at an early period in Greece, were derived from this source.

Beside Egyptian and Phoenicia, it is possible that the Phrygians may be entitled to some share in the honour of having contributed toward the cultivation of Greece. In the intricate legends of the Greek Archipelago we find names of fabulous beings, of a nature akin to the Telchines, and apparently standing in nearly the same relation to the Phrygians as the Telechines to the Phoenicians. Such are the Corybantes, and the Idaean Dactyls, who are connected on the one hand with the arts, on the other with the worship, of Phrygia. It might even be a not untenable hypothesis, to suppose that Pelops, if he indeed was a foreigner, belonged to the same stock; especially as we hear of Idaean Dactyls at Pisa. But perhaps it may not be necessary to go as far in order to explain the common story, without absolutely rejecting it. As the Pelasgians belonged no less to Asia than to Europe, so Pelops and his sister Niobe, who is the daughter of the Argive king Phoroneus as well as of the Lydian Tantalus (for it is idle to distinguish these mythical personages), may, perhaps, with equal truth be considered as natives of either continent: and this appears to have been, in substance, Niebuhr's solution of the difficulty.* We will not attempt to pierce further into the night of ages: we will only suggest that some traditions of the tribes which first settled in Greece may have been retained and transmitted in an altered form as accounts of subsequent expeditions and migrations: though what has been said, seems sufficient to show that the received opinion as to the foreign colonists had an independent historical groundwork.

---

*   He observes (*Kleine Schriften*, p. 370 note), 'The migration of Pelops signified nothing more than the affinity of the peoples on both sides of the Aegean'.

History and Mythology

The Heroes and Their Age

Of Thirlwall's predecessors, Clinton and Mitford were happy to treat the legends of the 'Heroic Age' as historical fact. Goldsmith, avoiding discussion of the historicity of Homeric epic, had demonstrated extremes of incredulity. Chapters 5 and 6 of Thirlwall's history clearly owe their rationale to German scholarship, in particular the application to epic poetry of Niebuhr's principle that mythology contains a kernel of historical truth and can inform the historian of 'the general condition of society, its institutions, manners and opinions'. Accordingly, the stories of Heracles represent memories of the infant civilisation's struggles against nature. In another section (not included here; vol. i, pp. 143–8), the myth of the Argonauts is said to indicate 'an opening intercourse between the opposite shores of the Aegean' (149).

The period included between the first appearance of the Hellenes in Thessaly, and the return of the Greeks from Troy, is commonly known by the name of the *heroic* age or ages. The real limits of this period cannot be exactly defined. The date of the siege of Troy is only the result of a doubtful calculation, and from what has already been said, the reader will see that it must be scarcely possible to ascertain the precise beginning of the period; but still, so far as its traditions admit of any thing like a chronological connection, its duration may be estimated at six generations, or about two hundred years. We have already described the general character of this period, as one in which a warlike race spread from the north over the south of Greece, and founded new dynasties in a number of little states; while, partly through the impulse given to the earlier settlers by this immigration, and partly in the natural progress of society, a similar state of things arose in those parts of the country which were not immediately occupied by the invaders; so that everywhere a class of nobles entirely given to martial purposes, and the principal owners of the land—whose station and character cannot perhaps be better illustrated when compared to that of the chivalrous barons of the middle ages—became prominent above the mass of the people, which they held in various degrees of subjection. The history of the heroic age is the history of the most celebrated persons belonging to this class, who, in the language of poetry, are called *heroes.* The term *hero* is of doubtful origin, though it was clearly a title of honour; but, in the poems of Homer, it is applied not only to the chiefs, but also to their followers, the freemen of lower rank, without however being contrasted with any other, so as to determine its precise meaning. In later times its use was narrowed, and in some degree altered:* it was restricted to persons, whether of the heroic or of after ages, who were believed to be endowed with a superhuman, though not a divine, nature, and who were honoured with sacred rites, and were imagined to have the power of dispensing good or evil to their worshippers; and it was gradually combined with the notion of prodigious strength and gigantic stature. Here however we have only to do with the heroes as men. The history of their age is filled with their wars, expeditions, and adventures, and this is the great mine from which the materials of the Greek poetry were almost entirely drawn. But the richer a period is in poetic materials, the more difficult it usually is to extract from it any that are fit for the use of the historian; and this is especially true in the present instance. Though what has been transmitted to us is perhaps only a minute part of the legends which sprang from this inexhaustible source, they are sufficient to perplex the inquirer by

---

*   In Homer, it is used as the German *Rechen* in the Nibelungenlied. So too in Hesiod (*Op et D.* 155–71), all the warriors before Thebes and Troy seem to be included in the name. Afterwards it was limited to the most eminent persons of the heroic age; not however to distinguish them from their own contemporaries, but to contrast them with the men of a later and inferior generation.

their multiplicity and their variations, as well as by their marvellous nature. The pains taken by the ancient compilers to reduce them to an orderly system, have only served, in most cases, to disguise their original form, and thus to increase the difficulty of detecting their real foundation. It would answer no useful purpose to repeat or abridge those legends, without subjecting them to a critical examination, for which we cannot afford room: we must content ourselves with touching on some which appear most worthy of notice, either from their celebrity, or for the light they throw on the general character of the period, or their connection, real or supposed, with subsequent historical events.

We must pass very hastily over the exploits of Bellerophon and Perseus, and we mention them only for the sake of one remark. The scene of their principal adventures is laid out of Greece, in the East. The former, whose father Glaucus is the son of Sisyphus, having chanced to stain his hands with the blood of a kinsman, flies to Argos, where he excites the jealousy of Proetus, and is sent by him to Lycia, the country where Proetus himself had been hospitably entertained in his exile. It is in the adjacent regions of Asia that the Corinthian hero proves his valour by vanquishing ferocious tribes and terrible monsters. Perseus too has been sent over the sea by his grandfather Acrisius, and his achievements follow the same direction, but take a wider range: he is carried along the coasts of Syria to Egypt, where Herodotus heard of him from the priests, and into the unknown lands of the South. There can be no doubt that these fables owed many of their leading features to the Argive colonies which were planted at a later period in Rhodes, and on the south-west coast of Asia. But still it is not improbable that the connection implied by them between Argolis and the nearest parts of Asia, may not be wholly without foundation. We proceed however to a much more celebrated name, on which we must dwell a little longer—that of Hercules. It has been a subject of long dispute, whether Hercules was a real or a purely fictitious personage; but it seems clear that the question, according to the sense in which it is understood, may admit of two contrary answers, both equally true. When we survey the whole mass of the actions ascribed to him, we find that they fall under two classes. The one carries us back to

the infancy of society, when it is engaged in its first struggles with
nature for existence and security: we see him cleaving rocks, turning
the course of rivers, opening or stopping the subterraneous outlets
of lakes, clearing the earth of noxious animals, and, in a word, by
his single arm effecting the works which properly belong to the
untied labours of a young community. The other class exhibits a
state of things comparatively settled and mature, when the first
victory has been gained, and the contest is now between one tribe
and another, for possession and dominion; we see him maintaining
the cause of the weak against the strong, of the innocent against the
oppressor, punishing wrong, and robbery, and sacrilege, subduing
tyrants, exterminating his enemies, and bestowing kingdoms on his
friends. It would be futile to inquire, who the person was to whom
the deeds of the former kind were attributed; but it is an interesting
question, whether the first conception of such a being was formed
in the mind of the Greeks by their own unassisted imagination,
or was suggested to them by a different people,—in other words,
whether Hercules, viewed in this light, is a creature of the Greek
or of foreign mythology.

It is sufficient to throw a single glance at the fabulous adventures
called the *labours* of Hercules, to be convinced that a part of them
at least belongs to the Phoenicians, and their wandering god, in
whose honour they built temples in all their principal settlements
along the coast of the Mediterranean. To him must be attributed
all the journeys of Hercules round the shores of Western Europe,
which did not become known to the Greeks for many centuries after
they had been explored by the Phoenician navigators. The number
to which those labours are confined by the legend is evidently an
astronomical period, and thus itself points to the course of the sun
which the Phoenician god represented. The event which closes the
career of the Greek hero, who rises to immortality from the flames
of the pile on which he lays himself, is a prominent feature in the
same Eastern mythology, and may therefore be safely considered
as borrowed from it.* All these tales may indeed be regarded as

---

* See Boettiger, *Kunst-Mythologie*, 37. Mueller, in the *Rheinisches Museum*,
iii, 28.

additions made at a late period to the Greek legend, after it had sprung up independently at home. But it is at least a remarkable coincidence, that the birth of Hercules is assigned to the city of Cadmus; and the great works ascribed to him, so far as they were really accomplished by human labour, may seem to correspond better with the art and industry of the Phoenicians, than with the skill and powers of a less civilised race. But in whatever way the origin of the name and the idea of Hercules may be explained, at least in that which we have distinguished as the second class of legends relating to him, he appears, without any ambiguity, as a Greek hero; and here it may be reasonably be asked, whether all or any part of the adventures they describe, really happened to a single person, who either properly bore the name of Hercules, or received it as a title of honour.

We must briefly mention the manner in which these adventures are linked together in the common story. Amphitryon, the reputed father of Hercules, was the son of Alcaeus, who is named first among the children born to Perseus at Mycenae. The hero's mother, Alcmena, was the daughter of Electryon, another son of Perseus, who had succeeded to the kingdom. In his reign, the Taphians, a piratical people who inhabited the islands called the Echinades, near the mouth of the Achelous, landed in Argolis, and carried off the king's herds. While Electryon was preparing to avenge himself by invading their land, after he had committed his kingdom and his daughter to the charge of Amphitryon, a chance like that which caused the death of Acrisius stained the hands of the nephew with his uncle's blood. Sthenelus, a third son of Perseus, laid hold of this pretext to force Amphitryon and Alcmena to quit the country, and they took refuge in Thebes: thus it happened that Hercules, though an Argive by descent, and, by his mortal parentage, legitimate heir to the throne of Mycenae, was, as to his birthplace, a Theban. Hence Boeotia is the scene of his youthful exploits: bred up among the herdsmen of Cithaeron, like Cyrus and Romulus, he delivers Thespiae from the lion which made havoc among its cattle. He then frees Thebes from the yoke of its more powerful neighbour, Orchomenos: and here we find something which has more the look of a historical tradition, though it is no less poetical in its form. The king of Orchomenos had been killed, in the sanctuary of Poseidon at Onchestus, by a Theban. His successor, Erginus, imposes a tribute on Thebes; but Hercules mutilates his heralds when they come to exact it, and then marching against Orchomenus, slays Erginus, and forces the Minyans to pay twice the tribute which they had hitherto received (Apollod. ii 4.11). According to a Theban legend, it was on this occasion that he stopped the subterraneous outlet of the Cephisus, and thus formed the lake which covered the greater part of the plain of Orchomenus (Paus. ix 38.7). In the meanwhile Sthenelus had been succeeded by his son Eurystheus, the destined enemy of Hercules and his race, at whose command the hero undertakes his labours. This voluntary subjection of the rightful prince to the weak and timid usurper is represented as an expiation, ordained by the Delphic oracle, for a fit of phrenzy, in which Hercules had destroyed his wife and children. This, as a poetical or religious fiction, is very happily conceived: but when we are seeking for a historical thread to connect the Boeotian legends of Hercules with those of Peloponnesus, it must be set entirely aside; and yet it is not only the oldest form of the story, but no other has hitherto been found or devised to fill its place with a greater appearance of probability. The supposed right of Hercules to the throne of Mycenae was, as we shall see, the ground on which the Dorians, some generations later, claimed the dominion of Peloponnesus. Yet, in any other than a poetical view, his enmity to Eurystheus is utterly inconsistent with the exploits ascribed to him in the peninsula. It is also remarkable, that while the adventures which he undertakes at the bidding are prodigious and supernatural, belonging to the first of the two classes above distinguished, he is described as during the same period engaged in expeditions which are only accidentally connected with these marvellous labours, and which, if they stood alone, might be taken for traditional facts. In these he appears in the light of an independent prince, and a powerful conqueror. He leads an army against Augeas, king of Elis, and having slain him, bestows his kingdom on one of his sons, who had condemned his father's injustice. So he invades Pylus to avenge an insult which he had received from Neleus, and puts him to death, with all his children, except Nestor, who was absent, or had escaped to Gerenia. Again he carries his conquering arms into Laconia, where he exterminates the family of the king Hippocoon, and places Tyndareus on the throne. Here, if any where in the legend of Hercules, we might seem to be reading an account of real events. Yet who can believe, that while he was overthrowing these hostile dynasties, and giving away sceptres, he suffered himself to be excluded from his own kingdom?

It was the fate of Hercules to be incessantly forced into dangerous and arduous enterprises: and hence every part of Greece is in its turn the scene of his achievements. Thus we have already seen him, in Thessaly, the ally of the Dorians, laying the foundation of a perpetual union between the people and his own descendants, as if he had either abandoned all hope of ever recovering the crown of Mycenae, or had forseen that his posterity would require the aid of the Dorians for that purpose. In Aetolia too he appears as a friend and a protector of the royal house, and fights its battles against the Thesprotians of Epirus (Apollod. ii 7.6). These perpetual wanderings, these successive alliances with so many different races, excite no surprise, so long as we view them in a poetical light, as issuing out of one source, the implacable hate with which Juno persecutes the son of Jove. They may also be understood as real events, if they are supposed to have been perfectly independent of each other, and connected only by being referred to one fabulous name. But when the poetical motive is rejected, it seems impossible to frame any rational scheme according to which they may be regarded as incidents in the life of one man, unless we imagine Hercules, in the purest spirit of knight-errantry, sallying forth in quest of adventures, without any definite object, or any impulse but that of disinterested benevolence. It will be safer, after rejecting those features in the legend which manifestly belong to Eastern religions, to distinguish the Theban Hercules from the Dorian, and the Peloponnesian, hero. In the story of each some historical fragments have most probably been preserved, and perhaps least disfigured in the Theban and Dorian legends. In those of Peloponnesus it is difficult to say to what extent their original form may not have been distorted from political motives. If we might place any reliance on them, we should be inclined to conjecture that they contain traces of the struggles by which the kingdom of Mycenae attained to that influence over the rest of the peninsula, which is attributed to it by Homer, and which we shall have occasion to notice when we come to speak of the Trojan war.

Thirlwall continues with a description of the historical and mythological elements of the stories related to Theseus, Minos and the Argonauts. Before going on to approach Homer as a source for social history, Thirlwall exposes his reader to debate about the historicity of the siege of Troy.

The reality of the siege of Troy has sometimes been questioned, we conceive, without sufficient ground, and against some strong evidence. According to the rules of sound criticism, very cogent arguments ought to be required to induce us to reject as a mere fiction a tradition so ancient, so universally received, so definite, and so interwoven with the whole mass of the national recollections, as that of the Trojan war. Even if unfounded, it must still have had some adequate occasion and motive; and it is difficult to imagine what this could have been, unless it arose out of the Greek colonies in Asia; and in this case its universal reception in Greece itself, is not easily explained. The leaders of the earliest among these colonies, which were planted in the neighbourhood of Troy, claimed Agamemnon as their ancestor; but if this had suggested the story of her victories in Asia, their scene would probably have been fixed in the very region occupied by his descendants, not in an adjacent land. On the other hand the course taken by this first (Aeolian) migration falls in naturally with a previous tradition of a conquest achieved by Greeks in this part of Asia. We therefore conceive it necessary to admit the reality of the Trojan war as a general fact; but beyond this we scarcely venture to proceed a single step. Its cause and its issue, the manner in which it was conducted, and the parties engaged in it, are all involved in an obscurity which we cannot pretend to penetrate. We find it impossible to adopt the poetical story of Helen, partly on account of its inherent improbability, and partly because we are convinced that Helen is merely a mythological person. The common account of the origin of the war has indeed been defended, on the ground that it is perfectly consistent with the manners of the age—as if a popular tale, whether true or false, could be at variance with them. The feature in the narrative which strikes us as in the highest degree improbable, setting the character of the persons out of the question, is the intercourse implied in it between Troy and Sparta. As to the heroine, it would be sufficient to raise a strong suspicion of her fabulous nature, to observe that she is classed by Herodotus with Io, and Europa, and Medea, all of them persons who, on distinct grounds, must clearly be referred to the domain of mythology. This suspicion is confirmed by all the particulars of her legend; by her birth;* by her relation to the divine Twins, whose worship seems to have been one of the most ancient forms of religion in the Peloponnesus, and especially in Laconia; and by the divine honours paid to her at Sparta, and elsewhere.† But a still stronger reason for doubting the reality of the motive assigned by Homer for the Trojan war is, that the same incident recurs in another circle of fictions, and that, in the abduction of Helen, Paris only repeats an exploit also attributed to Theseus. This adventure of the Attic hero seems to have been known to Homer; for he introduces Aethra, the mother of Theseus, whom the Dioscuri were said to have carried off from Attica, when they invaded it to recover their sister, in Helen's company at Troy. Theseus, when he came to bear her away, is said to have found her dancing in the temple of the goddess, whose image her daughter, Iphigenia, was believed to have brought home from Scythia; a feature in the legend which perhaps marks the branch of the Lacedaemonian worship to which she belonged. According to another tradition, Helen was carried off by Idas and Lynceus, the Messenian pair of heroes who answer to the Spartan Twins,—variations which seem to show that her abduction was a theme for poetry originally independent of the

---

* Homer describes her as the daughter of Jupiter, but does not mention her mother Leda, the wife of Tyndareus. The fable, that he was the daughter of Nemesis (Paus. i 33.7), sounds to us, who are only familiar with the later idea of Nemesis, as an allegorical fiction; but it may be quite as ancient as the other, perhaps originally the same as Hesiod's (Schol. Pindar *Nemean.* x 150) that she was a daughter of Oceanus and Tethys.

† Herod. vi 61. At Rhodes she was worshipped under the epithet *dendritis*, and a legend was devised to account for it (Paus. iii 19.10). Compare also the accounts of the temple which she dedicates to Illithyia (Paus. ii 22.6), of the temple of Aphrodite at Troezea (Paus. ii 32.7), with Plut. *Thes.* 20, 21.

Trojan war, but which might easily and naturally be associated with that event.

Thirlwall goes on to consider Helen as a mythological person, along with the historical view of the Trojan war.

In discussing the historical reality of the Trojan war, we have abstained from touching on a question connected with it, which is still a subject of active controversy,—the antiquity and original form of the poems which contain the earliest memorial of the event. We have thought it better to keep aloof for the present from this controversy; because, in whatever manner it may be decided, it does not seem to affect any of the opinions here advanced. However near the poet, if he is to be considered as a single one, may be supposed to have lived to the times of which he sings, it is clear that he did not suffer himself to be fettered by his knowledge of the facts. For aught we know, he may have been a contemporary of those who had fought under Achilles; but it is not the less true that he describes his principal hero as the son of a sea-goddess. He and his hearers most probably looked upon epic song as a vehicle of history, and therefore it required a popular tradition for its basis, without which it would have seemed hollow and insipid, its ornaments misplaced and its catastrophe uninteresting. But it is equally manifest that the kind of history for which he invoked the aid of Muses to strengthen his memory, was not chiefly valued as a recital of real events: that it was one in which the marvellous appeared natural, and that form of the narrative most credible which tended most to exalt the glory of his heroes. If in detached passages the poet sometimes appears to be relating with the naked simplicity of truth, we cannot ascribe any higher authority to these episodes than to the rest of the poem, and must attribute their seeming plainness and sobriety to the brevity of the space allotted to them, rather than to superior accuracy in the transmission of their contents. The campaigns of Nestor, the wars of Calydon, the expeditions of Achilles, probably appear less poetical than the battles before Troy, only because they stand in the background of the picture, as subordinate groups, and were perhaps transferred into it from other legends, in which, occupying a different place, they were exhibited in a more marvellous and poetical shape.

But though, when we are inquiring into the reality of persons and events, we can allow very little weight to the authority of Homer, there is another more important kind of truth, which we attribute to his poetry with a conviction which would not be at all shaken, even if it could be shown that he was separated from the scenes which he describes by a longer interval than has yet been assumed in any hypothesis. The kind of truth we mean is that which relates to the general condition of society, to institutions, manners and opinions. Of this kind of truth the poet's contemporaries were competent and unbiased judges. A picture which did not correspond to a state of things intelligible to them, they would have found unintelligible and uninteresting. We cannot ascribe to either of them the power of comprehending or to the poet the ambition of affecting, a learned propriety in his descriptions, and still less can it be supposed that he drew from any ideal model. It seems clear that the generation which he saw was not parted from that of which he sang by any wide break in thoughts, feeling, or social relations. Such a supposition would not only be groundless, but would be at variance with all that we know of the gradual progress of change in the earliest period of Greek history. There may perhaps be room for suspecting, that he has unwittingly passed over some gradations in the advance of society, that he has sometimes transferred to the age of his heroes what properly belonged to his own, and still oftener that he has heightened and embellished the objects which he touches; but there is no ground for the opposite suspicion, that he has anywhere endeavoured to revive an image of obsolete simplicity, or, for the sake of dramatic correctness, has suppressed any advantage in knowledge or refinement which his contemporaries possessed. What he represents most truly is the state of Grecian society near to his own day; but if we make due allowance for the effects of imperceptible changes, and for poetical colouring, we are in no danger of falling into any material error, in extending his descriptions to the whole period which we term the Heroic.

The Homeric world is not a region of enchantment, called into existence by the wand of a magician; it is at once poetical and real.

In confining our view to its real side, we do not break the charm by which it captivates the imagination. The historian's aim however is very different from the poet's: it is the province of the former to collect what the latter scatters carelessly and unconsciously over his way; to interpret and supply dark and imperfect hints. For the subjects on which the poet dwells with delight are not always the most interesting and instructive to the historical inquirer, though there are few in which his curiosity is absolutely disappointed. Homer is often minutely exact in describing artificial productions, and technical processes; while the social institutions, the moral and religious sentiments, of his age, as things universally understood, are never formally noticed, but only betrayed by accidental allusions. But the light which he affords is confined to the circle into which he draws us: it is only one period, and one stage of society, that he exhibits, and he is wholly silent as to the steps which led to it. When we desire to look back to an antecedent period, we are reduced to depend on traditions and indications, which are seldom so clear and authentic as his evidence with regard to his own age. They are not however on that account to be indiscriminately rejected; nor can his silence always be held conclusive as to things which, if they existed, must have come within his knowledge. From the materials furnished by the Homeric poems—examined, however, by the light of historical analogy, and compared with other accounts and vestiges—we shall now endeavour to trace the main features of the Heroic or Homeric form of society. The order on which we shall review them will lead us successively to consider the state of government, of manners, of religion, knowledge, and arts.

The Government and Manners of the Greeks in the Heroic Age

Thirlwall rejected Wolf's theory of a multiple authorship of the *Iliad*; he argued that it was most probably composed as a unity by one poet. For Thirlwall the *Iliad* and the *Odyssey* could profitably be read for the sake of what they can tell us about the 'infancy' of Greek society. In chapter 6 he investigated in turn the 'Government, Religion, Knowledge and Arts of the Greeks in the Heroic Age'.[1] He is interested not

only in the history of institutions and customs but also the experiences of private life; the chapter reflects the historiographical enthusiasm for the study of everyday life which emerged during the eighteenth century.[2]

The political institutions of the heroic period were not contrived by the wisdom of legislators, but grew spontaneously out of natural causes. They appear to have exhibited in every part of Greece a certain resemblance in their general outlines but the circumstances out of which they arose were probably not everywhere the same, and hence a notion of them, founded on the supposition of their complete uniformity, would probably be narrow and erroneous. The few scanty hints afforded to us on the transition from the obscure period which we may call the Pelasgian, to that with which Homer has made us comparatively familiar, do not enable us to draw any general conclusion as to the mode in which it was effected. We can just discern a warlike and adventurous race starting up, and gradually overspreading the land; but in what relation they stood to the former inhabitants, what changes they introduced in the ancient order of things, can only be conjectured from the social institutions which we find subsisting in the later period. These do not generally present traces of violent revolutions, and subjugating conquests, like those of which the subsequent history of Greece furnishes so many examples; yet it is natural to imagine that they took place occasionally, and here and there we meet with facts, or illusions, which confirm this suspicion. The distinction between slaves and freemen seems to have obtained generally, though not perhaps universally:* but there is no distinct trace that it anywhere

---

* The purchase and use of slaves indeed is repeatedly mentioned by Homer: the household of Ulysses is served by slaves, over whom their master exercises the power of life and death. But the use of such domestics was perhaps nowhere very common, except in the houses of the great, and in several parts of Greece, was not introduced till a later period. This is asserted in Herodotus (vi 137), of the Greeks in general, and of the Athenians in particular. The assertion is repeated by Timaeus (Athenaeus vi 86), with particular reference to the Locrians and Phocians. But when it is said that the Chians were the first Greeks who used purchased slaves (Theopompus in Athen. vi 88), this must be understood of a regular traffic, as on the other hand Pliny's *servitium invenere Lacedaemonii* (*NH* vii 56), applies only to the helots.

owed its origin to an invasion which deprived the natives of their liberty. As soon as war and piracy became frequent, captives, taken or bought, were employed in servile labours: chiefly, it would seem, those of the house; in those of husbandry the poor freemen did not disdain to serve the wealthier for hire. But a class of serfs, reduced to cultivate the land which they had once owned for the benefit of a foreign conqueror and either bound to it, or liable to be expelled at his pleasure, if it existed anywhere, must have been an exception to the general rule.* On the other hand a broad distinction is drawn between the common freemen and the chiefs, who form two separate classes. The latter are described by various titles, denoting their superior dignity, as, the best, the foremost, princes and elders; for this last epithet seems already to have been bestowed with relation rather to the functions of counsellors and judges than to their age. The essential quality of persons belonging to this higher order was noble birth, which implied nothing less than a connection with the gods themselves, to whom every princely house seems to have traced its origin. But though this illustrious parentage constituted one claim of the great to popular veneration, it would soon have been forgotten or neglected, unless accompanied by some visible tokens, which were not sought in pedigrees or records, but in personal advantages and merits. The legitimate chief was distinguished from the vulgar herd, of merely mortal origin, by his robust frame, his lofty stature, his majestic presence, his piercing eye, and sonorous

---

* Yet in the *Odyssey* (iv 176), Menelaus expresses his willingness to give a settlement to Ulysses and his followers, by ejecting his own subjects from one of the towns in his dominions, and planting the Ithacans in their room. This passage indeed has been condemned as spurious, because such despotic power seemed inconsistent with the ordinary relation between king and people in the heroic ages; and undoubtedly it would imply a kind of subjection very different from that in which the warriors who fought at Troy seem to have stood to their princes: yet, as a result of peculiar circumstances, it may not have been incredible; and the less, since Agamemnon, when he offers to transfer to Achilles seven towns inhabited by wealthy husbandmen, who would enrich their lord by presents and tribute, seems likewise to assume rather a property in them, than an authority over them (*Il.* ix 149). And the same thing may be intimated when it is said that Peleus bestowed a great people, the Dolopes of Phthia, on Phoenix (*Il.* ix 483).

voice, but still more by the virtues which these bodily endowments promised, by skill in warlike exercises, patience under hardship, contempt of danger, and love of glorious enterprises. Prudence in council, readiness in invention, and fluency of speech, though highly valued, were not equally requisite to preserve general respect. But though the influence of the nobles depended on the degree in which they were thus gifted and accomplished, it also needed the support of superior wealth. It was this which furnished them with the means of undertaking the numerous adventures in which they proved their valour, while their martial achievements commonly increased both their frame and their riches, by the booty which rewarded a successful expedition. If the arm of a single chief could often turn the fortune of a battle, and put to flight a host of common men, this was undoubtedly owed not solely to his extraordinary prowess, but to the strength of his armour, the temper of his weapons, the fleetness of the steeds, which transported his chariot from one part of the field to another, and secured for him the foremost place, whether in the flight or the pursuit.

The kingly form of government appears to have been the only one known in the heroic age. Its origin is ascribed by Aristotle to the free choice of the people, which first conferred the royal dignity on the man who had rendered some important service to the public, by the introduction of new arts, or by martial achievements, or who had collected a body of settlers, and assigned to them portions of his own or of conquered lands. The latter supposition, unless it carries us back to the very beginning of civil society, is only applicable to the case of a migration or invasion, which implies the previous acknowledgement of a prince or chief. But that the kingly office was originally bestowed by popular election, as the reward of personal merit, seems to be a conjecture which wants historical foundation. Nor do we find among the ancient Greeks any trace of a distinction as is said to have existed among the ancient Germans, between kings chosen for their illustrious birth, and commanders chosen for their valour: both qualities were expected to meet in the same person: in both the king was conspicuous among the nobles, as the latter were above the multitude. It is however probable, that the monarchical form of government arose from the patriarchical, with and out of the warlike and adventurous character of the heroic age. Where the people was almost always in arms, the office of leader naturally became permanent. The royal houses may sometimes have been founded by wealthy and powerful strangers, but it is quite as easy to conceive that they often grew by insensible degrees into reputation and authority. Homer mentions certain divisions of the nation, in a way implying that they were elements which entered into the composition of every Greek community. Nestor advises Agamemnon to marshal his army according to the larger or smaller bodies in which the families were collected, in order that each might derive aid and encouragement from the presence of its neighbour (*Il.* ii 362): not to be included in one is the mark of an outlaw or a homeless vagrant (*Il.* ix 63). It is probable that in the heroic age these tribes and clans were still regarded more as natural than as political associations, and that in a yet earlier period the heads of each exercised a patriarchical rule over its members. The public sacrifices, which in the remotest, certainly not less than in later times, formed the bond of their union were, it may be supposed, celebrated by the chief of the principal family, and these priestly functions seem to have been one of the most ancient branches of the regal office,* as they were retained the longest. The person to whom they belonged would naturally assume the rest as occasion required. But the causes which determined the precedence of a particular family in each tribe, and in a state, when several tribes were united in one body, may have been infinitely varied, and in almost all cases lie beyond the reach of historical investigation.

The nature and prerogatives of the heroic sovereignty however are subject to less doubt than its origin. The command in war, the performance of those sacrifices which were not appropriate to particular priests, and the administration of justice, are mentioned by Aristotle as the three main functions of heroic kings. It must have been from the discharge of the first that they derived the greatest part of their power. Their authority, if feeble at home, was strengthened by the obedience which they were able to exact in the field, and, if their enterprizes were successful, by the renown of their

---

* See the whole description of the sacrifice at Pylus, *Od.* iii.

exploits; in the division of the spoil their share was usually increased
by a present previously selected from the common mass. The
religious rites which they were entitled to celebrate in behalf of the
people, if they invested their persons with some degree of sanctity,
can have added little to their real influence. Nor was this greatly
increased by their judicial character; not merely because comparatively few occasions occurred to call it into action, but because it
did not belong to them exclusively. Notwithstanding the fabulous
reputation of Minos and Rhadamanthys, it must be inferred, from
the manner in which Homer describes and alludes to the administration of justice, that the heroic kings did not usually try causes
alone, and that in their decisions they expressed the judgment of
their assessors, if not of the multitude. In the representation of a
trial, which fills one compartment in the shield of Achilles, the
elders are seated on polished stones which were ranged, in a sacred
circle, in the market place; the crowd stands without, kept in order
by the heralds, but no king appears to preside. On the other hand,
among the royal prerogatives which Telemachus is said to retain in
the absence of Ulysses, the judicial office is expressly mentioned,
as a source of honour and profit; not however in a way implying
that he exercised it alone. Achilles, swearing by the sceptre which
he has received from the herald, speaks of it as passing through the
hands of judges in the discharge of their duty, just as we see it used
by those in the shield. The king seems only to have occupied the
most distinguished place on these occasions. So when Telemachus
convenes an assembly in Ithaca, he takes his seat in the market
place on his paternal throne, while the elders reverently make way
for him. They must be conceived here to occupy a circle, like that
of the judges in the scene on the shield: the ring of stones may be
fairly presumed to have been a common and permanent ornament
of the public places where all assemblies, judicial or deliberative,
were held, and it marks the ordinary limits of the kingly power. It is
evident that the kings took no measures, and transacted no affairs,
in their official capacity, without the assistance and the sanction
of the chiefs and the people. In the camp indeed Agamemnon
frequently summons a select council of the princes, who may be
considered either as his generals, or allies. But even there, on great

occasions, the whole army is assembled, and in peace there seems to have been no formal and regular distinction between a popular assembly, and a senate: every public meeting might be regarded in either light. The great men who formed the inner circle were the counsellors who debated; but no freeman was excluded from the outer space; and the presence of the multitude must have had some influence on all proceedings. Even at the trial the heralds do not prevent them from venting their feelings; and their clamour seems to have had the greater weight, in proportion as their interests were affected by the result of their deliberation (*Od.* iii 150).

Alcinous is described in the Odyssey as king of all the Phaeacians, and yet as only one of thirteen chiefs, who all bear the same title; he speaks of himself rather as the first among equals, than as if he belonged to a higher order. In Ithaca, though there was one acknowledged sovereign, many bore the name of king, and in the vacancy of the throne might aspire to the supreme dignity. There seems to be no good reason for doubting that these instances represent the ordinary relation of the kings to the nobles, nor for suspecting that they are less applicable to the earlier times, than to a period when the royal authority was on the decline: but here it may be especially necessary to remember the remark with which we set out, and to be on our guard against laying down any immutable rule and standard for the power of the heroic kings. Though their functions indeed were pretty accurately determined by custom, the extent of their influence was not regulated by the same measure, but must have varied according to their personal character and circumstances. The love and respect of the people, acquired by valour, prudence, gentleness, and munificence, might often raise the king above the nobles, by a much greater distance than his constitutional prerogatives interposed between them: though royalty might immediately confer little solid power, it furnished means, which a vigorous and skilful hand might apply to the purposes of personal aggrandisement. 'It is no bad thing for a man,' says Telemachus, 'to be a king; his house presently grows rich, and he himself rises to honour.' Some advantages arising from the discharge of the kingly office have been already mentioned; there were others, perhaps less brilliant, but more definite and certain. The most important of these was the domain, which, as it was originally the gift of the people, seems to have been attached to the station, and not to have been the private property of the person; for Telemachus is described as retaining the domains of Ulysses, among other rights of the crown, which he was nevertheless in danger of losing, if he should not be permitted to succeed his father (*Od.* xi 185); but even his enemy Eurymachus, who wishes to exclude him from the throne, declares that no one shall deprive him of his patrimony (*Od.* i 402). Presents appear to have constituted another part of the royal revenue, important enough to be mentioned by Agamemnon, as the chief profit to be expected from the towns which he proposed to transfer to Achilles; but whether they were stated and periodical, or merely voluntary and occasional, is uncertain.* Achilles brands Agamemnon with an epithet signifying that he was one of those kings who devoured the substance of his people; and Alcinous seems to assert a power very like that of taxing the Phaeacians at his pleasure.† The administration of justice seems always to have been requited with a present from the parties. The banquets to which the kings were invited, are more than once noticed, as a valuable, at least an agreeable, pertinent of their station (*Od.* xi 185; *Il.* xii 311).

The crown appears to have been everywhere hereditary, according to the general usage, though the observance of this usage might depend on the age and character of the person, whose birth gave him a claim to the succession. The ordinary practice is recognised even in the case of Telemachus, which forms a seeming exception to it. It is indeed represented as uncertain, whether the young prince shall finally wield his father's sceptre in his own right; but while the fate of Ulysses remains unknown, his son continues to enjoy the royal honours and revenues, and even Antinous admits, that his birth gives him a presumptive title to the throne. The uncertainty, in this instance, seems to have arisen, not from the want of an acknowledged law, or custom, to regulate the succession, but from the peculiar situation of the rightful heir. The general usage is confirmed by the cases in which the aged parent resigns the reins

---

* The *liparchai themistes*, *Il.* ix 156, may be considered as stated dues.
† *Od* xiii 14. It may, however, mean a purely voluntary contribution.

of government to his son, as Ulysses reigns over Ithaca in the lifetime of his father Laertes, and Peleus sinks into a private station,
in which he needs the protection of Achilles. Such instances prove
that personal vigour was necessary to maintain the royal dignity;
and in general the king's legal prerogatives, unless supported by the
qualities of the man, were probably a very feeble restraint on the
independence of the nobles. Most of the great families seem to have
resided in the same town which contained the royal mansion, which
frequently stood on a fortified height, though we also find frequent
mention of their sequestered rural habitations.* But it would appear
that a long absence from the town was unusual, and was regarded
as a kind of exile (*Od.* xi 198). Homer affords no glimpse of a mode
of life among the heroic nobles at all resembling that of the feudal
barons, nor of holds from which they sallied forth on predatory
excursions: there may be more room to imagine, that, at a distance
from the capital, they exercised a separate jurisdiction, as the heads
of their tribes or clans.

The word answering to *law* in the language of the later Greeks,
does not occur in the Homeric poems, nor do they contain any
allusion which might lead us to suppose that any assemblies ever
met for the purpose of legislation. Rights, human and divine (*dike*
and *themis*), were fired only by immemorial usage, confirmed and
expounded by judicial decisions: in most cases perhaps the judges
had no guide but principles of natural equity. These might have
been sufficient for such a stage of society, if they could have been
uniformly enforced. But unless where the king was able and willing
to afford protection and redress, the rich and powerful seem to
have been subject to no more effectual restraint than the fear of
divine anger, or of public opinion. These motives were both sufficient to check the licence of the suitors in the absence of Ulysses.
Phoenix in his youth had quarrelled with his father, and had
thought of murdering him; but some friendly deity withheld him,
by reminding him of the obloquy, the reproach, and the foul name
of parricide which he would incur by the deed. The state appears not
to have interfered in private differences, unless the parties agreed to

---

*   *Od.* xviii 358, xi 188, xxiv 208, iv 517.

submit their cause to a public tribunal; such a consent is expressly mentioned in the description of the trial in the shield of Achilles. The whole community however was interested in suppressing quarrels, which threatened to disturb the public peace, and must therefore have compelled one who had suffered a wrong to accept the compensation established by custom from the aggressor. Among a people of strong passions and quick resentment, where the magistrate did not undertake to avenge an injury offered to one of his subjects as an offence to himself, there would have been no end of bloodshed, had not a more peaceful mode of atonement been substituted by common agreement. Accordingly even the vengeance of a family which had been deprived of a kinsman by violence, might be redeemed at a stipulated price. Ajax, when he would set the implacable anger of Achilles in the strongest light, observes, that a man is used to accept a compensation from the murderer of his brother or his son, so that the one remains in his country, after having paid a heavy price, and the vindictive spirit of the kinsman who receives it is staid. An instinctive religious feeling, deeply rooted in the bosom of the Greek, though easily overpowered by the violence of his passions, a feeling which shrank from the stain of the kindred blood, as loathsome even to the gods, concurred with the motive of general expediency in introducing this usage: for that feeling, especially in earlier times, embraced all freemen who were connected together by the ties of civil society, the rights of intermarriage, and communion in public worship. From this feeling also arose a practice, which Herodotus describes as prevailing among the Lydians and Phrygians, as well as the Greeks,—that the manslayer withdrew into a foreign land, and did not return to his country, till he had been purified by some expiatory rites. Homer indeed, though he frequently notices this species of exile, nowhere speaks of religious ceremonies accompanying it; but at least the antiquity of the religious sentiment which they imply seems unquestionable.*
Legends which appear to be very ancient, since the custom they refer

---

* Whether such rites are distinctly alluded to by Homer, depends on the reading of *Il*. xxiv 482, where Mueller (*Dorians* ii 8.6 note m in the English translation) infers from the Scholiast that we ought to read *hagiteo* for *haphneiou*. But propitiary sacrifices are mentioned in *Il*. ix 500.

to is never mentioned in the historical period, describe a voluntary servitude as part of the expiation. It is clear that it would be easier to effect a compromise in the case of undesigned homicide, than of a deliberate murder; yet the voluntary exile seems to have been quite as usual in the former as in the latter. A kind of sanctity seems to have been attached to the person of the fugitive, and it was deemed almost sacrilegious to refuse him shelter.

Acts considered as offences against the community were probably of rare occurrence, and it was only in extraordinary cases that they were visited with capital punishment. Eurymachus, in the name of the suitors, threatens Halitherses with a mulct for his officious interference. It is apparently a sudden irregular burst of popular indignation to which Hector alludes, when he regrets that the Trojans had not spirit enough to cover Paris with a mantle of stones. This however was also one of the ordinary formal modes of punishment for the great public offences. It may have been originally connected with the same feeling—the desire of avoiding the pollution of bloodshed—which seems to have suggested the practice of burying criminals alive, with a scantling of food by their side. Though Homer makes no mention of this horrible usage, the example of the Roman vestals affords reason for believing that, in ascribing it to the heroic ages, Sophocles followed an authentic tradition. Religious associations seem also to have given rise to the practice, which as likewise common to Greece and Italy, of hurling offenders down a precipice: they were perhaps originally regarded rather as victims devoted to propriate the anger of the gods, than as debtors to human justice.

The mutual dealings of independent states were not regulated by sturdier principles than those of individuals. Consciousness of a distinct national existence, and of certain rights incident to it, manifested itself, not uniformly and consistently, but only on particular occasions, and under accidental impulses. It seems not to have exerted itself in restraining individuals in one community from attacking the members of another, between which and their own no hostility had been previously declared, or known to exist. The case however was different, when two states were not only at peace, but in alliance, or intimate amity, with each other. The people of Ithaca was violently incensed against the father of Antinous, and was with difficulty restrained from putting him to death, and confiscating his property, because he had joined the Taphian freebooters in molesting the Thesprotians, a friendly nation (*Od.* xvi 428). Piracy was everywhere an honourable occupation: and though restitution was sometimes demanded, in the name of the state, for piratical aggressions which injured persons of high station, it is probable that, when the sufferers were of inferior rank, they were left to right themselves as they could. The war between Pylus and Elis, in which Nestor performed his first feat of arms, is represented to have arisen from an unprovoked attack on the part of the Epeans, who took advantage of the defenceless condition in which their neighbours had been left by the invasion of Hercules. In this instance the Pylians retaliated by a sudden inroad into the Elean territory. In common cases, especially where the countries lay wider apart, it was perhaps more usual first to demand reparation. Heralds, who formed a distinct class, and whose office was accounted sacred, and seems often to have been hereditary, carried on communications between hostile states; but it does not appear that they were employed, like the Italian Fetials, to make formal declarations of war.

Partial associations among neighbouring states were very early formed, for purposes, partly religious, partly political, of which we shall have occasion to speak hereafter. The Trojan war was, or at least was very early represented as, a national enterprise, and at least the legend contributed to awaken the consciousness of a natural unity in the several members of the nation. The name of Hellen indeed, by which this unity was afterwards denoted, had not in the Homeric age become generally prevalent, though it seems then already to have been extended beyond the district of Thessaly, to which it was first confined, to the whole of Greece north of the Isthmus. Its place is most frequently supplied by that of Achaeans. Nor does the term *barbarous* appear to have been yet applied to nations, or to have implied any notion of intellectual or moral inferiority: in Homer it is only used as an epithet of language seemingly however to signify, not a merely a strange, but also an uncouth speech; as the rude sounds of the Sintians are mentioned with evident consciousness of a more harmonious language. But the poet seems to have felt the place which his people filled in the scale of nations, the advantage of their social state over a solitary Cyclopean life, and over the savage manners of the Sicels: and on the other hand, the higher rank which the Egyptians and the Phoenicians had attained in knowledge and the arts. The time was yet to come, though the poet himself was its harbinger, when the contrast between Greek and barbarian should be thought to swallow up all other distinctions in the human race.

The laws and institutions of a people can never be wholly separated from the history of its manners, and are most intimately connected with it in a period, when, as among the Greeks of the heroic age, law and custom have not yet been discriminated and are expressed by the same word. Still it is in the relations which afford the widest range for individual freedom that national character is most clearly unfolded. We shall here touch on a few, which may serve to mark the character of the Greeks, and the stage which society had reached among them, in the period which Homer describes.

The intercourse between the sexes, though much more restricted than by modern European usages, was perhaps subject to less restraint than in the later times of Greece. If it is entirely destitute of the chivalrous devotion which has left so deep a tinge in our manners, it displays more of truth and simplicity in the degree of respect which the stronger sex pays to the weaker. Before marriage, young persons of different sex and family saw each other only in public, and then at a distance, except when some festival might chance to bring them nearer to each other: as a picture of public rejoicing in the Iliad, exhibits youths and virgins of rank linked together in the dance, as well as promiscuously joining in a vintage procession (xviii 567, 593). But the simplicity of the heroic way of life not unfrequently drew the maiden out of doors to discharge various household offices, which were afterwards confined to slaves; for it was thought no more degrading to a young princess to carry her urn to the fountain,* than for her brother to tend his father's

---

*   *Od.* vii 20, x 107, xv 428; Pindar *Ol.* vi 67.

flocks and herds.* It was to an occasion still more homely, according to modern prejudices, that Ulysses is represented as owing his first meeting with the daughter of king Alcinous. And it seems to have been not unusual for young women of the highest quality to attend on the guests of the family in situations which appear strangely revolting to modern delicacy.† The father disposed of the maiden's hand with absolute authority: but yet it does not seem that the marriage contract was commonly regarded in the light of a bargain and sale (Cf. *Od.* xv 367 and xviii 279). Presents were interchanged, probably proportioned on both sides to the means of the parties. If the connection was dissolved by the wife's infidelity, her friends seem to have been bound to restore what they had received (*Od.* viii 318); and if the wife, or the widow (*Od.* iii 133), was forced, without her fault, to return to her father's house, she was entitled to carry her portion back with her. But in this age of heroic enterprise, wealth, and even rank or birth, did not perhaps, more powerfully recommend a suitor, than strength, courage, and dexterity in manly sports and martial exercises; and these qualities seem often to have been tried by a public competition, or by the undertaking of some difficult adventure (Apollod. l 9.12.1). It accords with this usage, that in many parts of Greece, as among the ancient Romans, the nuptial ceremony wore the show of a forcible abduction of the bride.‡

Homer has drawn a pleasing picture of maidenly simplicity, filial

---

*   *Od.* xiii 223 and Eustathius *Il.* vi 25.

†   Thus in *Od.* iii 464, Nestor's daughter is said to have assisted Telemachus in bathing, anointing, and dressing himself; and in *Il.* v 905, Hebe appears to render like services to Mars. In *Od.* vi 210, we find Nausicaa ordering her female attendants to attend of Ulysses for the same purpose; but the hero declines their assistance, expressly on the same move which, according to our feelings, should have prevented it from being offered. Yet almost immediately after, in the house of Alcinous, he gladly accepts from them the same attendance which his son is described as receiving from Pericaste. A comparison of these data seems to prove that the common usage cannot have included any thing grossly offensive, even to our more refined conceptions of decency.

‡   This may be inferred, not merely from the Spartan and Cretan usages, but from the religious rites and legends founded on this custom. It is interesting to observe the close resemblance between the Spartan usage described by Plutarch (*Lycurgus*, 15), and that of the modern Circassians related by Klaproth, *Tableau de Caucase*, p. 80.

tenderness, and hospitable kindness, in the person of the Phaeacian princess Nausicaa, one of his most amiable creations: yet he seems to dwell with still greater satisfaction on the matronly dignity and conjugal devotion, which command our respect and admiration in a Penelope, an Arete, and an Andromache. If, indeed, we should draw out notions as to the state of domestic society in the heroic age from these characters, we might be in danger of estimating it too favourably. But the poet himself furnished hints which may serve to correct this impression, especially when combined with certain mythical traditions, which, however fabulous in their origin, show the view which the later Greeks took of the manners of their ancestors. The stories of the loves of the gods, the adventures of a crowd of heroines, like Tyro, and Aethra, Creusa, and Coronis, seem clearly to intimate, that female purity was not very highly valued. Nausicaa calmly declares, that she herself disapproves of stolen interviews between maidens and their lovers, and that she is therefore the more desirous of avoiding the suspicions which she would certainly incur, if she were seen accompanied by a stranger on her return to the town. In like manner numberless tales of the heroic mythology, such as those of Helen, and Clytaemnestra, Antaea, Phaedra, and Alcmena, suggest the conclusion, that the faithlessness of the wife—which was undoubtedly often provoked, as in the family of Phoenix (*Il.* ix 450; cf. *Od.* i 433, *Il.* v 71), by the inconstancy of the husband—was not considered either as an event of rare occurrence, or an offence of great enormity. And here again the Homeric poems seem to confirm the inference, not only by the respect with which we find Helen treated by the family of her paramour, but by the manner in which she is introduced in the Odyssey, which still more plainly marks the wide difference between the feelings of the ancient Greeks, and those of modern civilised Europeans, in this respect. She there appears restored to her home and to her rank, enjoying the unabated confidence and esteem of her injured husband, and neither afflicted by the consciousness of her fault, nor blushing to allude to it.

One of the noblest and most amiable sides of the Greek character is the readiness with which it lent itself to construct intimate and durable friendships; and this is a feature no less prominent in the earliest than in the latest times. It was indeed connected with the comparatively low estimation in which female society was held; but the devotedness and constancy with which these attachments were maintained was not the less admirable and engaging. The heroic companions whom we find celebrated, partly by Homer and partly in traditions, which, if not of equal antiquity were grounded on the same feeling, seem to have but one heart and soul, with scarcely a wish or object apart, and only to live, as they are always ready to die, for one another. It is true that the relation between them is not always one of perfect equality: but this is a circumstance, which, while it often adds a peculiar charm to the poetical description, detracts little from the dignity of the idea which it presents. Such were the friendships of Hercules and Iolaus, of Theseus and Pirithous, of Orestes and Pylades: and though these may owe the greater part of their fame to the later epic, or even dramatic, poetry, the moral groundwork undoubtedly subsisted in the period to which the tradition referred. The argument of the Iliad mainly turns on the affection of Achilles for Patroclus, whose love for the greater hero is only tempered by reverence for his higher birth and his unequalled prowess. But the mutual regard which united Idomeneus and Meriones, Diomedes and Sthenelus, though, as the persons themselves are less important, it is kept more in the back-ground, is manifestly viewed by the poet in the same light. The idea of a Greek hero seems not to have been thought complete, without such a brother in arms by his side.

It was a natural effect of the unsettled state of society in this period, that every stranger was looked upon either as an enemy or a guest. If he threw himself on those among whom he came, no other title was requisite to insure him a hospitable reception. When a traveller appears at the threshold of a princely hall, the only anxiety of the master of the house is, lest he should have been kept waiting at his gate. No question is asked as to the occasion of his coming, unless he has partaken of the best cheer which the mansion can furnish: and then the inquiries addressed to him imply friendly curiosity, rather than suspicion or distrust. Indeed, it was scarcely possible that any disclosure of his condition and purposes could defeat his claim to friendly entertainment. When Telemachus arrives at Pylus by sea, after he has shared the banquet of the Pylians, Nestor asks him whether he is voyaging with any fixed object, or merely roving over the sea as a pirate, bent on indiscriminate mischief. When the character of a stranger was united with that of the suppliant, it commanded still greater respect. The stranger and suppliant, says Alcinous to Ulysses, stand in place of a brother to a man who has the slightest share of right feeling. It is elsewhere mentioned as a motive for observing the laws of hospitality, that the gods sometimes visit the cities of men in the likeness of strangers (*Od.* xvii 485). If the suppliant could seat himself at the hearth, his person was deemed particularly sacred, and his request could scarcely be rejected without impiety. Numerous occasions of this kind were supplied by the chances of war, domestic feuds, and sudden provocations, which in the quick temper of the Greeks, easily kindled a flame only to be quenched by blood. And these accidents appear frequently to have led to a close and permanent connection between families seated in distant lands, which might be transmitted through many genera-tions. In an episode of the Iliad, the ties of hospitality, which subsist between the houses of an Argive and a Lycian chief, are represented as of sufficient force to restrain them, though before personally unknown to each other, from a hostile conflict. An interchange of armour ratifies the agreement, which the two heroes make, to shun each other's path thenceforward in the battle.

The convivial usages of the Greeks present an advantageous contrast to the gross intemperance which prevails in the banquets of the northern Europeans at a corresponding period of their social progress. The guests took their places on seats which were ranged along the walls of the banqueting room, and a separate table was set before each. An ablution, such as is now practiced throughout the East, uniformly preceded the repast. The fare, even in the houses of the great, was of the simplest kind: in the luxurious palace of Alcinous the only preparations for a feast, described by a poet, consist of the sheep, the hogs, and the oxen, which are slaughtered for the occasion.* A guest sometimes sent a part of his portion, as

---

* On the fare of the heroes, see Athenaeus i 45; cf. *Od.* xxi 332, xix 113, 536; *Il.* xvi 747.

a mark of respect, to another table. After the cravings of nature had been satisfied, the bowls indeed were to be made in honour of the gods. But the glory of the feast was not held to depend on a lengthened carouse: its appropriate ornaments were the song and dance. The presence of the bard was almost indispensible at every great entertainment: but the time was not wholly spent in listening to his strains. Alcinous, at the conclusion of the banquet, leads out his guests, after they have been satiated with the lyre, and the song of Demodocus, in the hall, to an open place, where they first amuse themselves with trials of strength in gymnastic exercises. A space is then carefully levelled for a dance, which is exhibited by youths practised in the art, under the control of judges accustomed to preside over such public amusements, and accompanied by the bard with a sportive lay, which perhaps interpreted the movements of the dancers to the spectators. Finally, at the command of Alcinous, two other performers, of incomparable agility, execute an extraordinary feat of leaping and dancing, which terminates the entertainment amid a tumult of applause. Even the suitors, who are continually feasting at the expense of Ulysses, are never represented as drinking to excess:* and among the abusive epithets which Achilles, in the height of his passion, applies to Agamemnon, the foremost is, heavy with wine (compare *Od.* xix 122).

Hospitality among the Greeks was not confined to the opulent. It was not exercised only by such men as the wealthy Axylus, who had a house by the way-side, which he kept open to all comers. Eumaeus, though in a humble and dependent station, speaks of the relief which he affords to the distressed, as the object which he holds of the first importance, next to the necessary provision for his own wants (*Od.* xv 373). None but men callous to shame and piety, like the most boorish and ignorant of the Ithacan suitors, are capable of treating the poor and destitute with disrespect, and there are powers, both above and in the lower world, ever watching to avenge such wrongs (*Od.* xvii 475). No less amiable is the indulgence with which slaves, though wholly in the power of their masters, appear to

---

* Compare *Od.* I 150 ff. and xvii 605. There seems to be no ground whatever for the conjecture of Eustathius on *Od.* xx 391.

have been treated in well-regulated families. The visible approbation with which the poet mentions the kindness shown by Laertes and his wife to their domestics,* marks the general tone of feeling that prevailed on this subject among his countrymen. Even the severity with which Ulysses punishes the wantonness of his slaves, seems to imply that their condition left them a title to a certain degree of respect, which they could only forfeit by their own misconduct.

It is the more necessary, for the sake of justice, to observe all these indications of compassionate and benevolent affections in the Greek character, as it must be owned that, if the friendship of the Greek was warm, and his hospitality large, his anger was fierce, and his enmity ruthless. He was indeed rather resentful than vindictive; though easily provoked, he might be appeased without much difficulty. His law of honour did not compel him to treasure up in his memory the offensive language which might be addressed to him by a passionate adversary, not to conceive that it left a stain which could only be washed away by blood. Even for real and deep injuries he was commonly willing to accept a pecuniary compensation (*Il.* ix 635, 526). But as long as it lasted, his resentment overpowered every other feeling, was regardless of the most sacred ties, and rushed at once to the most violent excess. At a very early age Patroclus has killed his young playmate in a fit of passion, occasioned by a quarrel at their boyish game. Phoenix has had great difficulty in refraining from murdering his father, to revenge a curse which he had himself provoked by a deliberate injury. Ulysses, in one of his fictitious narratives of his own adventures, relates that he had lain in wait with a companion in the dark, and had assassinated a person who had shown a disposition to deprive him of his share in the booty brought from Troy. But even such examples are scarcely sufficient to prepare us for the extreme ferocity of the usages of war, which prevailed among the Greeks of the heroic age, and perhaps cannot be very well reconciled with other features of their social state, unless it be supposed that they had arisen in a still ruder period, and that custom had contributed to extinguish the sense of humanity, which on other occasions was

---

*   *Od.* i 432, xv 365, xviii 323, xxi 225.

quickly wakened. In battle, quarter seems never to have been given, except with a view to the ransom of the prisoner. Agamemnon, in the Iliad, reproaches Menelaus with unmanly softness, when he is on the point of sparing a fallen enemy, and himself puts the suppliant to the sword: and the poet describes the deed in language which shows that he approves of it. The armour of the slain constituted a valuable part of the spoil, and was uniformly stripped off by the conquerors. But hostility did not end here; the naked corpse became the object of an obstinate struggle; if it remained in the power of the enemy, it was deprived of burial, and exposed to the vultures and ravenous beasts; and was not unfrequently mutilated. It was indeed only distinguished persons who were subject to such treatment: an armistice was usually requested, and readily granted to the defeated party, for the purpose of celebrating the obsequies of their friends (*Il.* vii 409). But the indignities offered to the body of Hector by Achilles were not an extraordinary example of hostile rage: for Hector himself intended to inflict similar outrages on the corpse of Patroclus (*Il.* xviii 176 cf. xvii 39): and it is mentioned as a signal of respect paid by Achilles to Eetion, whose city he had sacked without any remarkable provocation, that after slaying him, he abstained from spoiling his remains, and honoured them with funeral rites. On the other hand the sacrifice which Achilles makes to the shade of Patroclus, of twelve Trojan prisoners, whom he had taken alive in the battle, for the purpose of slaughtering them at the funeral pile, was certainly not authorised by the established maxims of warfare, any more than the use of poisoned weapons, to which the poet alludes with manifest disapprobation (*Od.* i 263).

The fate of a captured city was fixed in an equally merciless spirit, and by a perhaps still more inflexible rule. All the males capable of bearing arms were exterminated: the women and children were dragged away, to be divided among the victors, as the most valuable part of the spoil. And the evils of slavery were no doubt often aggravated by a partition, which tore a family asunder, and scattered its members over distant quarters of a foreign land. Homer describes a scene which was probably familiar to his contemporaries, when he compares the flood of tears drawn from Ulysses by his painful recollections, with the weeping of a woman, torn from the body of her husband, who had just fallen in defence of his city, and hurried along by the captors, who quicken her steps by striking her back and shoulders with their spears (*Od.* viii 528). Yet the sanctuaries of the gods sometimes afforded an asylum which was respected on these occasions by the conquerors. Thus Maro, the priest of Apollo, was saved with his family from the common destruction, in which the Ciconians of Ismarus were involved by Ulysses; for he dwelt within the precincts sacred to the god: yet he redeemed himself by a heavy ransom. The priest of Apollo who occasions the quarrel in the Iliad, was not so fortunate: he loses his daughter in the sack of Thebe, and only recovers her through the extraordinary interference of the god.

Having investigated the political and social implications of the Homeric poems, Thirlwall goes on to examine what mythology says about the earliest manifestations of Greek religion, the connection between religion and morality and the traces of monotheism in Greek relgion. His assessment of Homeric civilisation is concluded with a discussion of the level of artistic cultivation that can be detected in the poems.

A
HISTORY OF GREECE.

BY

CONNOP THIRLWALL, D.D.

Bishop of St David's

FORMERLY FELLOW OF TRINITY COLLEGE. CAMBRIDGE.

VOL. II.

H. Corbould. Del.

E. Finden. sc.

Themistocles at the hearth of Admetus.

p. 383.

London.
PRINTED FOR LONGMAN, BROWN, GREEN & LONGMAN'S PATERNOSTER ROW
AND JOHN TAYLOR, UPPER GOWER STREET.

CHAPTER FOUR

Colonisation and Culture

The Colonies of the Greeks, and the Progress of Art and
Literature from the Homeric Age to the Persian War
(vol. ii, chapter 12, pp. 97–9, 103–5, 108–16, 127–9)   73

**In this chapter Thirlwall combines an investigation of Greek colonisation with
an investigation of the art and literature of the early Greeks, suggesting that the
former led to vigorous developments in the latter, as well as innovation in political
institutions. The inevitable shift from hereditary government to democratic
government begins in this period: the shift away from aristocracy, he claims, and the
spirit of competition between 'oligarchy' and 'commonalty', provided the essential
conditions for the blossoming of the 'Ionian genius'. In this section he considers for
the first time the potential benefits of federal government, which emerge more fully
in volume v as an important theme in his history.**

The migrations of Greek colonists were commonly undertaken with
the approbation and encouragement of the states from which they
issued; and it frequently happened that the motive of the expedition
was one, in which the interest of the mother country was mainly
concerned: as when the object was to relieve it of superfluous hands,
or of discontented and turbulent spirits. But it was seldom that the
parent state looked forward to any more remote advantage from the
colony or that the colony expected or desired any from the parent
state. There was in most cases nothing to suggest the feeling of
dependence on the one side or a claim of authority in the other. The
sons, when they left their home to shift for themselves on a foreign
shore, carried with them only the blessing of their fathers, and felt
themselves completely emancipated from their control. Often the
colony became more powerful than its parent, and the distance

between them was generally so great as to preclude all attempts to enforce submission. But though they were not connected by the bands of mutual interest, or by a yoke laid by the powerful on the weak, the place of such relations was supplied by the gentler and nobler ties of filial affection and religious reverence, and by usages, which, springing out of these feelings, stood in their room, and tended to suggest them, where they were wanting. Except in the few cases where the emigrants were forced, as outcasts, from their native land, they cherished the remembrance of it as a duty, prescribed not merely by nature, but by religion. The colony regarded its prosperity as mainly depending on the favour of the tutelary gods of the state to which it owed its birth. They were invited to share the newly conquered land, and the temples were commonly dedicated to them in the new citadel, resembling as nearly as possible, in form and position, those with which they were honoured in the mother country: their images here renewed the old model; and it is not improbable that the priests who ministered to them were sometimes brought from their ancient seats.* The sacred fire, which was kept constantly burning on the public hearth of the colony, was taken from the altar of Vesta in the council-hall of the elder state. The founder of a colony, who might be considered as representing its parent city, was honoured after his death with sacred rites, as a being of a higher order: and when the colony in its turn became parent, it usually sought a leader from the original mother-country, to direct the planting of the new settlement. The same reverential feeling manifested itself more regularly in embassies and offerings sent by the colony to honour the festivals of the parent city, and in the marks of respect shown to its citizens who represented it on similar occasions in the colony. But the most valuable fruit of this feeling was a disposition to mutual good offices in seasons of danger and distress.

With regard to the position of the colonists in their new country,

---

* The existence of this custom however rests only on an assertion of the scholiast of Thucydides ii 25, which may have been no more than an erroneous reference from his author's words; but it is in some degree confirmed by analogy, and perhaps by what Tacitus (*Annals* ii 54) says of the priesthood at Claros, which has been referred to this usage.

it must be observed, that they almost every where established themselves as conquerors, in a land already inhabited and cultivated, and partially if not entirely dispossessed its ancient owners. The terms on which they might live with those of the old inhabitants who were suffered to remain, would depend on an infinite variety of circumstances. But in general it may be safely presumed, that even where the first people was not reduced to bondage or absolute subjection, the conquerors would maintain a superior station in their political institutions. But between these classes many other gradations of rank were frequently introduced by the accession of new adventurers, who, though willingly received, could seldom be admitted on a footing of perfect equality with the first settlers. On the other hand, the maritime position and pursuits of the colonies, and the very spirit in which they were founded was highly unfavourable to the permanence of an aristocratical ascendency. A powerful and enterprising commonalty soon sprang up, and the natural tendency of the state toward a complete democracy could seldom be restrained, except by the adoption of a liberal standard of property as the measure of political rights.

As in the period of the early migrations which followed the return of the Heracleids, the monarchical form of government was almost every where prevalent in Greece itself, but it was very probably generally established in the colonies. But the causes just noticed, incident to their peculiar situation, tended, in the first instance, to restrict the power of the hereditary chiefs, and gradually to reduce it to a mere shadow, which itself finally disappeared. The history of Cyrene affords a remarkable illustration of the manner in which this change may have been effected in many other cases which are not recorded.

Thirlwall accounts for the colonisation of Cyrene and the Greek colonies on the west coast of Asia Minor, before turning to examine the organisation of the colonies.

No provision was made either for defence against foreign enemies, or for the maintenance of internal tranquility: there was no common treasure, nor tribunal, nor magistrate, nor laws. Yet it may have been very early, though the time is uncertain, that the Lycians set an example of the manner in which the advantages of a close federal union might be reconciled with mutual independence. They distributed their twenty-three cities into three classes: the cities of the first rank possessed three votes, those of the second two, those of the lowest one, and each contributed to a common fund in proportion to its weight in the common council. This was held, not in any fixed place, so as to raise one city to the rank of a capital, but in one appointed for the time by common consent. A supreme magistrate and other officers were here elected: and a court was instituted for the decision of all disputes that might arise between members of the confederacy: the cities contributing in proportion to their rank to fill the places in the national judicature and magistracy: in the same assemblies were discussed all questions relating to peace and war, and the general interests of the united states. Had the Greeks on the western coast of Asia adopted similar institutions, their history, and that of the mother country might have been very different from what it became.

But whatever ill effects may be attributed to their want of union, it does not seem immediately to have checked the growth or to have diminished the prosperity, of the several cities. They may perhaps have shot up the more vigorously and luxuriantly from the absence of all restraint. This advantage undoubtedly also resulted from the abolition of the monarchical form of government, which probably took place every where within a few generations after the first settlement, though the good was balanced by great evils. From the scanty fragments remaining of the internal history of the Asiatic colonies it may be collected, that they passed through the various stages of which we have given an outline in a preceding chapter, and that they suffered much from intestine discord. Thus it is related that Miletus, after the overthrow of a tyrannical dynasty, was split into two factions, designated by names which seem to indicate an oligarchy and a commonalty (Plut. *Q. Gr.* 32). The former gained the ascendant, but was forced to take extraordinary precautions to preserve it. Again we read of a struggle between the wealthy citizens and the commonalty, accompanied with the most horrible excesses on both sides.* It is uncertain whether this is the period to which Herodotus refers, when he speaks of a civil war which lasted for two generations at Miletus, and reduced it to great distress, and was at length terminated by the mediation of the Parians, who seem to have committed the government to those landowners who had shown the greatest moderation, or had kept aloof from the contest of the parties (Hdt. v 28). These convulsions took place within the same period in which Miletus rose to the summit of her greatness as a maritime state, and in which her colonies and her commerce were extending the limits of the Greek world, and opening an intercourse between its more distant regions. How far political changes were connected with the prime spring of that wonderful activity which was displayed by the Asiatic Greeks, more especially the Ionians in the seventh and sixth centuries before our era, can only be conjectured. It seems probable that the fall of the ancient aristocracies which succeeded the heroic monarchy and the emulation between a growing commonalty, and an oligarchy which grounded its political claims solely on superior wealth, were conditions, without which the Ionian genius would not have found room to expand itself so freely. On the other hand the inferior degree in which the Dorians and Aeolians were animated with the spirit of commercial adventure, may have been owing to their political institutions, not less than to a difference in their national character. It is however certain that in the two centuries just mentioned the progress of mercantile industry and maritime discovery was coupled with the cultivation of nobler arts, and the opening of new intellectual fields, in a degree to which history affords no parallel before the beginning of the latest period of European civilisation.

Having set the scene, Thirlwall goes on to discuss the consequences of the Greek exploration of the Mediterranean: the development of art and literature.

---

*   Athenaeus xii 524. Here the commonalty bears the name *Gerithes*—that of the remnant of the ancient Teucrians in the Troas (Strabo viii 559; Herodotus vii 43; Athenaeus vi 256). They are a rustic population, and crush the children of their adversaries to death on their threshing-floors; the opposite party revenges itself by burning them alive with their children.

Nearly at the same time that the Phocaeans were making their first excursions in the west of the Mediterranean, the country from which, according to general belief, Greece had in ancient times received the germs of her arts, religion and civility, but which had long been jealously closed against foreign settlers, was thrown open for permanent and friendly intercourse to the Greeks. About 650 BC a band composed of Ionians and Carians chanced in the course of a piratical expedition to land on the coast of Egypt, and were induced by great offers to enter into the service of Psammetichus, who established himself on the throne by their aid. He not only rewarded them with a grant of lands on the Nile, but gave all their countrymen free access to his dominions;* and, to promote their commerce with his subjects, consigned a number of Egyptian boys to their care, to be instructed in the Greek language, so as to form a permanent class of interpreters. His successors adhered to the same policy; and thus Greeks of various classes were drawn to Egypt, in the pursuit of knowledge as well as gain. Of the impression produced on an inquisitive and intelligent Greek by the sight of this wonderful land, which even by its ruins, and in its lowest state of degradation, has never ceased to inspire astonishment and awe, we are able to judge from the testimony of Herodotus. Even if the effects of the intercourse between the two nations had been limited to those of a purely material traffic, they would have been incalculably great, because to this traffic Greek literature was indebted for one of the most important outward conditions of its development— a cheap and commodious writing material for writing, which was supplied by the Egyptian papyrus—but undoubtedly these effects did not terminate here; though it is difficult to estimate them, and the opinions of learned men are divided as to their nature and extent.

Though we have not yet brought the political history of the Asiatic colonies down to the period at which we dropped that of the mother country, just before the beginning of the great struggle

---

* This account of the matter in Herodotus ii 154 is no doubt substantially correct, and yet it may not be a sufficient ground for rejecting the date assigned by Eusebius to the foundation of Naucratis, which according to him was founded by Milesians (*Ol.* vi 4), confirmed by the story in Athenaeus xv 18.

between Greece and Asia, as the present seems to be the most suitable place for taking a view of the progress of art and literature, which was so intimately connected with the rise of those colonies, we shall not scruple, for the sake of continuity, to trace it down to the Persian war.

We have seen that several arts, subservient either to the enjoyment of the great and affluent, or to the uses of religion, had been cultivated by the Greeks before the time of Homer with a considerable degree of civility and success: and it may easily be conceived that their progress kept pace with the advance of public and private prosperity. The increase of wealth and refinement appears to have been much more rapid in the Asiatic colonies, particularly in Ionia, than among the Greeks of the mother country, where it was not equally favoured by nature, and was long checked by the troubles which followed the Dorian conquest. The Ionian cities were probably at an early period distinguished by a degree of luxury before unknown to the Greeks; and hence Lycurgus is said to have visited the contrast between their magnificence and the Cretan simplicity (Plut. *Lyc.* 4). The same fact is indicated by the legend, that the daughter of Neleus, the founder, was seduced by one of the barbarians, and is most probably the ground of the picture which Homer has drawn of the Phaeacians, in whom it is scarcely possible to avoid recognising his Ionian countrymen. About the beginning of the Olympiads, the fall of Magnesia on the Maeander was ascribed by poets of the same century to the prevalence of effeminate habits (Athen. xii 29). We have seen however that the Ionians did not abandon themselves to indolence, and the active spirit which led them to pursue their commercial adventures into unknown regions, found employment at home in the arts by which their private and public life was cheered and adorned. Among the cities of Greece perhaps Corinth alone can be compared to them. There the overthrow of the Bacchiads was attributed to their luxury, which probably formed a contrast to the plainness and frugality that prevailed in the other Dorian states. But though the Dorian character and institutions were adverse to luxury, they did not exclude the highest degree of magnificence in works either consecrated to the gods, or designated for the service of the state. And hence even where, as at Sparta, the Dorian freemen were not permitted themselves to cultivate any of the arts, artists of various kinds were well received, and found abundant employment; and schools of art occur more frequently in Dorian than in Ionian cities. The first steps in the arts of drawing, of painting, of moulding figures in clay, were commonly attributed to the Corinthians, who, as they afterwards gave their name to one of the three orders of architecture, made the earliest improvement in the form of the Doric temple.* But Sicyon disputed the honour of some of these inventions with Corinth, and was more celebrated than her wealthier neighbour for her school of sculpture. Those of Argos and Lacedaemon, of Rhodes and Crete, and above all of Aegina, were fruitful and renowned, while that of Athens, though it boasted Daedalus as its founder, and transmitted his art in an uninterrupted succession of families, seems to have been barren in great works, as it was in illustrious names. But the Ionians were not behindhand either in the richness of their productions, or in the glory of new inventions. They began early to vie with one another in the magnitude and splendour of their sacred buildings, and consequently in all the arts which served to adorn them. The temple of Hera at Samos, the largest of all that Herodotus had seen, appears to have been begun in the eighth century BC, or early in the seventh. It was built in the Doric style, which soon after generally gave way in the Asiatic temples to the lighter Ionic. Its architect Rhoecus, a native of the island, was the father of Theodorus, who was equally celebrated as the builder of the Lemnian labyrinth, and the author of several memorable inventions. The most important was the art of casting metal statues, which before had been formed of pieces wrought with the hammer, and nailed together. Theodorus exerted his ingenuity in overcoming the difficulties presented by the nature of the ground, in laying the foundation of the great temple of Artemis at Ephesus.† It would seem too that the art of painting had made considerable progress in Ionia, while it was in its first rudiments at Corinth, if we may believe the account, that a picture of Bularchus was purchased at a high price in the eighth century

---

*   See Boeckh on Pindar, O. xiii 214.

†   Diog. Laert. ii 103. He suggested the use of charcoal for this purpose.

by the Lydian king Candaules,* and can reconcile this fact with the Corinthian tradition, that the earliest essays in colouring were made by Cleophantus, at the time of the overthrow of the Bacchiads.†

It will not be expected that we should enter into the history of the fine arts in their various branches, or that we should fill our pages with the names of the masters, and with the accounts preserved by the ancients of their works. Our object is only to point out the connection made between the progress of these arts, and that which the Greeks made during the same period in other spheres of intellectual exertion. And for this purpose it will be sufficient to observe the manner in which one art—the most important, as an indication of the genius of the people, of all those which were occupied with the creation of visible forms—which, to avoid the references to the nature of its materials implied in the word sculpture, is better termed statuary, rose within this period nearly to the summit of its perfection. We have already, in our view of the Homeric age, had occasion to notice a very difficult question, relating to the origin of this art—the uncertainty whether it sprang up, and was gradually formed, in Greece, or was introduced from the East in a stage of comparative maturity, at which it remained for centuries, fixed by the control of religion. It happens by a singular coincidence that the epoch at which the Greeks opened or renewed their intercourse with Egypt, was also that in which statuary was on the point of breaking through its ancient restraints, and of entering on a new career, in which it arrived, within little more than another century, at its highest point of attainable excellence. It is not surprising that two facts which in time came so nearly together, should have been thought to be related to each other as cause and effect. And hence it may seem a probable opinion that the Greek artists, as soon as they were able to visit Egypt, were instructed by the Egyptians in various technical processes which had been long familiar to them, but hitherto unknown to the Greeks, and that by

---

* Pliny *NH* vii 39; xxxv 34. It represented the destruction of Magnesia on the Maeander, probably that which it suffered from the Cimmerian tribe, the Treres, about *Ol.* 18. Candaules is said to have paid its weight in gold.

† Pliny *NH* xxxv 5. He, or another artist of the same name, was said to have followed Demaratus into Italy.

this fortunate assistance Greek art advanced at once from a degree of extreme rudeness to the same level which it had attained in Egypt through the persevering labour of numberless generations. There is a celebrated story, which has been thought to confirm this opinion; that the Samian Theodorus, and his brother Telecles, having studied in Egypt, on their return made a statue of Apollo, in such exact conformity to the rules which they had learnt, that the one half, which Telecles executed at Samos, tallied with the other, on which his brother had been employed during the same time at Ephesus, as exactly if the whole had been the work of one artist (Diodorus i 98). But if the truth of the story was certain, the inference would lose all its force, if, as there are strong reasons for believing, the two brothers flourished in the eighth century BC; and we should then be driven to a supposition, which the language of Herodotus seems directly to contradict—that Egypt had been visited by Greek artists before the reign of Psammetichus. Independently however of the evidence which the Homeric poems afford, to elevate our conceptions of the earlier state of Greek art, descriptions have been left to us of several elaborate works, which, though their date cannot perhaps be precisely ascertained, appear to belong to the period preceding the opening of a regular intercourse with Egypt, and would prove that the Greeks cannot have been much indebted to the Egyptians during this period for instruments or processes of art. A tenth of the profits made by Colaeus in his voyage, which we have already mentioned, to Tartessus, was dedicated, probably not long after, to Hera, in the shape of a huge vessel of brass, adorned with figures of griffins round its border, and supported by three colossal statues (Herodotus iv 152). The magnificent coffer of cedar wood covered with groups of figures, some of the same wood, others of ivory, others of gold, which was consecrated at Olympia by the Cypselids, was said to be the very same in which the infant Cypselus had been concealed from the search of the Bacchiads, and, if so, had been no doubt long one of the family treasures.* The colossal throne of Apollo at Amyclae, which was constructed for the Spartans by a company of artists from Magnesia on the Maeander, and was

---

*   Paus. v 17.5; and Thiersch, p. 167 n. 66.

richly adorned with sculptures, seems with great probability to be referred to the eighth century BC, in which, after Magnesia had been destroyed by the Cimmerians, these artists may have taken refuge, and sought employment in Greece.*

It seems at all events certain that there were other causes, which operated much more efficaciously than the intercourse with Egypt, to urge the rapid progress of statuary in the century preceding the Persian wars. Among these causes might be mentioned the preference which was generally given to brass and marble over the ancient material, wood, which henceforth, when employed, was commonly overlaid with the more precious substances, as ivory and gold. This change arose in part out of the invention of Theodorus, which gave a new command over metals. The use of marble for statues is said to have been introduced in the fiftieth Olympiad by two Cretan artists named Dipaenus and Scyllis, but was probably most promoted by the closer alliance with architecture into which statuary began to be brought, and by the increased sumptuousness of the temples, in which, as in that of Delphi, when rebuilt by the Alcmaeonids, marble frequently took the place of ordinary stone. It may however be conceived that the technical rules taught by the Egyptians had first enabled the Greeks to treat the harder material with ease and freedom. But this substitution, though an important step, did not of necessity involve any change of style, and would not of itself have prevented the art from remaining stationary at the stage to which it had been carried by the Egyptians themselves. A cause of still greater efficacy was the enlargement which it experienced in the range of its subjects, and the consequent multiplicity of its productions. As long as the statues were no longer confined to the interior of temples, and no more were seen in each sanctuary than the idol of its worship, there was little room and motive for innovation; and on the other hand there were strong inducements for adhering to the practice of antiquity. But insensibly piety or ostentation began to fill the temples with groups of gods and heroes, strangers to the place, and guests of the power who was properly invoked there. The deep recesses of their pediments were peopled

---

* Thiersch, p. 176 n. 83.

with colossal forms, exhibiting some legendary scene, appropriate to the place or occasion of the building. The custom, which we have already noticed, of honouring the victors at the public games with a statue—an honour afterward extended to other distinguished persons—contributed perhaps to still the same effect. For, whatever restraints may have been imposed on artists in the representation of sacred subjects, either by usage or by a religious scruple, were removed when they were employed in exhibiting the images of mere mortals. As the field of art was widened to embrace new objects, the number of masters increased: they were no longer limited, where this had before been the case, to families or guilds: their industry was sharpened by a more active competition and by richer awards: as the study of nature became more earnest, the sense of beauty became quicker and steadier; and so rapid was the march of the art, that the last vestiges of the arbitrary forms which had been hallowed by time or religion had not yet disappeared, when the final union of truth and beauty, which we sometimes endeavour to express by the term *ideal*, was accomplished in the school of Phidias.

After a commentary on early Greek poetry, there follows a review of early Greek historiography, the style of which might betray a veiled criticism of his own predecessors.

The early Greek poetry was designed for exhibition, more or less public, and it was late before any one appears to have thought of writing, without any view to recitation, for the satisfaction of individual readers. This could only be the case when instruction, not pleasure, was the immediate end proposed; and hence the rise of a prose literature among the Greeks coincides with that of historical inquiry and philosophical speculation. When the object of the authors was no longer to work on the feelings and the imagination, but simply to convey knowledge or reasonings, they naturally adopted the style of familiar discourse, which was gradually ennobled and refined, till in the art of composition it equalled the most elaborate productions of the national poetry. If we may rely on the tradition of later times as to a point which we must have always been obscure, Pherecydes, a native of the isle of Syros, who flourished about the middle of the sixth century BC, was the first prose-writer:* his work seems to have been partly mythical, partly philosophical. Cadmus of Miletus is said first to have applied prose to an historical subject.

When however we speak of a rising spirit of historical inquiry in the period preceding the Persian wars, we must be careful to limit our notions on this head with due regard to the character of the people, and the circumstances of the age. The first essays at historical composition among the Greeks appear to have been subordinate on the one hand to poetry, on the other to the study of nature. The works of the early historians, so far as we can judge of them from the general accounts of Strabo and Dionysius of Halicarnassus, and from the fragments, or slight notices, which have been preserved of their contents, seem to have been in part professedly mythological, and to have given, perhaps in a more connected form, and with some traditional supplements, the substance of a large portion of the epic cycle. It is apparently to this class that Strabo alludes (i 34), when he says, that Cadmus, Pherecydes, and Hecataeus, only got rid of their poetical predecessors, but in other respects adhered to them so closely, as even to retain the character of their diction. But there was another, and perhaps a larger class of works, which might have been more properly referred to the head of geography or topography than to that of history, in which the description of a country, or a city, served as a thread to connect its traditions. It must have been this class that Dionysius had in view (*De Thuc. Jud.* v), when he spoke of the historians who preceded Herodotus, as confining themselves to local limits, and contenting themselves with simply recording the legends, whether sacred or profane, or each region or district, however incredible, in a style which, though concise and artless, was clear and not ungraceful. Though we must not construe this language so strictly as to suppose, that these historians never interposed their own judgment on the matters which they related, it is certain that the faculty of historical criticism, which indeed was never very generally awakened among the Greeks, and never attained any high degree of vigour, was long almost entirely dormant. In the selection and arrangement of their materials, they

---

*   Plin. *NH* vii 57; Apuleius *Flor.* 130 ed. Bip.

were probably governed, in most cases, by no higher principle than the desire of gratifying patriotic vanity, or the popular taste for the marvellous. But whenever they aspired to the more difficult and glorious task, of unravelling any of those mythical webs which must often have perplexed them, they could scarcely fail to aggravate the real confusion, by a false show of an artificial harmony and order. It is doubtful how far they commonly descended into the later political vicissitudes of the countries which they described. But before the Persian wars the Greeks did not suspect the importance of their own history, and it was not till long after that either its highest interest, or its practical uses began to be distinctly understood.

A
HISTORY OF GREECE.

BY
THE REV: CONNOP THIRLWALL,

Late Fellow of Trinity College, Cambridge.

VOL. III.

*Pericles bursting into tears, as he places the
funeral garland on his dead Son.*

London:
PRINTED FOR LONGMAN, BROWN, GREEN, & LONGMANS, PATERNOSTER ROW,
AND JOHN TAYLOR, UPPER GOWER STREET.

Periclean Athens

In these chapters, Thirlwall investigates the political career of Pericles, and associates the blossoming of Athenian culture with the emergence of democracy and the Athenian empire. Thirlwall does not approve of the growth of private munificence in the fifth century, but he appears to think that democracy before the Peloponnesian War was admirably steered by Pericles. His main reservation about Athenian democracy, the preponderance of the lower classes, is saved for a later chapter (see below, ch. 32). Thirlwall's place in the historiography of Athenian democracy has been investigated in the work of K.Demetriou.[1] On political matters, Thirlwall was a pragmatist: he accepted democracy in the ancient and modern worlds; he inclined towards the view that the emergence of democracy was an inevitable surge that neither could nor should be stemmed. He discussed the reform bill of 1867 in a charge of 1869:

> Whether this change is a mere momentary fluctuation which may be expected to subside, or is a mighty stream of tendency, which no human power can arrest of control, if it is unmistakably marked with the character of a natural social development, then however much we may see in it to deplore or dream, still, as believers in a superintending Providence, we cannot look upon it as merely evil; and instead of mourning over it, or ... wasting our strength in a vain attempt to stem the tide which is carrying all before it upon earth ... we shall hold it our duty to deal with it in a loving and hopeful spirit.[2]

Democracy in the Age of Pericles

While Themistocles and Aristides were occupying the political stage, an extraordinary genius had been ripening in obscurity, and was only waiting for a favourable juncture to issue from the shade into the broad day of public life. Xanthippus, the conqueror of Mycale, had married Agariste, a descendant of the famous Cleisthenes, and had left two sons, Ariphron and Pericles. Of Ariphron little is known beside his name: but Pericles, to an observing eye, gave early indications of a mind formed for great things, and a will earnestly bent on them. In his youth he had not rested satisfied with the ordinary Greek education, but had applied himself, with an ardour which was not even abated by the lapse of years, nor stifled by his public avocations, to intellectual pursuits, which were then new at Athens, and confined to a very new circle of inquisitive pursuits. His birth and fortune afforded him the means of familiar intercourse with all the men most eminent in every kind of knowledge and art, who were already beginning to resort to Athens as a common seat of learning. Thus, though Pythoclides taught him to touch the cithara, he sought the elements of a higher kind of music in the lessons of Damon, who was believed to have contributed mainly to train him for his political career: himself no ordinary person; for he was held up by the comic poets to public jealousy, as a secret favourer of tyranny, and was driven from Athens by the process of ostracism. But Pericles also entered with avidity into abstrusest philosophical speculations, and even took pleasure in the arid subtleties of the Eleatic school, or at least in the ingenuity and the dialectic art with which they were unfolded to him by Zeno. But his principal guide in such researches, and the man who appears to have exercised the most powerful and durable influence on his mind and character, was the philosopher Anaxagoras, with whom he was long united in intimate friendship. Not only his public and private deportment, and his habits of thought, but the tone and style of his eloquence were believed to have been formed by his intercourse with Anaxagoras. It was commonly supposed that this effect was produced by the philosopher's physical speculations, which, elevating his disciple above the ignorant superstition of the vulgar, had imparted to him the serene condescension and dignified language of a superior being. But we should be loth to believe that it was the possession of such physical secrets as Anaxagoras was able to communicate, that inspired Pericles with his lofty conceptions, or that he was intoxicated with the little taste of science which had weaned him from a few popular prejudices. We should rather ascribe so deep an impression to the distinguishing tenet of Anaxagorean system, by which the philosopher himself was supposed to have acquired the title of *Mind* from his contemporaries. The doctrine of an ordering intelligence, distinct from the material universe, and ruling it with absolute sway, was striking from its novelty, and peculiarly congenial to the character of Pericles. Such was the supremacy which Athens exercised over the multitude of her dependent states, and such the ascendancy which he felt himself destined to obtain over the multitude at Athens.

It was undoubtedly not for the mere amusement of his leisure that Pericles had enriched his mind with so many rare acquirements. All of them were probably considered by him as instruments for the use of the statesman: and even those which seemed most remote from all practical purposes, may have contributed to the cultivation of that natural eloquence, to which he owed so much of his influence. He left no specimens of his oratory behind him, and we can only estimate it, like may other fruits of Greek genius, by the effect it produced. The few minute fragments preserved by Plutarch, which were recorded by earlier authors because they had sunk so deep in the mind of his hearers, seem to indicate that he loved to concentrate his thoughts in a bold and vivid image: as when he called Aegina the eyesore of Piraeus, and said that he descried war lowering from Peloponnesus. But though signally gifted and accomplished for political action, it was not without much hesitation and apprehension that he entered on a field, where he saw ample room indeed for the display of his powers, but also many enemies and great dangers. The very superiority of which he could not but be conscious, suggested a motive for alarm, as it might easily excite suspicion in the people of views adverse to their freedom: and these fears were heightened by some circumstances, trifling in themselves, but capable of awakening or confirming a popular prejudice. His personal appearance was graceful and majestic, notwithstanding a remarkable disproportion in the length of his head, which became a subject of inexhaustible pleasantry for the comic poets of his day (Plut. *Per.* 3, 14): but the old men who remembered Pisistratus, were struck by the resemblance which they discovered between the tyrant and the young heir of the Alcmaeonids, and not only in their features,* but in the sweetness of voice, and the volubility of utterance, with which both expressed themselves. Still, after the ostracism of Themistocles, and the death of Aristides, while Cimon was engaged in continual expeditions, Pericles began to present himself more and more to the public eye, and was soon the acknowledged chief of a powerful party, which openly aimed at counteracting Cimon's influence, and introducing opposite maxims into the public counsels.

To some of the ancients indeed it appeared that the course of policy adopted by Pericles was entirely determined by the spirit of emulation, which induced him to take a different ground from that which he found already occupied by Cimon: and that, as Cimon was at the head of the aristocratical party which had been repre-sented by Aristides, he therefore placed himself in the front of that which had been led by Themistocles. The difference between these parties after the revolution by which the ancestor of Pericles had undermined the power of the old aristocracy, was for some time very faintly marked, and we have seen that Aristides himself was the author of a very democratical measure which threw the first offices of the state open to all classes of the citizens. The aristocracy had no hope of recovering what it had lost; but, as the commonality grew more enterprising, it became also more intent on keeping all that it had retained, and on stopping all further innovation at home. Abroad too, though it was no longer a question, whether Athens should continue to be a great maritime power, or should reduce

---

* The contemporaries of Pisistratus seem to have discovered a striking likeness between his head and that of a statue of the god Dionysus, which was therefore supposed by some to have been sacrilegiously designed by the artist as a portrait of the mortal, and was looked upon as a specimen of the tyrant's arrogance (Athen. xii 533). Hence, probably not without a malicious allusion to the scandal about Aspasia, Hermippus, in one of his comedies, entitled Pericles King of the Satyrs (Plut. *Per.* 33).

her navy to the footing of the old *naucraries*, and though Cimon himself had actively pursued the policy of Themistocles, there was room for great difference of opinion as to the course which was to be followed in her foreign relations. The aristocratical party wished, for their own sake at least as much as for that of peace and justice, to preserve the balance of power as steady as possible in Greece, and directed the Athenian arms against the Persian empire with the greater energy, in the hope of diverting them from intestine warfare. The democratical part had other interests, and concurred only with that part of these views which tended towards enriching and aggrandising the state.

It is difficult wholly to clear Pericles from the charge of having been swayed by personal motives in the choice of his political system, as it would be to establish it. But even if it were certain that his decision was not the result of conviction, it might as fairly be attributed to a hereditary prepossession in favour of the principles for which his ancestors had contended, and which had probably been transmitted in his family, as to his competition with Cimon, or to his fear of incurring the suspicion that he aimed at a tyranny, or unconstitutional power; a suspicion to which he was much more exposed in the station which he actually filled. But if his personal character might seem better adapted to an aristocratical rather than a democratic party, it must also render us unwilling to believe, that he devoted himself to the cause of commonalty, merely that he might make it the instrument of his own ambition. There seems to be much better ground for supposing that he deliberately preferred the system which he adopted, as the most consistent, if not alone reconcilable, with the prosperity and safety of Athens: through his own agency in directing and controlling it might be a prominent object in all his views. But he might well think that the people had gone too far to remain stationary, even if there was any reason why it should not seize the good which lay within its reach. Its greatness had risen with the growth of the commonalty, and, it might appear to him, could only be maintained and extended by the same means: at home by a decided ascendancy of the popular interest over that of the old aristocracy, and every other class in the state; abroad by an equally decided supremacy over the rest of Greece.

The contest between the parties seems for some time to have been carried on, without much violence or animosity, and rather with a noble emulation in the service of the public, than with assaults on one another. Cimon had enriched his country with the spoil and ransom of the Persians; and he had also greatly increased his private fortune. His disposition was naturally inclined to liberality, and he made a munificent use of his wealth. Several great works were wanting for the security of the city, and little had yet been done for its embellishment. The southern wall of the citadel was built with the treasure which Cimon brought home from Asia, and the plans of Themistocles were brought nearer to their accomplishment, by preparations which were now made for joining the city to its harbours, by walls carried down on the one side to Phalerus, on the other to Piraeus. The laying down of the foundations of these walls was itself an arduous and expensive work, on account of the marshy ground which they crossed; and Cimon himself executed the most difficult part with magnificent solidity at his own charge. He also set the example of adorning the public places of the city with trees, and by introducing a supply of water converted the Academy, a spot about two miles north of the city, from an arid waste, into a delightful grove, containing open lawns and courses for the exercises of the young, shady walks for the thoughtful, a scene of wholesome recreation for all.

This kind of expenditure was wise and noble: but it was coupled with another, mischievous in its tendency, and seemingly degrading both to the benefited and the benefactor. Cimon, it is said, not only like Pisistratus invited all who would to partake of the fruits of his fields and orchards, but threw down the fences, that none might scruple to enter. He not only gave the usual entertainments expected from the rich, to the members of his deme, but kept a table constantly open to them. When he went out into the streets he was commonly attended by a number of persons in good apparel, who when they met with any elderly citizen scantily clothed, would insist on exchanging their warm mantles for his threadbare covering. It was the office of the same agents respectfully to approach any of the poorer citizens of good character, whom they might see standing in the market-place, and silently to put some small pieces of money into their hands. There were some, Plutarch innocently observes, who decried this liberality as flattery of the mob, and the trick of a demagogue:* but such slander is, he thinks, amply refuted by the fact, that Cimon was the leader of the aristocratical and Laconian party, and one of the few Athenians whose incorruptible integrity raised them above all suspicion of venality, or of ever acting from selfish motives. And he adds a story of the magnanimity with which Cimon had rejected a present offered to him by a foreigner who needed his protection. It might perhaps be alleged with more colour of truth, that the ordinary relation subsisting at this period between the rich and poor at Athens, rendered such good offices so common, that they could not fairly be attributed even to ambition, much less to any meaner motive. It is true that the state of things had undergone a great change at Athens in favour of the poorer class, since Solon had been obliged to interpose, to protect them from the rigour of creditors, who first impoverished, and then enslaved them. Since this time the aristocracy had found it expedient to court the commonalty which it could no longer oppress, and to part with a portion of its wealth for the sake of retaining its power. There were of course then, as at all times, benevolent individuals, who only consulted the dictates of a generous nature: but the contrast between the practice which prevailed before and after the age of Solon, seems clearly to mark the spurious origin of the ordinary beneficence. Yet Isocrates, when he extols the bounty of the good old times, which prevented the pressure of poverty from being ever felt, speaks of land granted at low rents, sums of money advanced at low interest (*Areop.* 12), and asserts that none of the citizens were then in such indigence, as to depend on casual relief (*ibid.* 38). Cimon's munificence therefore must have been remarkable, not only in its degree but in its kind: and was not the less that of a demagogue, because he sought popularity, not merely for his own sake, but for that of his order and his party.

---

* Plutarch, *Cimon* 10. In his life of Pericles, 9, he seems himself to adopt the same view. With regard to the removal of the fences, Plutarch's statement is not confirmed by Theopompus (Athenaeus xii 533), and may therefore be suspected of exaggeration.

Such was the light in which it was viewed by Pericles; and some of the measures which most strongly marked his administration were adopted to counteract its effects. He was not able to rival Cimon's profusion, and he even husbanded his private fortune with rigid economy, that he might keep his probity in the management of public affairs free from both temptation and suspicion. His friend Demonides is said first to have suggested the thought of throwing Cimon's liberality into the shade, and rendering it superfluous, by proposing a similar application of the public revenue.* Pericles perhaps deemed it safer and more becoming, that the people should supply the poorer citizens with the means of enjoyment out of its own funds, that that they should depend on the bounty of opulent individuals. He might think that the generation which had raised their country to such a pitch of greatness, was entitled to reap the fruits of the sacrifice which their fathers had made, in resigning the produce of the mines of Laurium to the use of the state. Very early therefore he signalised his appearance in the assembly by becoming the author of a series of measures, all tending to provide for the subsistence and gratification of the poorer class at the public expense. We do not stop to describe these measures, because they will find a more appropriate place in a general view of the administration of Pericles. But we must here observe that, while he was courting the favour of the multitude by these arts, he was no less studious to command its respect. From his first entrance into public life, he devoted himself with unremitting application to business: he was never to be seen out of doors, but on the way between his house and the seat of council: and, as if by way of contrast to Cimon's convivial tastes, declined all invitations to the entertainments of his acquaintance—once only during the whole period he broke through this rule, to honour the wedding of his relative Euryptolemus with his presence—and confined himself to the society of a very select circle of intimate friends. He bestowed the most assiduous attention on the preparation of his speeches, and so little disguised it, that he used to say he never mounted the *bema*, without praying that no inappropriate word might drop from his lips. The impression thus

---

*   Plutarch, *Pericles* 9 on the authority of Aristotle.

produced was heightened by the calm majesty of his air and carriage and by the philosophical composure which he maintained under all provocations.* And he was so careful to avoid the effect which familiarity might have on the people, that he was sparing even in his attendance at the assembly, and reserving his own appearance for great occasions, carried many of his measures through the agency of his friends and partisans. Among them the person whose name is most frequently associated with that of Pericles was Ephialtes, son of Sophonides, a person not much less conspicuous for his rigid integrity than Aristides himself, and who seems to have entered into the views of Pericles with disinterested earnestness, and fearless to have borne the brunt of the conflict with the opposite party.

The Athenian Empire and Athenian Culture

Pericles, to describe his policy in a few words, had two objects mainly in view throughout his public life: to extend and strengthen the Athenian empire, and to raise the confidence and self-esteem of the Athenians themselves to a level with the lofty position which they occupied. Almost all of his measures may be clearly referred to one or the other of these ends. There are only a few as to which it may seem doubtful whether they can be reached to any higher aim than that of establishing his own power, and whether they must not be regarded as a sacrifice by which, at the expense of his principles, he purchased that popularity which was the indispensable condition of success in all his undertakings.

There follows an account of the Athenian empire in the 440s BC.

The condition of an Athenian citizen acquired a new dignity and value, when he was considered as one of the people which ruled a great empire with such absolute sway. But as it was one object which Pericles had constantly in view, to elevate the Athenians

---

* Plutarch tells a story—characteristic if not true—of a rude fellow, who after railing at Pericles all day, as he was transacting business in public, followed him after dusk with abusive language to his door, when Pericles ordered one of his servants to take a light, and conduct the man home.

to a full consciousness of their lofty station, as members of the sovereign state, and to lead them to look upon their city not merely as the capital of Attica, but as the metropolis of their extensive dominions, it was also one of his chief cares to present the contrast which might sometimes arise between the public character and the private circumstances of his fellow citizens, from becoming too glaring, or too general. One great class of measures which formed a prominent feature in his system, served the double purpose of providing many individuals with the means of subsistence, and of securing and strengthening the state. With this view numerous colonies were planted during his administration in positions where they might best guard and promote the interests of Athens. And the footing on which a great part of these colonists stood, while it preserved the closest connection between them and the mother country, rendered the relief thus afforded to their indigence so much the more acceptable. They were treated as Athenian citizens who had obtained grants of land in a foreign country, where they might fix their residence or not, as they thought fit, but without in either case renouncing their Athenian franchise.* There can be no doubt that the greater number of colonists shifted their abode and very seldom returned to exercise their ancient franchise. But still it must have been but rarely, and under peculiar circumstances, that they altogether dropped the character and feelings of Athenians.

There follow details of other Athenian colonies.

The anxiety of Pericles to raise the value of the Athenian franchise, was still more distinctly proved by a law which he caused to be enacted at an early period in his administration, confining the rights of citizenship to persons whose parents were both Athenians. This law was not called into extensive operation before the year BC 444, nearly at the same time with the foundation of Thurii. But this year the Libyan prince, Psammetichus, who was a master of a large part of Lower Egypt, having sent a present of corn to be distributed

---

* *Klerouchoi*, thus distinguished from *apoikoi*, colonists parted from the mother country.

among the Athenian people, a rigid security was instituted to try the titles of those who claimed a share of the largess. The result was that nearly 5000 persons were declared to be aliens, and, it is said, suffered the penalty appointed by a rigorous law for those who usurped the privilege of a citizen, being sold as slaves. The number of the citizens who passed through this ordeal amounted to very little more than 14,000. But even after this reduction, and while the colonies were drawing off a part of the residue, Pericles was obliged to make it one of his leading objects to provide for the subsistence of those who were left, and the extraordinary expenditure which he directed was destined mainly, though not exclusively, to this purpose. Thus a squadron of sixty galleys was sent out every year, and was kept at sea eight months, partly indeed to keep the crews in training, but not without a distinct view to the advantage which a large body of citizens derived from the pay, which probably supported them during the remainder of the year. But still more ample employment was furnished to the poorer class by the great works which were undertaken at the proposal of Pericles, and carried on under his eye, for the defence and embellishment of the city, and which have rendered his accession to power an epoch no less important in the history of the arts, than in that of Attica itself.

The great plan of Themistocles, which Cimon had prosecuted by the erection of Long Walls, was completed under the administration of Pericles, by the construction of a third wall, within the first two built, which ran parallel and near to that which joined the city to Piraeus, and served the purpose of keeping the communication open, even if either of the outer walls happened to be surprised by an enemy.* The ravages of the Persians, and the gratitude due to the gods who had delivered the city, imposed a religious obligation of replacing the defaced or demolished temples, at Athens, Eleusis, and in other parts of Attica, and of adding new ones, all on a scale of magnificence corresponding to the increased power and opulence

---

* This view of the subject, which is that of Dr. Arnold (*Thucyd.* ii 13) and Mueller (Ersch and Grueber's Encyclopaedia, art. *Attika*), seems decidedly preferable to the opinion of Col. Leake and Kruse (*Hellas* ii. 152), who hold that the *dia mesou teichos*, mentioned by Plato (*Gorgias* 455), was a transverse wall which joined the two long walls together.

of the state. The whole summit of the Rock was covered with sacred buildings and monuments, among which the greater temple of the tutelary goddess, the Parthenon, rose supreme in majesty and beauty. An ornamental fortification called the Propylaea, which covered the western side—the only one not quite precipitous—of the citadel, formed an approach worthy of the marvellous scene to which it gave access. Edifices of a different kind were required, as well for the theatrical and musical entertainments of the people, as for the reception of multitudes assembled on graver occasions. A theatre adapted to this purpose, as well as to the new form of the drama, had been begun before the time of Pericles. He added one designed for the performance of music, thence called the *Odeum*, with a pointed roof, shaped it is said in imitation of the tent of Xerxes, and constructed out of the masts of Persian ships. In the planning and adorning of these buildings some of the greatest architects and sculptors Greece ever produced—the unrivalled Phidias with his two scholars, Alcamenes and Agoracritus, Ictinus, and Callicrates (architects of the Parthenon), Mnesicles (architect of the Propylaea), Callimachus,* Coroebus,† Metagenes,‡ Xenocles and others—found ample exercise for their genius and talents. But according to Greek usages and taste architecture and sculpture were intimately allied with a long train of subordinate arts, which gave employment to the skill and ingenuity of a multitude of inferior workmen. Thus not only was the colossal image of the goddess, which was the principal object of worship in the Parthenon, formed of ivory and gold, but the same precious metal was profusely employed in the decoration of the sculptures which adorned the exterior of the temple, and which were also relieved by the most brilliant colours. The groups which filled its pediments, while they roused the strongest feelings of Attic religion and patriotism by the subjects which they repre-sented, and satisfied the severest taste by the harmony of the design, also dazzled the eye as gorgeous pictures,§ lighted up by the sky of

---

*   Inventor according to Vitruvius of the Corinthian order; he also executed a golden lamp, and a brazen palm-tree for the temple of Athene *Polias*.

†   He began the temple at Eleusis which was continued by Metagenes.

‡   He added the roof with a circular aperture (*opaion*) to the *Anaktoron*.

§   See Brønsted, *Reisen*, ii, 164.

Attica, and rendered the more striking by the simple purity of the marble frames in which they were set and of the colonnades which supported them. Hence, as Plutarch observes, so long as these vast undertakings, which required so many arts to be combined for their execution, were in progress, it was scarcely possible that a hand which needed work could be left idle in Athens. As a variety of costly materials, gold, and brass, and marble, and ivory, and ebony and cedar, were frequently demanded for different parts of the same work, so many classes of artists or craftsmen whose labours were more or less mechanical—a distinction to which the Greeks seem to have attached less importance than we do*—were needed to concur in working them up. And while carpenters, and masons, and smiths, and turners, and dyers, and carvers, and gilders, were thus employed at home, a great number of trades were set in active exercise to procure their materials, and to transport them by land and sea. Every art could marshal a host of dependants whom it maintained. It must however be observed, that though in every branch of industry which required a high degree of intelligence, the Attic workman might commonly be sure of being preferred at least to all foreigners who were not Greeks, in those which depended upon mere manual labour he was constantly brought into a disadvantageous competition with the slaves, and could not fail to be supplanted, or reduced to the most indigent condition, unless he had the means of becoming an owner of some whom he could employ in the same manner. This was an evil against which even the lavish expenditure of Pericles, judiciously as it was applied, could only afford a temporary or partial relief. For a time however the large sums which were distributed through so many channels diffused

---

* In the passage to which we here allude, *Pericles* 12, Plutarch—as is observed by Thiersch, *Epoch*, p. 102—classes a number of arts together, without making any distinction between those which we regard as liberal professions, and others which we treat as mechanical. Thiersch shows from Lucian (*Somn.* 1) that the epithet *basaunos* was applied no less to Phidias, or Polycletus, than to a common mason. But they seem to have been brought down to this level only in contrast with the higher dignity of political or military functions, according to the sentiment which Plutarch expresses, *Pericles* 2; as Aeschylus thought little of his poetry in comparison of having fought at Marathon.

general prosperity. The rapidity with which the new buildings were completed was no less marvellous than the perfection of art which they exhibited. The Propylaea, the most expensive of all,* and the most laborious, as well on account of the difficulties of the ground, as the manufacture of the structure, were finished in five years. During the whole period of this extraordinary activity there must have been a comparative scarcity of labour at Athens.

We shall shortly return to this subject for the purpose of presenting it under another point of view. For the present it leads us to consider some other modes of expending the public money, which exhibit the administration of Pericles in a much less favourable light, because they appear to serve no higher end than a temporary gratification of individuals, by which they were as little benefited as the state itself. It was, as we have seen, in his competition with Cimon for public favour, and to counteract the disadvantage under which he was placed by the slenderness of his private fortune, that Pericles was induced to adopt these measures. But this motive cannot be admitted as an excuse for his conduct if he courted popularity to the manifest detriment of the common weal. And this is a charge from which it is scarcely possible wholly to acquit him. But on the other hand he seems to have been often too harshly judged, and to have borne the blame of a later state of things, which, though it arose out of his system, was not a necessary result of it, and was one which he could not easily have forseen.

Pericles did not introduce that strong passion for public amusements, which in the end consumed so large a part both of the fortunes of individuals and of the revenue of the state of Athens. But he appears to have increased the number of spectacles by new festivals, sacrifices, processions, musical and gymnastic exhibitions; he probably heightened their attractions by new refinements of art; and he made them accessible to all the citizens without distinction, instead of being reserved for the more affluent. In the period when a wooden theatre still sufficed for the Attic drama, the public safety had appeared to require that a small sum should be paid for

---

* See Col. Leake, on the cost of the works of Pericles, *Topography of Athens*, 416.

admission, which was originally gratuitous; and this continued to be exacted after the stone theatre had been built. Pericles removed this imposition from the poorer class by law, which enabled them to receive the amount from the treasury, and this restored to them an enjoyment of which some had been deprived without sufficient reason, or which they were compelled to purchase by an inconvenient sacrifice. This was in itself a harmless and reasonable indulgence, and may have appeared the most economical expedient for attaining the object proposed. But it would have been better to have revived the free admissions; for the precedent thus set was extremely liable to abuse, and in fact opened the way for a profuse distribution of money, under the pretext of enabling the poorer citizens to enjoy various festivals, and led to the establishment of the fund called *Theoricon*, which drained the vitals of the commonwealth, and absorbed resources urgently demanded for the public service, to be squandered away in frivolous entertainments. What part of this evil may be justly imputed to Pericles, could only be ascertained if we knew how many steps he himself advanced beyond the first application of the theoric allowance. But his views scarcely had any thing in common with those of the demagogues who succeeded him; and the recreations which he procured for the people operated rather as a spur to industry than a temptation to idleness. Another innovation of a similar nature which is ascribed to him seems to have been attended with a train of pernicious consequences which he could not have anticipated. He introduced the practice of paying the jurors for their attendance on the courts of justice (*misthos dikastikos*); a provision, which—putting out of the question the cases which filled the tribunals with suitors—was no more than equitable. The remuneration which he assigned for the loss of time on these occasions was extremely moderate,* and could not have encouraged the taste for litigation which was gradually unfolded to a mischievous excess in the Athenian character; but the sum was afterwards tripled, and became one of the heaviest items on the Attic civil list. This however was not perhaps the worst effect of

---

* An obolus, the sixth of a drachma, equivalent to about fourteen pence of our currency, according to the calculation of Col. Leake, *Topography of Athens*, 416.

the measure; for it seems probable that it suggested another—which has sometimes been erroneously attributed to Pericles himself—the payment of attendance in the popular assembly (*misthos ekklesiastikos*); a regulation which became more and more pernicious as he burden which it laid upon the state was more sensibly felt.

We can understand how Plato (*Gorgias* 515), even though he was only looking at the remote consequences of these measures, which had become visible in his own day, might introduce Socrates saying, 'I hear that Pericles made the Athenians a lazy, cowardly, talkative, and money-loving people, by accustoming them to receive wages'. But we find no sufficient ground for the remark of a modern author, that Pericles despised the multitude whom he pampered.* This might have been the case with Pisistratus or Cimon. But as Pericles had nothing to give, and could only persuade the people to dispose of treasure, which—whether by right or by wrong—had in fact become its own, so it is certain that in the manner of expenditure, his private taste coincided with that of the public. The interest which the Athenians in general took in the master-pieces of art which even today in their ruins still attract the admiration of the civilized world, is evinced by two well known stories, which show that Pericles followed as well as guided the popular inclination. When the question was agitated in the assembly, whether marble or ivory should be employed in the statue of the goddess, and Phidias, the sculptor, recommended marble as cheaper material, the assembly on that very ground recommended ivory. On another occasion when Thucydides, the rival of Pericles, complained of the enormous expense to which he had subjected the state by the monuments erected at his suggestion, he is said to have offered to defray the coast, if he might be allowed to inscribe them with his name. The offer, it is true, if it had been accepted, could not have

---

* Boeckh, *Staatsh*. ii, 13. The high authority which Boeckh has so well earned by his learning and candour, entitles even a passing, and perhaps hasty remark of his, to more attention than is due to all the attempts, which for the last 40 years have been systematically made in our own literature—the periodical as well as the more permanent—for political and other purposes, to vilify the Athenians. But it is not very easy to reconcile B's remark with the admission which he makes in the next sentence.

been made good. But it was probably only meant to signify the firm reliance which Pericles placed on the liberality of his countrymen; and it seems to have answered his purpose, by reminding them of the lustre which these splendid works reflected on their own renown.* He was desired to proceed as he had begun, and to draw without sparing from the public treasury. Whether the age of Pericles is not degraded, when it is compared with other celebrated periods in the history of mankind, which resemble it in the successful cultivation of the arts, and whether in this respect it does not stand on an eminence which has never yet been approached, is a question on which opinions may differ. But at least it is distinguished by one very important feature. The magnificence which adorned it was not like that of a Lorenzo, or a Leo, it was not supplied from the coffers either of a wealthy citizen or a prince, to gratify the taste of a small circle of cultivated minds, nor was it like the magnificence of the Caesars, who expended a part of their immense revenues for the diversion of slaves; still more strongly was it contrasted with that of the selfish and narrow-minded despot, whose whole life expressed his maxim: I am the state;† it was not the magnificence of Pericles, but that of the Athenian people. That Pericles despised this people, even while he was providing for the least intellectual of its entertainments, we are as little able to believe, as, when we contemplate the remains of the works executed to gratify its taste, it is in our power, whatever we may think of its failings or vices, to despise it.

These works served two main ends, which were important enough to have justified the application of the treasure expended on them, had it but come by fair means into the hands of the Athenians. And even the fugitive amusements which were shared by the whole people under the superintendence of Pericles, contributed at least toward one of these ends. All of them tended continually to refine

---

* It is construed in a very different manner by Drumann, *Geschichte des Verfalls der griechischen Staaten*, p. 238, as a low, impudent trick, an interpretation for which we can find no better ground than the violent aversion which this writer takes every opportunity of expressing to the character and conduct of Pericles.
† *L'état, c'est moi.* The reader who wishes to feel rightly on this subject should compare Plutarch's *Pericles*, 12, 13, with Saint Simon's remarks on the magnificence of Louis XIV. *Mémoires*, tom. xiii, pp. 84–90.

that matchless purity of taste by which the Athenians were long distinguished, and which must have been an important element in their political prosperity, through the influence which it could not fail to exert on their manufactures and commerce. But the public buildings answered a still higher end, by exalting and endearing the state in the eyes of its citizens. Their exceeding magnificence, the more striking from its contrast to the extreme simplicity of all private dwellings (Dem *Aristoc.* 206–8 and *Meid.* 158), expressed the magistracy of the commonwealth, before which the greatness of the most eminent individual shrank into nothing. They were at the same time monuments of the past and pledges of the future. The Parthenon and Propylaea might be considered as trophies of Marathon and Salamis. They displayed the fruits of the patience and fortitude with which Athens had resisted the barbarians. They indicated the new station to which she had risen, and the abundance of the means she possessed for maintaining it. It is probable that the complacency with which the Athenians contemplated them from this point of view, was seldom embittered by the reflection, that this magnificence was in part founded upon wrong and robbery. It is true that in the account which all nations have to render at the bar of history, there is probably not one which can appear with clean hands to impeach the Athenians on this head. We must not however on this account shut our eyes upon the real nature of their conduct. And it may be useful to remember, that not only their greatness was unstable in proportion as it rested on violence and fraud; but—as one of the most splendid monuments of the Medicean age was the occasion of an irreparable calamity to the power which raised it—so the great works which the Athenians now adorned their city, both contributed to alienate and provoke the allies at whose expense they were executed, and to elate the people with that extravagant pride and confidence in its own strength and fortune, which hurried it on to its ruin.

Before the Persian war Athens had contributed less than many other cities, her inferiors in magnitude and in political importance, to the intellectual progress of Greece. She had produced no artists to be compared with those of Argos, Corinth, Sicyon, Aegina, Laconia and of many cities both in the eastern and western colonies. She could boast of no poets so celebrated as those of the Ionian and Aeolian schools. But her peaceful glories quickly followed and outshone that of her victories, conquests, and political ascendancy. In the period between the Persian and the Peloponnesian wars, both literature and the fine arts began to find to Athens as their most favoured seat. For here, above all other parts of Greece, genius and talents were encouraged by an ample field of exertion, by public sympathy and applause, as well as by the prospect of other rewards, which however were much more sparingly bestowed. Accordingly it was at Athens that architecture and sculpture reached the highest degree of perfection which either ever attained in the ancient world, and that Greek poetry was enriched with a new kind of composition, the drama, which united the leading feature of every species before cultivated in a new whole, and exhibited all the grace and vigour of the Greek imagination, together with the full compass and the highest refinement of the form of the language peculiar to Attica.

Thirlwall argues that drama had its roots in lyric poetry.

The drama was the branch of literature which peculiarly signalised the age of Pericles; and it belongs to the political no less than to the literary history of the times, and deserves to be considered in both points of view. The steps by which it was brought through a series of innovations to the form which it presents in its earliest extant remains, are still a subject of controversy among antiquarians; and even the poetical character of the authors by whom these changes were effected, and of their works, is involved in great uncertainty. We have reason to believe that it was no want of merit, or of absolute worth, which caused them to be neglected and forgotten, but only the superior attraction of the form which the drama finally assumed. Of Phrynichus in particular, the immediate predecessor of Aeschylus, we are led to conceive a very favourable opinion, both by the manner in which he is mentioned by the ancients who were acquainted with his poems and by the effect which he is recorded to have produced upon his audience. It seems clear that Aeschylus, who found him in undisputed possession of the public favour (Aristoph.

Ran. 908), regarded him as a worthy rival, and was in part stimulated by emulation to unfold the capacities of their common art by a variety of new inventions (Aristoph. *Ran.* 1295). These however were so important, as to entitle their author to be considered as the father of Attic tragedy. This title he would have deserved, if he had only introduced the dialogue, which distinguished his drama from that of the preceding poems, who had told the story of each piece in a series of monologues. So long as this was the case, the lyrical part must have created the chief interest; and the difference between the Attic tragedy, and the choral songs which were exhibited in a similar manner in the Dorian cities, was perhaps not so striking as their agreement. The innovation made by Aeschylus altered the whole character of the poem; raised the purely dramatic portion from a subordinate to the principal rank, and expanded it into a richly varied, and well-organised composition. With him, it would seem, and as a natural consequence of this great change, arose the urge which to us appears so singular, of exhibiting what was sometimes called a *trilogy*, which comprised three distinct tragedies, at the same time.*

It is a question still agitated by learned men, but one as to which we can scarcely expect to find any decisive evidence, whether, as in one instance furnished by his remaining works, he always, at least after an early period in his dramatic character, constructed the three tragedies of each trilogy into one great whole, which might be compared to some of Shakspeare's historical plays. The supposition is at least perfectly conformable to his genius, fills up a chasm which would otherwise be mysterious in the history of the drama, and, as far as it can, is confirmed by the remains of the poet's numerous lost works. Aeschylus paid no less attention to the exhibition of tragedy as a spectacle, for the purpose of heightening the effect of his poetry by scenic illusion. It was for him that Agatharchus painted the first scene which had ever been made to agree with the

---

*   So much at least seems clear, notwithstanding the widely different interpretations given to the statement of the Scholiast of Aristophanes (*Ran.* 1122), about Aristophanes and Apollonius, by Welcker, *Aeschylische Trilogie* 504, and by Gruppe, *Ariadne* (the quaint title of an interesting book on the history of Greek tragedy), p. 41.

rules of linear perspective, and thus led to a scientific investigation of its principles.* It need not however be supposed that the imagination of an Athenian audience was less capable of apprehending the poet's description, and of filling up his outlines with colours of its own, than that of Shakspeare's contemporaries. But the more fastidious taste of the Athenians seems to have required that, while the higher faculties were gratified, the eye and the ear should perceive nothing which tended to disturb this impression. They were perhaps less easily satisfied in this respect, the more familiar they became with the masterpieces of sculpture, and the difficulty was greater as the scene was exposed to the broad light of day. The decoration of tragedy became a very heavy charge, which fell almost entirely upon wealthy individuals; but the charm of the entertainment increased in proportion, and was the more generally felt. Aeschylus—who himself according to a long established custom, bore a part in the representation of his own plays—not only superintended the evolutions of his choruses with the most anxious attention but is recorded to have invented several minute additions to the theatrical wardrobe; and at Athens this was not thought unworthy of honourable mention in the life of a man who is known to us as one of the most sublime and original of poets.

Comments on the language of Aeschylus and Sophocles are followed by speculations on the intention of Attic tragedy.

The Attic tragedy was not merely a spectacle for the multitude, or a study for lovers of literature and art, but was capable of being applied to moral, or religious, and political purposes. The general impression which Aeschylus appears to aim at, if we may properly attribute any such objects to him, is rather of a religious than a moral nature. His persons are for the most part raised too far above the sphere of real life to awaken much moral sympathy. He

---

* Vitruvius, *Praef. lib.* vii. this seems to contradict Aristotle, who, *Poet.* 10, attributes the introduction of scene painting to Sophocles. Hence it has been supposed that Agatharchus may have been employed for one of the latest representations of Aeschylus. But it is possible that his was a first essay which was carried to perfection in the time of Sophocles.

sometimes represents man as the helpless sport of an inscrutable destiny; sometimes as the victim of a struggle between beings of a superior race; and such views may aspire to an undefined sense of religious awe, but cannot convey a practical lesson. Yet his darkest scenes are not without some gleams of light, which seem to fall from a higher and clearer region, and disclose partial intimations of a providential order of compensation and retribution, in which truth and justice will finally triumph. In the poetry of Sophocles this tendency is still more conspicuous; there dim forebodings brighten into a more cheerful hope, or suggest instructive warnings—the more efficacious as his persons are not too far removed from the common level of humanity—to rebuke the excesses of passion, the wantonness of power, the presumption of security, in which men forget their mortal condition, and trample upon laws human or divine. We have already mentioned an instance in which Aeschylus employed the drama as a political engine—to support the sinking authority of the Areopagus. There were perhaps few cases in which a tragic poet so distinctly disclosed a political object; still fewer in which he aimed at affecting the course of events. Aeschylus seems to have been the last who ventured to bring the men of his own time upon the stage. In the play which celebrated the battle of Salamis, he had followed the example of Phrynichus, who was not deterred by the reception he met with, when he exhibited the fall of Miletus, from treating another contemporary subject more grateful to the feelings of his audience. But Aeschylus seems not to have been content with the simple theme of his extant drama; there is ground for suspecting, that he connected it on the one hand with the earliest struggles between Europe and Asia, on the other with the recent victory gained by the Sicilian Greeks over the Carthaginians at Himera, and represented both events as the fulfilment of ancient prophecies, and as pledges of the lasting triumph which fate had decreed to Greece over all the power of the barbarians. With these few exceptions the scene of Greek tragedy was always laid in the heroic age, and its subjects were almost wholly confined to the circle traced by the epic poets. Yet allusions to living persons and passing occurrences were by no means rare, and were easily introduced. No extraordinary dexterity was needed to adapt the ancient legends to the new relations between Athens and other Greek states, and to cherish the feelings which happened to prevail in the public mind by a historical parallel. But in all these cases the object seems to have been rather to display the poet's ingenuity, than to produce any practical effect on his audience, or to influence the management of public affairs.

A
HISTORY OF GREECE.

BY

THE REV. CONNOP THIRLWALL,

Late Fellow of Trinity College Cambridge.

VOL. IV.

Death of Socrates.

London
PRINTED FOR LONGMAN, ORME, BROWN, GREEN & LONGMAN'S, PATERNOSTER ROW,
AND JOHN TAYLOR, UPPER GOWER STREET.

CHAPTER SIX

The Decline of Athens

Athens after the Peloponnesian War (vol. iv, chapter 32,
pp. 210–24, 244–7)   113

The idea that Athens fell into moral degeneracy over the course of the Peloponnesian War would come as no shock to a reader in the 1830s. Accounts of ancient history customarily narrated the decline as well as the rise of civilisations.[1] As a historian working within the Liberal Anglican tradition, Thirlwall reinforced that view of history. He has few good words to say about the successors of Pericles and he used their ascendancy to illustrate the degeneracy of Athenian society. However, his argument that the sources depict them in a false light opened the way for Grote's defence of the demagogues. Thirlwall finds room here for sober remarks on the constitution of Athens, informed by the work of Schoemann.[2] Notably, the sources that Thirlwall uses in his analysis of Athenian society after the Peloponnesian War are Aristophanes and [Xenophon]'s Constitution of the Athenians, as well as the forensic speeches of Lysias, through which he traces the emergence of oligarchical resentment towards democracy by the end of the fifth century BC. The use of the Attic orators for writing social history was not new: it was advocated by Macaulay in the 1820s[3] and had already been seriously developed by Gillies, who wrote in 1778: 'The works of the two orators [Lysias and Isocrates] together, exhibit an interesting picture, not only of the foreign wars and negotiations, but of the private lives and behaviour of this celebrated nation.'[4]

The state of Athens after the expulsion of the Thirty was in some respects apparently less desolate than that in which she had been left after the battle of Plataea. It is possible indeed that the invasions of Xerxes and Mardonius may have inflicted less injury on her territory than the methodical and lingering ravages of the Peloponnesians during the Peloponnesian War. But in 479 the city, as well as the country, had been, for a part of two consecutive years, in the power of an irritated enemy. All that it required both for ornament and defence was to be raised afresh from the ground. Yes, the treasury was empty: commerce had probably never yet yielded any considerable supplies, and it had been deeply disturbed by the war; the state possessed no dependent colonies or tributary allies, and was watched with a jealous eye by the most powerful of its confederates. Nevertheless it was impossible for an Athenian patriot to compare the situation and prospects of his country at these two epochs without a sigh. In 479 Athens was a mistress of a navy which gave her the pre-eminence over all the maritime states of Greece, and enabled her to carry her arms against any part of the enemy's coasts, to which she might be invited by the prospects of plunder or conquest; and a little vigour and prudence was sufficient to secure the city itself against the hostility of Sparta. The exertions and sacrifices by which she had weakened herself, had also made her formidable to the barbarians, and had won for her the admiration, goodwill, and confidence of the Grecian world. In 403 the city indeed stood untouched, except so far as the temples had been deprived of their ornaments and treasures by domestic spoilers. But its magnificence only attested the past greatness which seemed to have sunk for ever. All the sources of public and private wealth, except such as depended on a poor and wasted territory, and on the industry of individuals, were dried up. Not only were all those branches of the revenue which arose out of the sovereignty once exercised by Athens completely cut off—the influx of tribute, a great part of the fees of justice, the expenditure of the numerous foreigners who were drawn as suitors to the imperial city—but Athenian citizens whose property lay abroad, as appears to have been the case with a large class,* were either wholly deprived of it, or were obliged in their turn to prosecute their claims, under the most disadvantageous circumstances, at foreign tribunals. Commerce had not only been interrupted by the blockade but had sustained still greater detriment from the tyranny of the Thirty, which had crushed or scared away the most opulent and industrious of the aliens, and the cloud which continued to hang over the prospects of the state, even after freedom

---

* Andoc. *de Pace* 15; [Xen.] *Ath. Pol.* i 19; Xen. *Symp.* iv 31.

and tranquillity had been restored, tended to discourage those who might have been willing to return. The public distress was such that it was with the greatest difficulty that the council could produce ways and means for the ordinary expenses (Lys. *Nicom.* 19–20). Even the ancient sacrifices prescribed by the sacred canons were intermitted, because the treasury could not furnish three talents for their celebration:* and the repayment of a loan of two talents which had been advanced by the Thebans, probably in aid of the exiles (Plut. *Lys.* 27), was so long delayed through the same cause, that hostilities were threatened for the purpose of recovering the debt. The navy of Athens had now sunk to a fourth of that which she had maintained before the time of Solon, and it was limited to this footing by a compact which could not be broken or eluded without imminent danger; Piraeus was again unfortified: the arsenal was in ruins: even the city walls needed repairs, which could not be undertaken for want of money; and on all sides were enemies who rejoiced in her humiliation, and were urged both by their passions and interests to prevent her from again lifting up her head.

We have already endeavoured to point out the connection of the principal steps which led to this calamitous reverse, and we traced them to the policy though not so as to exclude the operation of causes which no human foresight could have guarded against. We must now take a nearer view of the manner in which this system worked, and of the changes it underwent during this period; and we shall be led to contemplate some features in the intellectual progress of Athenian society, which were intimately connected with this portion of its political history.

Pericles made few, if any, innovations in the Athenian constitution. The importance of the changes which he introduced into the jurisdiction of the Areopagus has probably been much exaggerated through the heat of the contest which they had excited at the time. But the influence of his administration continued to be long felt—perhaps we may say never ceased to manifest itself—in the spirit

---

* Lys. *loc. cit.* Bremi on this passage, and Schneider on [Xen.] *Ath. Pol.* iii 8, conclude from it that three talents was the whole sum allowed by Solon for the public sacrifices of the year. Boeckh considers it as the cost of a single sacrifice, *Public Economy of Athens* ii, 12.

of the government, and the views and the tastes of the people. The power of the popular assembly, on which his own was founded, had already in his lifetime reached its utmost extent, and was henceforth only capable of restriction. But the composition and character of the Assembly were considerably affected by the events of the war, and by the manner in which it was conducted under his system. We have already observed that one of the consequences which arose from the ravages of the pestilence, was that foreigners found it easy to gain admission to the franchise, either by legal means or through artifice and connivance. The latter class of cases appears to have been the commonest, as is indicated by the great number of distinguished persons whom we find charged with this kind of fraud; and it is probable that these new citizens crept in chiefly from the lower ranks. What proportion they bore to those of genuine Attic blood, it is impossible to determine. But the same facility either of evading the law, or of obtaining the franchise by favour of the people seems to have subsisted throughout the war. A much more important change however in the elements of which the assembly was ordinarily imposed was produced by the measures of Pericles, which drove a large part of the rural population into the city, where few could find employment, and most of them sank into the lowest class of the Athenian populace. The number of citizens of the higher and middle order who were usually absent from Athens in the fleets, armies, and garrisons, must likewise be taken into account, when we are estimating the effects of the war on the character of the assembly; and it may be added that the weight of the public burdens was continually depressing all private fortunes, except those which were raised by dishonest arts, to a lower level, and reduced many to indigence. That in the course of the war the poorer class began to preponderate, seems to be indicated by an innovation which took place probably toward the end of this period, though we do not know either its precise date, or any thing more of its author, Callistratus, than his name, which was one common to several Athenians of this age.* To him is ascribed the introduction of pay for attendance in the assembly; and whether the object of this measure was to provide

---

* See Boeckh, *Public Economy of Athens*, ii, 14.

for the more regular transaction of public business, or merely to gratify the multitude, it was alarming as a symptom, and baneful in its consequences. The remuneration which each member of the sovereign body received for the exercise of his functions, under the law of Callistratus, was no more than a single obolus. It would seem to follow that the persons to whom this trifling sum held out such an attraction as might be expected to secure their presence, formed either a majority or a very considerable part of every Assembly.

We may however be in danger of drawing very erroneous inferences from these facts, if we do not bear in mind, that at Athens the wealthy citizens possessed few peculiar advantages of education, and that poverty was accounted an evil indeed but not a disgrace.* The poorest Athenian had means of refining his taste, cultivating his understanding, and acquiring information concerning public affairs, superior to those enjoyed by the great mass of persons in the middle class among ourselves. The Assembly, the courts of justice, the market-place, the *lesche*, were so many schools of practical knowledge, as well as of eloquence and wit, which were open to all alike, and were perhaps most frequented by the lowest class. And in fact it is not to the ignorance or incapacity of the sovereign body that the mistakes committed in the management of the war are to be ascribed. There is another point connected with this subject in which prejudices have sometimes been entertained, which it may be useful to correct. The character of Pericles was so noble, that the sway which he exercised was no less honourable to the people than himself. But among the popular leaders who succeeded him we find several who are represented as men of low, and even servile origin, mean condition, slender abilities, coarse manners, and profligate conduct. And their ascendancy may be thought to prove the growing degeneracy of the people, or the predominance of a similar class of persons in the Assembly. But there are two errors which we have to guard against with respect to these demagogues. In the first place, it is probable that we are used to view them in a false light, and that they were not in general so despicable as, through the force of certain associations, we are apt to consider them. Many of them indeed

---

* So Pericles in Thuc. ii, 40.

were engaged in trade. Thus Lysicles and Eucrates, who rose for a short time to some degree of political eminence immediately after the death of Pericles, dealt, the one in cattle (Schol. Aristoph. *Eq.* 132), the other in flax and bran (Schol. Aristoph. *Eq.* 129, 253, 254): Cleon was a tanner, Hyperbolus a lamp-maker (Schol. Aristoph. *Eq.* 1301), Cleophon a manufacturer of lyres. Their occupations afforded a topic of ridicule to their contemporaries and are often treated as a sufficient evidence of their unfitness for the part which they took in public business. Some of their names indeed cannot be rescued from infamy. Hyperbolus labours under the charge not only of political profligacy, but of private dishonesty in the exercise of his trade;* and the epithet which Thucydides applies to him (Thuc. viii 73), implies that he was capable of any baseness: nor have we any reason to believe that his want of probity was covered by any shining or useful talents. But as far as we know there was nothing in his station or in that of the rest to exclude the highest qualifications of the Athenian statesman. It seems rather to deserve notice as a proof of the tenacity of aristocratical prejudices, that, in such a state as Athens, no earlier instance occurs in which the candidates for public favour came forward from the same rank: that the people could be expected to join in the laugh raised at the expense of the demagogues on this ground: and that even after the Peloponnesian war, Andocides should be found deploring the dishonour which had befallen his hereditary mansion when during his absence it was inhabited by Cleophon the *lyre maker* (And. *Myst* 146). But it must be remembered that, according to the expression of the Roman satyrist, Lysias and Demosthenes were brought up at the forge (Juvenal x 130). Cleon himself was probably no contemptible orator, and Thucydides did not scruple to put a very artful and dignified harangue in his mouth: and if Lysicles, by means of a union which he contracted with Aspasia after the death of Pericles, became in any sense the first of the Athenians (Aeschines the Socratic in Plut. *Per.* 24), notwithstanding the meanness of his extraction his mind cannot have been previously uncultivated.

---

* He is said to have mixed lead with the copper of his lamps, to cheat his customers, Schol. Ar. *Nub.* 1061.

The contrast therefore between Pericles and the demagogues who succeeded him may not have been in this respect so glaring as has been commonly supposed.* On the other hand the nature of their popularity has frequently been misrepresented, and the extent of their power overrated. The influence of Pericles was founded partly indeed on the measures by which he courted popular favour—which would have been equally agreeable if they had been proposed by any other man—but still more on the rare qualities of his genius and his character: on his eloquence, his military talents, his political experience, his prudence, his integrity, his serenity and greatness of soul. It was thus that he was enabled permanently to control the Assembly, and sometimes successfully to resist its declared wishes. No man ever appeared after him at the head of affairs combined so many claims to general confidence and respect. But with regard to the demagogues who succeeded him in the period which we are now reviewing, it is clear that, with one exception, none of them possessed any personal influence or was indebted for the degree of favour he enjoyed to any other instruments than the arts with which he flattered the passions of the people. The Athenians seem very well to have understood the character of their servants and courtiers, and even when they were following the worst guidance, not to have bestowed their good will and esteem upon unworthy objects. Nicias and Cleon, though neither of them in any respect equalled Pericles, may be considered as representing, one the better, the other worse side of his public character and policy. The boisterous, impudent, dishonest, ferocious, demagogue often, perhaps generally, prevailed in the assembly over the calm, prudent, and upright statesman; but it was not because he stood highest in public opinion. As the history of the Sicilian expedition shows that the merits of Nicias were at least not underrated, so the scene which gave occasion to the expedition against Sphacteria, proves that the people were not blind to Cleon's worthlessness. The tradition that the ostracism fell

---

* It deserves to be remarked, that the Scholiast of Aristophanes, in a note which seems to have been drawn from good sources (*Pax* 680) observes that it was with Hyperbolus the Athenians began to commit the administration of their affairs to worthless persons who would thus seem to include Lysicles, Eucrates, and Cleon himself.

into disuse, because it was universally considered as degraded when it had been used to expel Hyperbolus, indicates perhaps still more strongly the estimation in which he was held. Such men were only favourites with the multitude, because they ministered fuel to its vices. The man whose personal influence was the greatest, the only one who was regarded with a feeling of fondness, which even the deepest injuries could not entirely extinguish, was a demagogue of a very different stamp, the noble, refined, accomplished Alcibiades. It would be hard to reproach the Athenians with a partiality which Socrates was not ashamed to acknowledge; yet the counsels of Alcibiades led them into measures more injurious to their interest and their honour, than any which were ever proposed by Cleon, or Hyperbolus, or Cleophon: for he was the author of the Sicilian expedition, and the Melian massacre.

But it was the very calamity of the times that no extraordinary abilities, or eminent merit of any kind, were needed to pursue the track which had been opened by Pericles; the vilest and feeblest demagogue might easily go beyond him in the same course, and could thus gain the ear of the assembly, and acquire an habitual ascendancy over it. The smallest of the evils which ensued was, that the people grew more and more extravagant in its aims, elated with a more presumptuous confidence, more impatient of resistance to its will, and more furious in its resentment against those who opposed it. A still more pernicious result was, that the public affairs were conducted on a false principle, that the real and permanent interests of the whole commonwealth were postponed to the apparent and temporary advantage of a class, the largest indeed, but still only one, which was thus placed in a hostile position toward the wealthier citizens, who felt themselves burdened and aggrieved, and became on that account objects of a well-founded distrust, as disaffected to a government in which they had so little share, and from which they suffered so harsh treatment.* Even in time of peace the rich

---

* A humorous picture of the advantages which poverty enjoyed over wealth at Athens is given by Xenophon in his *Banquet*, iv 30, under the person of Charmides (probably a different person from the cousin of Critias) who had experienced both conditions, having been deprived of his property abroad and of the enjoyment of his estates in Attica by the war. This has been treated as a

Athenian was somewhat heavily taxed for the mere amusement of the less opulent, under the system of *liturgies*: the name given at Athens to those public services which demanded both money and personal attention and which was often accompanied with much trouble and anxiety, from the contributor. We will not trespass on a field of antiquarian learning which has been very fully and ably explored, to repeat any of the details belonging to this copious subject. We shall only observe that the theatrical, musical and gymnastic exhibitions, and other recreations connected with the religious festivals, which at Athens were more numerous than in any other Greek city (*De Rep. Ath.* iii 1), were all so many occasions on which some or other of the wealthy citizens,—according to an order determined by the law, which provided for the equable distribution of the burden, as well as for the performance of the duty,*—were responsible, with their purse and their time, for some essential part of the entertainment expected by the people. Yet the weight of this impost, though it was sufficient to press sensibly even on the largest fortunes, was relieved by its graceful and liberal form: by the opportunity which it afforded of exercising a refined taste, by the emulation excited, the applause, and reputation, which were earned by the successful competitors. But the pressure of the war taxes, which fell upon the rich in various shapes, both in the expense of military and naval equipments, and in extraordinary pecuniary contributions (*eisphorai*), which were levied whenever the treasury was exhausted, was still heavier, and was not mitigated by so many alleviating circumstances: though undoubtedly the trierarchy was not without its honours and advantages, to counterbalance its cost, cares and toils. At the same time the value of their estates in Attica was greatly reduced by the enemy's ravages, which, in the latter years of the war, entirely deprived them of the enjoyment of their landed property (Lysias 7.6). Their losses were embittered by the reflection, that it was not to the public good, but chiefly to the ambition and cupidity of the demagogues, that their patrimonies

---

very important testimony by several writers who have neglected to mention that at the end of Charmides being asked by his host whether he does not pray that he may never be rich again, answers: 'Not so; I am very ready to run the risk'.
* By the *diadikasia* (*De Rep Ath* iii 4) and the *antidosis*.

were sacrificed. The motives which led such demagogues as Cleon to promote the continuance of the war, are manifest enough, and have been already pointed out. To the people of all classes, upon a sober view of their own interests, peace should have appeared much more desirable (Aristoph. *Pax* 619). But they were urged to prosecute the court by a variety of inducements, which, in every posture of public affairs, furnished plausible arguments to the advocates of war. It was sometimes jealousy of Sparta, sometimes resentment against her or her allies, sometimes the prospect of conquests which promised an increase of revenue, that afforded a ground for rejecting pacific overtures, or for renewing hostilities: and even when the need of peace became most pressing, when nothing could be reasonably hoped, and the worst was feared, from war, there was still a motive by which the assembly might be deterred from sheathing the sword; and it was of such a nature as to appear strongest when all others failed. For it was in seasons of danger and distress that suspicions of treasonable designs were most readily entertained, and that there was really most reason to feel some anxiety for the safety of the constitution. This indeed seems to have been very early a common topic with the demagogues and sycophants; though we do not think the humorous exaggeration of the comic poet, from whom we learn this fact,* sufficient ground for believing that the people lived in a continual feverish dread of conspiracies against its liberty.† But a vague opinion had at length prevailed, so as to be publicly assumed as an acknowledged truth, that a state of war with Sparta was, if not absolutely necessary, at least the most favourable to the security of the democracy;‡ and whoever raised his voice for peace, exposed himself to the imputation of oligarchical principles, and perhaps of an intention to use the negotiation with the enemy as a cover for a treasonable correspondence. The people was thus entangled in a maze, from which it could scarcely be extricated without a

---

*　Arist. *Vesp* 488, 502; *Eq.* 236.

†　We could have wished for some better proof than the passages quoted from Aristophanes, for Wachsmuth's assertion (*H.A.I.* 2 p. 154) 'the people was always dreaming of conspiracies, and the loss of its absolute power: the words, *dissolution of democracy (katalusis tou demou)* produced a feverish uneasiness'.

‡　And. *de Pace* 2.

violent convulsion; the precautions taken to guard against the machinations of the disaffected, tended to increase their number and their malignity.

We have already observed, that the Council of Five Hundred, though, according to the design of Solon's institution, it was to prepare all the measures which passed through the Assembly, really exercised very little control over its proceedings, because a proposal sent down from the Council might be modified at the pleasure of the sovereign body,* and it even appears that a decree might be first moved in the Assembly, and then be sent up to receive the formal sanction of the Council, which could not be withheld; or at least that the Assembly took upon itself to prescribe the subjects which the Council should propose in the usual form for its deliberation.†
Still there was one important part of Solon's constitution which seems hitherto to have remained almost untouched: the business of legislation, including the revision of laws, still continued to be committed to a select body drawn from the Heliaea, and it does not appear that the Assembly had deliberately attempted to encroach upon its province, though it is probable that decrees were sometimes passed, which would more properly have been called laws.‡ The security afforded by this institution against rash innovations and the excessive multiplication of the laws, was indeed extremely valuable, though imperfect. But its beneficial effects were in a great

---

* To satisfy the law which directed that every decree of the assembly should be preceded by a resolution of the council (*probouleuma*) on the subject, it was only held to be necessary, that the Council should make a proposition on which the Assembly might deliberate. But the Assembly was not bound to simply to adopt or reject the proposed measure, but might immediately pass a decree of a totally different nature. To the examples of such a proceeding given by Schoemann (*De Com. Ath.* p. 98) from a later period, may be added that of the decree moved by Euryptolemus (Xen. *Hell.* i 7.37) in direct opposition to that which had been sent down from the council for regulating the trial of the generals after the battle of Arginusae.

† So we find the Assembly decreeing that the council should bring in a proposal (*probouleusasan esenegkein*) for regulating the proceedings against the generals (Xen. *Hell.* i 7.7) in direct opposition to that which had been sent down from the council for regulating the trial of the generals after the battle of Arginusae.

‡ Such, according to Xenophon's description (*Hell.* i 7.21) was the decree of Connonus.

measure counteracted by the vicious administration of the laws in the courts of justice, which introduced uncertainty and confusion into all the relations and transactions of private life, and contributed more than any other cause to the public disasters, while it corrupted the character of the people. Solon, when he regulated the constitution of the tribunals, seems to have thought it desirable that every citizen of mature age should from time to time be called upon to discharge the functions of a juror, and to have apprehended no danger from the great number of persons who were to be invested with them at the same time, but rather to have considered this as an additional safeguard against venality and fraud. And in fact it was not until near the end of the war, that verdicts were obtained by direct bribery: a practice which appears to have had its origin in the oligarchical associations which began to be formed, or to acquire a new character, in that period.* But Solon relied on the authority of the magistrates, the simplicity and notoriety of the laws, and above all the public spirit and pure intentions of the large assemblies whom he entrusted with the administration of justice. He calculated on the state of things which existed in his own day, but which was afterwards entirely changed, when the judicial duties of the presiding magistrates became merely formal; when the numerous body which was drawn indiscriminately from all classes, and therefore chiefly from the lowest, to decide a cause affecting life or property without appeal and without responsibility, was left wholly to its own discretion, which was neither enlightened nor controlled by any superior; when the laws became multifarious and complicated; but especially when the spirit of the people had begun to degenerate, had contracted a wrong bias, had lost its early reverence for truth and right, and had become capable of sacrificing them to its interest and its passions.

The corruption of the Athenian courts of justice probably began

---

* Diodorus, xiii 64 and Aristotle (in Harpokration, *Dekazon*) refer the origin of the practice to Anytus, whose case was probably the first in which it was known to have been used. At the time when the treatise *De Rep. Athen.* was written, the multitude of the jurors was considered as a sufficient obstacle to it. Yet according to Schneider's highly probable correction of the passage iii 7 the terms *dekazein* and *sundekazein* were then already current.

with that great extension of their business which took place when
the greater part of their allies had lost their independence and
were compelled to resort to Athens for the determination of all
important causes. At the same time the increase of wealth and the
enlargement of commerce, multiplied the occasions of litigation at
home. The taste of the people began to be more and more interested in forensic proceedings, even before it was attracted toward
them by any other inducement. The pay of the jurors introduced by
Pericles strengthened this impulse by a fresh motive, which, when
Cleon had tripled its amount, acted more powerfully, and on a
larger class. A considerable number of citizens then began to look
to the exercise of their judicial functions as a regular source of both
pleasure and profit. Several very pernicious consequences arose from
this bent of mind, when it prevailed in the majority. It created a
prepossession in favour of the party who brought his case before the
court, and particularly of the persons who most frequently appeared
there as claimants or accusers. It fostered a habit of viewing judicial
business as a pastime, and of paying more attention to the manner
in which a cause was conducted than to its merits. The taste of an
Athenian audience on all literary subjects was correct and fastidious;
it was keenly sensible of all the beauties of expression, and could
not tolerate a deviation from the strictest propriety of language. But
among the Athenians, as among the Greeks in general, the faculty
of weighing the force of arguments and evidence was rare, and it
was little cultivated by the practice of the popular tribunals. Even
in their best mood the Athenians came to the hearing of a cause
with a disposition too like that with which they took their places
at the theatre to compare the compositions of the rival poets; and
in later times at least a skilful advocate seized every opportunity
of interspersing his pleading with long poetical quotations.* Such
hearers were easily dazzled by eloquence, and when their attention

---

* Spengel (*Artium Scriptores*, 20) observes that if we judge from the remains of
the orators, we should believe that this practice did not begin much before the
age of Demosthenes; a large class of cases hardly admitted of it; and no instances
of it are found either in Lysias and Andocides, much less could they be expected
in Isaeus. But the taste of the Athenian courts in the time of Aristophanes is
sufficiently proved by his allusions in the *Vesp.* 579.

had been diverted from the state of the question by the art of the orator, it was never recalled to the point at issue by the presiding magistrate, whose duties were confined to the preliminaries of the trial and reception of the verdict.

But the prevalence of this frivolous habit was not the worst fault of the Athenian courts. In the most important class of cases, the criminal prosecutions, they were seldom perfectly impartial, and their ordinary bias was against the defendant. This general tendency to rigour, which appeared both in their verdicts and judgments, arose, independently of the cause which has been already mentioned, from the desire of exercising their power in the manner which rendered it most formidable, and which raised the importance of all the individuals who shared it ([Xen.] *Ath. Pol.* i 18; Aristoph. *Vesp.* 554). Even this propensity however was not so odious as another motive by which it appears to have been frequently seconded. The juror in the discharge of his office did not forget his quality of citizen, and was not indifferent to the manner in which the issue of a trial might affect the public revenue, and thus he leaned towards decisions which replenished the treasury with confiscations and pecuniary penalties, while they also served to terrify and humble the wealthy class, which he viewed with jealousy and envy. It was more especially in trials for political offences that these motives most frequently co-operated in their full force to the defendant's ruin. A large fortune was both an object of cupidity, and of itself raised a suspicion of disaffection toward the democracy, which was sufficient to cover many defects in the evidence brought against the possessor, unless he could show that he had reduced his income by voluntary and liberal sacrifices for the public benefit. This iniquitous prejudice was not only the cause of many unjust sentences, but subjected the rich to a kind of persecution, which was continually threatening their peace, even if it did not actually assail them. For on this notorious temper of the courts was grounded the power of the infamous sycophants who lived by extortion, and generally singled out, as the objects of their attacks, the opulent citizens of timid natures and quiet habits, who were both unable to plead for themselves and shrank from a public appearance. Such persons might indeed procure the aid of an advocate, but they commonly thought it better to purchase the silence of the informer—unless they could shelter themselves by such an expedient as that which Socrates suggested to his friend Crito—* than to expose themselves to the risk and the certain inconvenience of a trial. The resident aliens were not exempt from this annoyance; and, though they were not objects of fear or jealousy, they were placed under many disadvantages in a contest with an Athenian prosecutor.† But the noble and affluent citizens of the subject states, above all, had reason to tremble at the thought of being summoned to Athens, to meet any of the charges which it was easy to devise against them, and to connect with an imputation of hostile designs or disloyal sentiments, and were ready to stop the mouths of the orators with gold (*Pax* 622). The states themselves might often find it necessary to gain the protection of a powerful demagogue against the oppressive demands of the sovereign city, as we know Cleon was once bribed by some of the islanders to exert his influence to relieve them from an extraordinary impost: and the commanders of the Athenian squadrons, especially those who were employed in collecting contributions from the allies, had unbounded opportunities of enriching themselves by the terror which their presence inspired.

There is no room for doubt as to the existence of the evils and vices we have been describing, though the most copious information we possess on the subject is drawn not from purely historical sources, but from the dramatic satires of Aristophanes. But there may still be a question as to the measure of allowance to be made for comic exaggeration, or political prejudices, in the poet; and it seems probable that the colours in which he has painted his countrymen are in some respects too dark. If we should be willing to believe that the people, instead of being blinded by the demagogues, acted on a Turkish system toward them, and connived at their peculation and extortion in the prospect of afterwards reaping the fruits of their crimes while it punished the delinquents (Aristoph. *Eq.* 1117 ff.), we

---

* It is not clear that the thought was new; but the expedient cannot have been very frequently employed before.

† Cleon in Aristoph. *Eq.* 347, seems to treat the management of a cause against an alien as the easiest kind of practice in which a rising sycophant usually acquired the rudiments of his art.

should still require stronger evidence to satisfy us, that what we have considered merely as a bias which perverted the administration of justice, was accompanied with a distinct consciousness of its nature and tendency, and that the Athenian courts in all their proceedings deliberately obeyed the foulest motives, and must be looked upon as dens of robbery and murder. That the mass of the people had not sunk to this degree of depravity, may we think be inferred from the grief and indignation which it is recorded to have shown on some occasions, where it had been misled into an unjust sentence, by which it stained itself with innocent blood: as Callixenus, who however was not worse than other sycophants, though he was among those who returned after the expulsion of the Thirty, and enjoyed the benefit of the amnesty, died, universally hated, of hunger. This conclusion will be confirmed by facts which we shall soon have to relate. The Athenian character had undoubtedly been much corrupted by the influence of the most unfavorable circumstances to which the virtue of a nation was ever exposed, which may perhaps all be traced to the first signal breach of faith and justice by which the contributions of the allies had been diverted into the Athenian treasury; but still the portrait in which Parrhasius endeavoured to represent the lights and shades with which it was singularly chequered, was probably not less applicable to the people in this than in any other stage of its history: if it was fickle, passionate, often unjust, it was still always capable of mercy and pity; a compound of generosity and meanness, and of numberless other contrasts, which by turns excited regard and indignation, admiration and contempt in the beholder (Pliny *NH* xxxvi 10).

The danger with which the state had been threatened by the disastrous event of the Sicilian expedition had, as we have seen, awakened a spirit of more sober reflection, which appeared not only in the measures immediately adopted for the public safety, but in the patience with which the people afterwards listened to proposals for a reform of the constitution, and submitted to that limitation of the democracy which was retained after the oligarchy of the Four Hundred had been overthrown. But the calamitous issue of the war, the sufferings of the siege, and of the terrible period which ensued, were still more adapted to direct general attention towards the causes of these evils, and to produce an earnest inquiry after a remedy for the inward disorders out of which they had mainly risen. And accordingly after the expulsion of the Thirty there was not wanting in the body of the people a strong disposition to profit by past experience, to correct abuses, and to guard against their recurrence. Perhaps if the past could really have been buried in oblivion, or the feelings which it excited could have been perfectly allayed, it might not have been difficult to devise measures which would have secured a better state of things for the future, without either the sacrifice of liberty, or any material encroachment on popular rights. The immediate source of evil, as seems to have been almost universally felt and acknowledged, lay in the predominance of the demagogues and sycophants (Lys. 25.27). To prevent the revival of their sway, it would have been necessary above all things to reform the constitution of the courts of justice, and at least to give property so much weight in them, as would have sufficed to counterbalance the influence of mercenary motives. Another safeguard against popular levity would have been contained if the qualification required for admission to the Council had been newly regulated on a like principle, and its prerogatives enlarged, so as to enable it more efficaciously to direct the proceedings of the Assembly. If to such measures had been added some provision for the more economical application of the public revenue, and for compelling the poorer citizens to resort to pursuits of honest industry for their subsistence, the Assembly might perhaps have been safely left in possession of its ancient functions. The government would then have become a polity, while it would have preserved one of the most essential and valued characters of a pure democracy.

Changes of this kind might perhaps have been practicable if there had been wisdom and virtue enough in the leading men to make a patriotic use of the opportunity for salutary innovation which presented itself at the close of the war. But after the revolution which has been described in the preceding chapter, the time for such an attempt had gone by. The people had been taught that the worst abuses of the old democracy were light in comparison with the excesses of an oligarchical dynasty. Their experience in the artifices of the oligarchical faction led them to consider every limitation of the political privileges as a step toward the bondage from which they had just escaped (cf. Lyc. *Leoc.* 124–5). To part with any portion of their power, and especially to transfer it to the class to which their late oppressors belonged, would at this juncture have been deemed the height of frenzy. The first condition of future prosperity, even in the judgement of upright and enlightened men, was to keep the old constitution entire: the second, to restore it to its primitive purity, and to adopt such precautions as were consistent with its safety, against the abuses which had crept into its practice. Such appears to have been the tone and the feeling which prevailed for some time after the civil war. The termination of the Anarchy— as the year of the Thirty was called, to mark that the Archon was not legally appointed—was to be the beginning of a new period, a reign of law and order, under which the pests which had long afflicted and dishonoured the commonwealth were never to be seen again. Nor were these mere empty professions accompanied by no attempt to carry them into effect. The sincerity of the people's intentions manifested itself, if not in the most judicious manner, yet by several unequivocal proofs.

Thirlwall postulates that the revival of the law-code illustrated a respect for antiquity and good government, as did the success of the amnesty. He then goes on to investigate the oligarchic feelings that had arisen by the end of the fifth century.

There was, as we learn from Lysias, a whole class of prosecutions, which arose immediately out of the wants of the treasury. It appears that a new board of magistrates under the title of Syndics (Harpokration s.v. *Syndikoi*) was appointed immediately after the Anarchy, to receive informations about property due to the state. When the property of a delinquent had been confiscated, if it did not prove equal to the expectations which had been formed of its amount, his nearest relatives and most intimate friends incurred the suspicion of having secreted a part of it, and became liable to a charge which it was generally extremely difficult to repel. So after Ergocles, the defendant in the case already mentioned, had been put to death for peculation and treason, his kinsman and friend Philocrates, was accused of embezzling his property, and in the

speech composed by Lysias for the occasion, is called upon to prove
either that others were in possession of it, or that the judgment
under which Ergocles had suffered was unjust. But two facts which
are incidentally disclosed in the speech are more important than the
case itself. Ergocles, it is said, had deposited three talents with his
advocates, which they were to retain if he gained his cause; and at
the time of his trial his friends had publicly boasted that they had
purchased 1500 votes in Piraeus and 1600 in the city. In another case
of a like nature the client of Lysias is able to give seemingly very
clear proofs that the property which he was accused of embezzling
did not exist; he was also able to plead the extraordinary liberality with which his family had contributed to the public exigencies
and had relieved the distress of individuals; for his father had not
only discharged the most expensive liturgies, but had portioned out
several poor girls, had ransomed captives, and defrayed the cost of
the burials, and had thus spent the greater part of a large fortune;
yet he thinks it necessary to deprecate the adverse prejudices of the
court with the remark, that it would be not only for the honour
but for the interest of the people that he should be permitted to
retain this small remnant that was left of his family property, which
would still be employed as before in the public service (Lysias 19).
The same ground is taken by the speaker in another case, which is
much more remarkable on account of the parties interested, though
it is not equally intelligible. The brother and son of the unfortunate
Nicias had, as we have seen, been put to death by the Thirty, though
it was generally believed that, if they had been willing, they might
have shared the power of the oligarchs. Their children had been
presented to Pausanias, to incline him toward the cause of the exiles,
or to afford him a pretext for embracing it. Yet, many years after the
Anarchy, we find the son of Eucrates pleading to avert the confis-
cation of his father's property. And it appears that his patrimony
had been claimed by the treasury shortly after the restoration of
the democracy; that it had then been successfully defended, but
was now again threatened; under what title or colour we are unable
to discover. Lysias however makes his client, after having urged the
claims of his family on the public gratitude, appeal to the interest of
the people, which he considers as represented by the court. 'If you

were really gainers by unjust confiscations,' he argues, 'there would be some ground for disregarding our pleas. But such proceedings must tend to disturb that concord which you have acknowledged by your public acts to be the greatest of blessings'. And then he adds another argument similar to that of the orator's client in the last mentioned case: 'Our property, if confiscated, will be wasted by those who claim it for the treasury; if left in our hands it will be expended in the public service.'

These instances appear to betray a very low tone of public morals, though they may for the most part be referred to the abuse of a principle, which was recognised in every Greek state, that the interests of individuals were in all cases to be sacrificed to the public good. But the comedies of Aristophanes exhibit his fellow-citizens in a still more unfavourable light, as well as by his general complaints of their degeneracy, as by a variety of particular and personal allusions. We perceive that gross vices had become so common that they were scarcely thought to need concealment; and the habits and character of the women are objects of unsparing and indiscriminate satire. The corruption was probably deep and widely spread; though as poverty was the source of many misdeeds to which the affluent were never tempted the higher and middling classes may have retained much of the ancient and purity of manners. But the influence of the men whose character and station might have enabled them to check the evil tendencies of the age, and even to enlighten and direct the rest of the community, was not proportioned to their numbers, and was not always exerted for salutary ends. Some were prevented by timidity or by their love of quiet or by the want of the talents or the physical powers required for appearing as speakers in the Assembly or the tribunals, from taking a part in public business.* Many, irritated or disheartened by their political disadvantages, kept sullenly or despondingly aloof from the great body of their fellow-citizens, nourishing a secret hatred to the constitution, and anxiously waiting for an opportunity of overthrowing it, and avenging themselves for past injuries and humiliation. The spirit

---

*   Such was the case with Charmides, who needed the exhortations of Socrates to encourage him to enter into the public life (Xen. *Mem.* iii 7 and with the persons mentioned by Xenophon *Mem.* i 2.48).

which prevailed in a large part of the higher order of citizens is illustrated by many passages, and indeed by the whole tenor of the treatise or fragment, preserved among the works of Xenophon under the title of *the Athenian Commonwealth*. Its value in this respect is the same, whether Xenophon or any one else, was the author; for it was probably written during the Peloponnesian war, and apparently before the end of the Sicilian expedition. The whole is one bitter sarcasm, and in every sentence breathes the rancorous scorn with which the writer regarded the government and the mass of the people. According to his view the contrast between the upper and lower classes is equivalent to that between vice and virtue. The rich are the worthy, the excellent, the wise: the poor are ignorant and depraved. Hence the two classes are irreconcilably hostile to each other. All the world over the best class is adverse to democracy, and is therefore oppressed by the other, when this happens to gain the upper hand. The common people will not be governed by the counsels of the wise and virtuous, because, ignorant and foolish as they are, they still have sense enough to know that the good men are their mortal enemies, and if they were trusted with power, would very soon deprive them of their liberty (i 4–9). Such is the strain in which the book opens, and proceeds to the end; it breathes the spirit of the oath which in the time of Aristotle was taken by the members of the ruling body in some of the Greek oligarchies: I will be hostile to the commonalty, and will do it all the harm in my power by my counsels (*Politics* v 7.19); and one reason for doubting that it has been rightly attributed to Xenophon, is, that in his other works, which were all written later, he nowhere betrays such violent oligarchical feelings. There are also indications that it was written at a distance from Athens (i 2.10), and therefore most probably by an exile. But still it may justly be considered as representing the sentiments of a large body of Athenians, the same who constituted the strength of the Four Hundred and of the Thirty.

There were however others who though very much dissatisfied with the existing state of things, were willing to accept and even eagerly sought the highest offices under the democratical government, some from common motives of ambition, others with dishonest and malignant designs. Xenophon has reported a conversation between

Socrates and the younger Pericles, which must have taken place
during the Peace of Nicias.* Nicias had either been elected general,
or aspired to the office. Yet Socrates, after having endeavoured to
convince him that the Athenians are not so incurably degenerate as
he thinks them, delicately reminds him, that he has not yet qualified
himself for the station which he covets; and Pericles admits the justice
of the reproof. Nicias affords an example of a better spirit, which,
though rare, was not wholly wanting in any period of Athenian
history. Though he both saw and suffered from the defects of the
government, he served his country zealously and faithfully, and, as
far as we can judge, without any oblique aim. Such was probably
also the case with his brother Eucrates, Conon, Diomedon, Leon,
and perhaps with several others among the generals and statesmen
who have already been named. But a still higher praise seems to
belong to the poet Aristophanes, and his genius, wonderful as it is,
is less admirable than the use which he made of it. He, whose works
have furnished the most abundant materials for all the repulsive
descriptions of his contemporaries which have been given in modern
times, never ceased to exert his matchless powers in endeavours to
counteract, or remedy, or to abate, the evils which he observed.
He seems to have neglected no opportunity of giving wholesome
advice in that which he judged the most efficacious form; and only
took advantage of his theatrical privilege to attack prevailing abuses,
and to rouse contempt and indignation against the follies and vices
which appeared to him most intimately connected with the worst
calamities and the dangers of the times.

---

*   *Mem.* iii 5. The date is determined by the state of public affairs described
in the fourth section.

A
HISTORY OF GREECE,

BY

THE REV. CONNOP THIRLWALL,

Late Fellow of Trinity College Cambridge.

VOL. V.

H. Corbould, Del.   E. Finden, sc.

The Death of Epaminondas.

London:
PRINTED FOR LONGMAN BROWN GREEN, & LONGMANS PATERNOSTER ROW,
AND JOHN TAYLOR UPPER GOWER STREET.

Greece and Philip II

The Greeks failed to learn what Thirlwall thought of as the lesson of the Peloponnesian War: that unity and coalition government was the best way of ensuring a secure future. By failing to unite thus they became easy prey for the Macedonians, who went on to impose their own version of federalism. Thirlwall's work has long been recognized as the first account of the struggle between Philip and Demosthenes which reasons with both the Athenian and Macedonian sides.[1] His comparison of Philip II of Macedon with a Russian autocrat reflects the widespread scholarly habit of imagining Philip as a modern figure,[2] as either saviour or enemy of the civilised world. Even in the twentieth century, this habit has endured.[3] The strength of Thirlwall's account is its ability to combine awareness of the gloomy prospects of Greece at the time of the battle of Mantinea with recognition of the talents and contributions of *both* Demosthenes and Philip.

Greece after Mantinea and the Early Years of Philip

To an enlightened and patriotic Greek the prospects of his country must have appeared more gloomy after the battle of Mantinea than at any previous epoch. The most desirable of all conditions for Greece would have been, to be united in a confederacy, strong enough to prevent intestine warfare among its members, and so constituted as to guard against all unnecessary encroachment of their independence. This was the mark toward which the aims of the nation would have been most wisely directed. But though the Amphictyonies, particularly that of Delphi, afforded not only a hint, but a ground-work, which might have been enlarged and adapted to this purpose: though the Lycian colonies exhibited an admirable example of a similar union: though the Persian invasion held out such a strong motive, and a fair opportunity for such an undertaking, it is doubtful whether the thought had ever occurred to a single Greek statesman; and it is probable that, if it had been suggested itself, it would have been rejected as a chimera. The next good to this would have been the supremacy of some Grecian state, powerful enough to enforce peace, but not to crush liberty. Nearly such had been that which Sparta exercised over the Peloponnesian confederacy before the Persian war. And, for a few years after, the division of power between Sparta and Athens might have seemed to promise the attainment of the blessing, in a different form indeed, but in one which afforded better security for freedom than could have been enjoyed under the sway of either alone. But the restless ambition of Athens soon destroyed the equipoise on which these hopes rested, and plunged the nation into greater calamities than it would probably have incurred, if all its states had been left absolutely independent of each other. The only benefit which could have compensated for the evils of the Peloponnesian war, would have been the conviction, which it ought to have produced, of the necessity of national union under a mild but firm federal government. But the lessons of the past were lost upon those whose conduct was chiefly to determine the future. Sparta was not warned by the example of Athens; she threw away a golden opportunity of establishing her own ascendancy on the tranquillity and happiness of Greece, forfeited the confidence of her allies, and proved, for the instruction of those who might have fancied that the misrule which Athens exercised abroad was connected with the peculiar character of her domestic institutions, that the dominion of an oligarchy might be still more oppressive to its foreign dependants than that of a democracy. Thebes in her turn, even under the administration of Epaminondas—though probably without any fault on his part—

wasted the sympathy and admiration which she had attracted by the wounds she suffered, and by the energy with which she avenged them, through her tyrannical treatment of the Boeotian towns, and the spirit in which she had interfered in the affairs of the Peloponnesus. The time had passed by, when the supremacy of any state could either have been willingly acknowledged by the rest or imposed upon them by force.

The hope of any favourable change in the general condition of Greece was now become fainter than ever. The immediate result to be expected, unless some extraordinary interference should avert it, was that she would gradually waste her strength away in a series of domestic wars. It was however possible that this lingering decay might be interrupted by a sudden revolution, which might subject her either to some native tyrant, such as Jason or Dionysius, or to a foreign yoke. But at the time which our history has now reached, no danger of this kind could be thought near enough to disturb that sense of general security which had prevailed ever since the Persian wars, and which had permitted and encouraged each state and party to concentrate its attention on its own affairs, and to look with indifference on all occurrences which did not affect its particular and immediate welfare. Notwithstanding the destructive struggles of so many generations, Greece was still in the prime of her vigour. The forces which had been brought into the field at the battle of Mantinea, if they had been arrayed on one side, might have defied the attack of any power then known to the Greeks. Toward whatever side they might turn their view, they could descry no reasonable ground for apprehension. In the west all the efforts of Carthaginians had been baffled by the resistance of Syracuse. In the east the Persian empire had owed its safety to the divisions of the Greeks, and their mercenaries formed the strength of its armies. There was indeed a danger, and very near at hand; but it was one which no human sagacity could yet have perceived and the quarter from which it arose, was perhaps the last to which a statesman would have looked for the enemy who was to crush the independence of Greece. The state of Macedonia, the seat of the new power which was destined soon to become so formidable, had hitherto been such as but very slightly to attract the attention of the

Greeks, and still less to awaken their fears. Since the close of the Peloponnesian war we have but rarely found occasion to mention it at all, and, whenever its name had occurred, we have seen it rather passively than actively connected with Grecian politics.

Thirlwall now gives an account of the Macedonian monarchy and the nature of Philip's education.

It is perhaps less probable that the house of Polymnis, the father of Epaminondas, should have been chosen for his residence, as Diodorus relates, than that of Pammenes, according to Plutarch's statement:* and the fable of his Pythagorean studies—worthy of Diodorus—is below criticism.† But a certain tincture of philosophy was at this time deemed almost an indispensable requisite in a liberal education. The fame of Plato, who had no doubt many admirers and disciples at Thebes, could not but engage Philip's attention, and awaken his curiosity. We do not undertake to determine, whether the relations subsisting between Thebes and Athens, during his stay in Greece, were such as to permit us to suppose that he visited Athens, or became personally acquainted with the founder of the Academy. But it seems an almost inevitable inference from a fact attested by contemporary evidence, that some kind of communication took place during this period between Plato and Philip, which impressed the philosopher with a favourable opinion of the prince: and it is not too bold, if it be not an indispensable conjecture, that Philip's

---

* The French author who supposed that, on account of the poverty of Polymnis, a public pension was assigned to defray the expense of Philip's education, perceived the difficulty, but was not happy in his expedient for removing it.

† It did not deserve the elaborate discussion which Wesseling has bestowed on it in his note on xvi 2. The main fact, which is the only point of importance—Philip's residence as a hostage at Thebes—is not at all affected by the discrepancies which he notices. This is another instance which ought to teach us caution in drawing arguments from the silence of the orators. It is certainly remarkable that no allusion occurs in any of them to this period of Philip's life—especially as Dio Chrysostom (ii p. 248 Reisk) mentions a report, which, if it had been current in the time of Demosthenes, might have afforded a topic for invective; but no intelligent critic will think this is a sufficient reason for questioning the fact.

esteem and admiration for Aristotle, of which he afterwards gave so remarkable a proof, had its origin in an acquaintance formed at the same epoch. Speusippus, Plato's kinsman and favourite scholar, related that, by Plato's recommendation conveyed through Euphraeus, Perdiccas was induced to bestow a principality by the way of apanage on his brother, who was consequently in possession of it, and in Macedonia when the throne became vacant. The authority of Speusippus must be deemed sufficient to place the substance of this account—the grant itself, and his uncle's recommendation—beyond question; nor is there anything in the slightest degree improbable, or inconsistent with the known characters and situation of the parties, in any one of the particulars. Only it may be necessary to observe, that it does not follow that Philip's return to Macedonia was effected through Plato's mediation, or that Plato had been previously in correspondence with Perdiccas. The king had no reason to be jealous of his brother;* and after the death of Ptolemy, the Thebans, as we have already remarked, could not have wished to detain him. It is therefore probable enough that the term of three years assigned to his stay at Thebes, though not on the best authority, is not far from the truth. It would be the part of his life which intervened between the age of sixteen and twenty.

It was undoubtedly not the study of philosophy either speculative or practical that chiefly occupied Philip's attention during this period. To the society in which it was passed he may have been mainly indebted for that command of the Greek language which enabled him both to write and speak it with a degree of ease and elegance not inferior to that of the most practised orators of the day. But the most important advantages which he gained from his stay at Thebes, were probably derived from the political and military lessons with which the conversations of generals and statesmen like Epaminondas, Pelopidas, and their friends, could not fail to abound. It was by them that the art of war had been carried to the highest point it had yet reached in Greece; or rather they, more particularly Epaminondas, had given it a new form: and the details of

---

*   It is merely arbitrary conjecture of Flathe's (i p. 48) that Philip's desire to obtain the government of a Macedonian province, had provoked a misunderstanding between him and Perdiccas, which was adjusted by Plato's meditation.

their battles and campaigns would be eagerly collected by an intelligent and ambitious youth. Thebes was at this time the centre of
political movements: the point from which the condition, interests
and mutual relations of the Greek states might be most distinctly
surveyed. Here too were to be gained the clearest ideas of the state
of parties, of the nature and working of republican especially of
democratical institutions: here probably Philip learned many of
those secrets which often enabled him to conquer without drawing
the sword. And as he was placed in one of the most favourable
positions for studying the Greek character, so the need which his
situation imposed on him of continual caution and self-control must
have served very greatly to sharpen his natural sagacity, and to form
the address which he afterwards displayed in dealing with men, and
winning them for his ends. What were the impressions made upon
his taste and feelings by his residence at Thebes, it would be vain
to inquire; but it is remarkable that there are parts of his political
conduct which it is not easy to explain, except on the supposition
that he viewed Athens with a certain degree of predilection; which
inclined him, where his own interest allowed liberty of choice, to
favour her at the expense of her Boeotian rival.

Nature had gifted him with almost every quality that could fit
him for the station which he was destined to fill: a frame of extraordinary robustness, which was no doubt well trained in the exercises
of the Theban palaestras: a noble person, a commanding and prepos-
sessing mien, which won respect and inspired confidence in all who
approached him: ready eloquence, to which art only applied the
cultivation requisite to satisfy the fastidious demands of a rhetorical
age: quickness of observation, acuteness of discernment, presence of
mind, fertility of invention, and dexterity in the management of men
and things. There seem to have been two features in his character,
which, in another station, or under different circumstances, might
have gone near to lower him into an ordinary person, but which
were so controlled by his fortune as to contribute not a little to his
success. He appears to have been by his temperament prone to almost
every kind of sensual pleasure. But as his life was too busy to allow
him often to indulge his bias, his occasional excesses wore the air
of an amiable condescension. So his natural humour would perhaps

have led him too often to forget his dignity in intercourse with his inferiors. But to Philip, the great king, the conqueror, the restless politician, these intervals of relaxation occurred so rarely, that they might strengthen his influence with the vulgar, and could never expose him to contempt. From that he was secured by the energy of will, which made all his faculties and accomplishments of mind and body, and even his failings, as well as what may be called in a lower sense his virtues—his affability, clemency, and generosity—always subservient to the purposes of his lofty ambition. A moral estimate of such a man's character is comprised in the bare mention of this ruling passion, and cannot be enlarged by any investigation into the motives of particular actions; and it is scarcely worth while to consider him in any other light than as an instrument of Providence for fixing the destiny of nations.

Greece in the Fourth Century BC

The comparisons drawn by Thirlwall, more often than not, reflected a pessimistic view of the modern world. Thirlwall blamed decline in the public spirit of fourth-century Greece on the preponderance of mercenaries at the time. In his second edition, he added the comment that the Greek mercenaries were comparable to 'English sailors in the time of war, when they receive their prize-money and wages', who 'are encouraged to waste the earning in a few days (vol.v, p.280).'[4] *The Times* of Thursday May 29th 1856 reported the calmer side of such celebrations:

Peace Rejoicings, Liverpool, May 28th

The demonstrations to-morrow will include reviews of the local pensioners and the Royal Lancashire Artillery Militia; a regatta on the river by the Royal Mersey Yacht Club; large processions of school children, with flags, banners, and bands of music; a great display of bunting in the streets; and pleasure trips to Wales and the Isle of Man. Illuminations and fireworks are discouraged in consequence of the failures and casualties on the occasion of the visit of the Duke of Cambridge. All returned soldiers from the Crimea, in the town, will be treated by the Mayor to a hot dinner of roast beef and plum-pudding, a pint of ale, and a shilling each. The public buildings in the

town and some of the dock warehouses will be thrown open to the public, and two free performances on the great organ will be given in the course of the afternoon. The banks will close at 11 O'Clock, and business operations will be generally suspended.

These expeditions of Alexander [of Pherae] are significant in more than one point of view: partly as they show that Athens was not so completely mistress of the seas, as she had been in former times; and partly as an example of piracy on a large scale. This was an evil which henceforward continued to increase: but it was connected with another, one of the main causes of the ruin of Greece which has already been slightly noticed, and will now claim more particular attention. We have frequent occasion to mention the mercenary bands, which from the beginning of this century take a more and more prominent part in Grecian warfare. It was no doubt the long continuance of the Peloponnesian war, and the troubles which ensued that called them into existence;* but it was not in the wars of Greece alone that they found employment, nor, it would seem, did they hold out the strongest temptation to needy adventurers to enter upon this course of life. Higher pay and richer plunder were to be found in Asia, where the disturbed state of the Persian empire created almost continual occasions for the services of Greek auxiliaries, whose superiority in arms was universally acknowledged by the barbarians. Hence the number of persons who devoted themselves to an occupation which attracted ardent spirits by its dangers and vicissitudes, as well as the more sordid by the prospect of gain and pleasure, was constantly increasing;[5] there was no state which might not carry on the war with such troops, if it could only find means of maintaining them: and their regular training and experience perhaps gave them an advantage over the native militia of most cities. By Sparta and Thebes, which assiduously cultivated the art of war, and grounded all their pretensions to political pre-eminence on their military strength, they were very sparingly employed. But Athens began early to make frequent use

---

* The Arcadians mentioned by Herodotus (viii 26: *oligoi tines*) are, as Wachsmuth remarks, an earlier example of the practice; but it is one which does not affect the general truth of the observation in the text.

of them, and by degrees fell into the practice of employing them oftener than her own citizens, and sometimes alone.

The pernicious effects of this system soon became manifest in a variety of ways. A greater number of citizens remained at home, not however engaged in useful industry, but subsisting chiefly on the pittances granted for their attendance at the assembly and the tribunals, and on the largesses which many of the numberless festivals brought with them, along with the shows and the pleasures of the day. And this was no doubt the main motive which led to the preference of mercenaries for military service. On the other hand these men communicated their dissolute habits to the citizens who served in the same camp, and thus contributed to corrupt the manners of the city more deeply than ever. These may perhaps be considered as the most direct causes of that visible increase of dissipation and licentiousness, which struck a Greek historian of this period in the character of Athenian society (Theopompus ad Athenaeum xii 43; cf. Justin vi). But in a political point of view the most important effect of this change of system was that which it produced on the Athenian generals, who collected and commanded these mercenary troops in the service of the commonwealth. They were led to consider themselves very nearly in the same light as the men who made the collecting and commanding of such forces a profession and to adopt their views, and follow their example. The mercenary leaders, whatever might be the variety of their talents and characters, all perfectly resembled one another in one point. They had broken the ties which bound them to their native cities: they were under no control, and had nothing to hope and fear from their fellow-citizens: their sole object was to secure their independence, and to establish themselves in opulence and power elsewhere. There were two roads by which they were often able to attain this object. The foreign princes into whose service they entered were frequently willing to attach them to their interests by a domestic alliance, and an honourable settlement.* Thus it was that Seuthes would have detained Xenophon, offering him the hand of one of his daughters, and one of his most valuable towns near

---

* Another point of resemblance to the Italian *condottieri*.

the coast. Several other instances of this kind will shortly occur
to us. Another very common mode of accomplishing their wishes,
was to seize some fortified town, and to erect a tyranny in it. So
Charidemus, after he had quitted the Athenian service, crossed over
to Asia, and made himself master of the towns of Scepsis, Cebren
and Ilium (Dem. *Aristoc.* 154). He was encouraged to make this
attempt by the unsettled state of the province, which was an object
of contest between two rival Persian satraps. But like opportunities
were frequently offered on the coast of Asia, which held out the
strongest temptations to these adventurers, by the fertility of the
soil, and the wealth of the cities. The orators of this age represent
such acts of violence as having become an ordinary practice. 'You
know', the speaker says in an oration of Demosthenes delivered
in 352, that all these chiefs of mercenaries make it their claim to
take possession of Greek cities and to rule in them, and that they
go ravaging about, and everywhere conducting themselves as the
common enemies of all those who wish to live in freedom according
to their own laws' (Dem. *Aristocrates* 139). Isocrates represents the
inhabitants of the Asiatic coast as the principal sufferers, and enters
into details, which show that the treatment they received from the
freebooters into whose power they fell, was usually marked by the
foulest excesses of wantonness and cruelty.

It is however hardly possible to read the account which the
same author, in a passage to which we have referred a few pages
back, gives of the exploits of Timotheus, without observing, that
the main points which distinguished the Athenian general from
such men as Charidemus, were on the one hand his loyalty and on
the other the natural gentleness and moderation of his character,
which prevented him from inflicting any wanton wrong. But in
other respects he conducted his operations very much after the
manner of the mercenary chiefs, and was not scrupulous as to the
means of finding pay for his troops. It was to be supposed that other
generals placed in a like situation would be much less careful of the
interests of Athens and would pay much less regard to the feelings
of the Greeks who might be subject to their pleasure. Accordingly
we find that Iphicrates and Chabrias spent much of their time in
foreign service, and not only without any respect to the interests

of Athens, but sometimes in direct opposition to them. At a time when it was very desirable for Athens to cultivate the friendship of the Persian king, Chabrias, without asking permission from the people, accepted the command of the forces with which the revolted Egyptians were making war against him. He was compelled indeed to return by a threatening decree which was passed in compliance with the remonstrances of the Persian court (Diodorus xv 29); but he was a man of such dissolute and expensive habits, contracted most probably in his campaigns in the east, that even the liberty of Athens did not satisfy him, and he resided as much as he was able abroad (Theoph. *ad Athen.* xii 43). Iphicrates ventured still more openly to drop the character of an Athenian citizen, when it would have imposed an inconvenient restraint upon him. He not only entered onto the service of Cotys, and married one of his daughters, but aided him in several acts of unequivocal hostility against his country. Yet he was suffered to retain the awards which had been bestowed upon him for his past deserts, apparently on the same ground which rendered the Athenians so indulgent to Charidemus. Chares, whom we have hitherto had but little occasion to notice, but who will hereafter be seen taking a very prominent part in the history of these times, seems to have been inferior in military and political abilities to the three men just mentioned, and much less under the restraint of any motives of patriotism or honour. He was too indolent and too much addicted to pleasure to be keenly sensible to the spur of ambition, and was perfectly reckless as to the choice of the means by which he might gratify his inclinations. Of him, as well as of Timotheus, Chabrias and Iphicrates, it was observed by Theopompus, that he preferred sojourning in foreign parts to living at Athens: and that Sigeum, near the mouth of the Hellespont, was his ordinary residence. The historian indeed puts this remark in a general form, as applying to all the eminent men of Athens: and attributes the fact to the intractable temper of the people. But as the examples he adduced all belong to this period—except that of Conon which is manifestly irrelevant—we may be allowed to believe that that cause was not one which had existed long before, and at least not in a slighter degree, but one peculiar to this age: and it may be most easily traced to the change which we have been noticing in the Athenian military system. As the commander of a mercenary force, an Athenian general, as long as he could keep his troops together, possessed almost absolute authority, as far as his power reached. As the chief witnesses of his conduct were strangers, who were generally benefited by his worst proceedings, he was seldom liable to be called to account at home, unless he very grossly betrayed or thwarted the interests of the commonwealth. The Athenians were not capable of feeling much concern for the sufferings of others, and were easily induced to connive at a wrong by which they did not lose, still more easily at one by which they gained. They paid little heed to the complaints of their allies, so long as their contributions were regularly brought in, still less to those of any other foreigners. Chares adopted an expedient, which, if not absolutely new, seems never to have been so largely employed before, to contain impunity and favour with the people. He spent a part of the sums which he received, and which ought either to have been paid into the treasury, or applied to the service of the state, to gain some of the venal orators, and to influence the proceedings of the tribunals. By these arts, and by promises which became proverbial from the readiness with which he made and broke them (*Charetos hyposcheseis*, Suidas), he was able to squander the public money on his dissolute pleasures, and still to be accounted a useful and trusty servant of the commonwealth.

In a country like Greece the increase of piracy was necessarily connected with such a military system as we have described. Every freebooter was, or might easily have become a pirate; as Charidemus is said to have begun his career as the captain of a pirate vessel (Dem. *Aristoc.* 148). Athens, as mistress of the sea, and chief of a great maritime confederacy, ought to have removed this nuisance, or at least was bound to protect her allies from it. But her negligence, or that of her commanders, who were themselves often engaged in a kind of warfare not much more legitimate, suffered it to gain ground, until, as we shall see in the sequel, it acquired a certain degree of political importance.

It is easy to conceive that out of this state of things many causes of discontent may have arisen to alienate the members of the confederacy of Athens. Among them we may notice an abuse which had crept into naval service. It became not unusual for the citizens on whom the duties of the trierarchy devolved, to transfer them to those who were willing to undertake them at the lowest rate. By such a bargain the trierarch, who always received a certain sum from the state, might often be a gainer, independently of the exemption he enjoyed from personal trouble and risk. The other part was commonly, it seems, a needy adventurer, whose object it was to get all he could by rapine and extortion. The trierarchs indeed were liable to be called to account for the misconduct of their substitutes (Dem. *de Coron. Trier.* 9 ff.); but the lawfulness of the practice seems hardly to have been disputed; and the cases in which it was attended with danger to them, were not those in which the evils it produced fell upon the allies of Athens. It may well be supposed that they were the more sensitive to injuries and encroachments on their rights, as she was no longer the formidable power she had once been: and that the leading states watched the manner in which she observed the stipulations of the league, with a jealousy quickened by their sense of their own importance. As to any particular provocation however offered to any of them, history is silent; it is chiefly from some general allusions of Isocrates that we are able to collect, that the exactions of the Athenian generals, for the support of their mercenary troops, were among the principal causes of a war, which broke out in the year 357 between Athens and her allies, from whom it took the name of the Social War. But before we enter upon the history of this war, we must relate some transactions which immediately preceded it, and perhaps contributed in some degree to hasten its outbreaking.

After an account of the outbreak and duration of the Social War, Thirlwall discusses the orator Isocrates, as a background to his statement about social changes in fourth-century Athens.

While the negotiation with the allies was pending, or soon after the peace, Isocrates wrote what we would call a pamphlet in the form of a speech intended to be delivered in the assembly held to deliberate on the treaty. The work is of considerable value as a historical document, though it affords less information than might have been expected from it with regard to the war. Isocrates was a rhetorician by profession: the framing of sentences, and the turning of periods, was the great business of his long life: the only one in which he was very successful; in that he attained to the highest skill labour could give, and amassed great wealth as a teacher. But he appears to have been a hearer of Socrates, was disgusted with the Sophists, and had little taste for the ordinary subjects of their disputations; he was thus led to apply his art to morals and politics, not like most of the Socratic school in the discussion of general principles, but in practical precepts and counsels. He was the first Greek writer who employed his pen on questions which arose out of passing events ([Plutarch] *Vit. X Orat* 837b). He seems to have believed that nothing but the weakness of his voice, and the shyness and timidity of his character, prevented him from taking a leading part in the public debates (*Panathen.* 12–13; *Philip* 93). But it is very doubtful whether any strength of lungs, or hardness of brow, could have rendered discourses such as he has left acceptable to an Athenian assembly, at least after it had learnt from Demosthenes, what real eloquence was. He valued himself not a little on his political sagacity, as to which a stronger mind than his own has entertained a widely different opinion.* But he was a respectable, well-meaning man; he deplored the evils which afflicted Greece, and thought he saw a remedy; but seems to have given little heed whether it might not prove worse than the disease. His general notion was union under a single chief; which however he wished to reconcile with liberty and independence. How inconsistent the plan which he proposed was with the combination of these objects, will appear in the proper place.

The advice however which he gives on the occasion of the peace seems indisputably good: and every Athenian patriot must have regretted that the people was so little disposed to follow it, and that even in the most elegant diction, and the most graceful periods, there is not a charm strong enough to eradicate ambition and cupidity, especially when confirmed by long indulgence, from

---

* Niebuhr *Kl. Schrift*, p. 474, and in the *Philological Museum*, ii, p. 492, 'at least in his old age a thoroughly bad citizen, as well as an ineffable fool'.

the human beast. Its effect may have been somewhat impaired by the ambiguity of the language in which it is conveyed, which, he himself admits, had a repulsive, paradoxical sound (*On the Peace* 77, 80). He exhorts the Athenians to cease to aim at the command of the sea, and appeals to history, both their own and Sparta's, to prove that this dazzling object of competition had only been a source of the greatest calamities to every power that had acquired it. He had spoken with the highest approbation of the peace of Antalcidas, so far as it provided for the independence of the Greeks, and had recommended that this should be adopted as the basis of the treaty under discussion (20): so that it might have been supposed that he wished to see the connection between Athens and her allies totally dissolved. This however, it appears from the sequel, was not his meaning. On the contrary it is that she may be again at the head of a confederacy as extensive as that which she had presided over in the days of Aristides (91, 92), that he desires she should renounce the command of the sea. All that he means by the command of the sea, is an unjust domination grounded upon and maintained by force. He would have a confederacy, in which all the members should be perfectly free, willingly submitting to the supremacy of Athens, paying none but voluntary contributions, and exempt from all kinds of molestation and encroachment. His proposition therefore, when distinctly understood, was not so paradoxical as it sounded. It was nothing more than had been done when the Athenian confederacy was revived; and all that was necessary to comply with his advice, was to return and adhere to the terms then laid down. How, if the people had been really desirous of this, it was to recover the confidence of its allies, is a question which he does not discuss.

Even as to the manner in which those terms had been violated, he affords very scanty information. He hints, rather than expressly asserts, that the Athenians had suffered their citizens to acquire property in the islands, against the spirit at least of the self-denying resolution, by which they had renounced all cleruchial possessions (6). He speaks also of arbitrary exactions, which have been already mentioned, and represents the allies as entirely abandoned to the discretion of the Athenian generals (160). He is however more explicit as to the domestic causes of the evil, which he is aware must be removed before any salutary change can be made in the foreign policy of the state. The people must discard its dishonest counsellors, must employ men of acknowledged probity both at home and abroad: it must cease itself to be indolent, voluptuous, rapacious, ambitious, greedy of flattery, and impatient of reproof. Hard conditions, and certainly surpassing the power of such rhetoric as that of Isocrates to bring to pass; for the old abuses, which had been repressed by the public calamities, and partially reformed, had sprung up again during the more tranquil and prosperous period that followed, with fresh luxuriance, and in new, more extravagant, and odious shapes. The city was again infested with a swarm of sycophants, more shameless, active, and venomous than in former times. The needy, idle, throng which lived upon the fees of legislation, government, and justice, viewed the men whose calumnious charges gave it most opportunities of exercising its judicial functions, as its greatest benefactors (156). The wealthy were exposed to continual vexation: Isocrates does not scruple to assert that they led more wretched lives than the indigent (154). Here however his own example shows how cautiously his general descriptions must be received. He complains much of the annoyance which he himself had suffered from the sycophants; and certainly his wealth, his incapacity for public speaking, his connection with Timotheus, and other distinguished citizens, and with foreign princes, and his avowed political sentiments, must all have conspired to point him out as one of the most signal objects for their attacks. Yet in the ninety-fifth year of his age he could look back upon a life of almost undisturbed prosperity, with no other regret than that he had been debarred by his natural defects from more active participation in public business (*Panathen.* 9–13). So too it can only be considered as a rhetorical exaggeration, that he represents the vilest, most profligate, and senseless demagogues, as the most popular. Had things come to this pass, no room would have been left for the influence of the able and upright men, whom we shall find for several years ordinarily taking the lead in public affairs. The real ground of this statement was probably that the same decay of public spirit which appeared in the growing neglect of military exercises, and the evasion both of foreign and home service, betrayed itself in the assembly by the levity and haste with which important matters were often handled, and the applause with which indecorous sallies of gaiety were received. This want of earnestness—which however might easily seem greater than it really was in an Athenian audience—was a subject of complaint with Demosthenes also.

In this piece Isocrates notices an innovation, which appears to him pregnant with pernicious consequences, or at least as a symptom of degeneracy, but which admits of being viewed in a different light. He speaks of it in a way which shows that he was only intent upon an antithesis; but the fact he alludes to is more clearly described and illustrated by Plutarch (*Phocion* 7). In earlier times all the great men of Athens combined the characters of the general and the statesman in one person. In the period at which we have now arrived, they were beginning to be more and more separated from each other. Many of the orators never saw the camp: the generals rarely ascended the *bema*. This practice was the effect, partly of the progress of eloquence, and the wider range of rhetorical studies, which demanded a longer preparation, and more laborious exercises, partly of the new military system, which, as we have seen, tended to draw the generals away from Athens. Phocion is remarked as one of the last Athenians in whom the two characters were still blended. According to modern notions this division of military and civil duties might be thought a great gain for the service of the state. Whatever evil sprang from it seems to have arisen from the corruption of the age. The responsibility both of the generals and the ministers—as we may call them—of the republic, was lessened; and it was easy for men like Chares to find advocates, apparently disinterested, to defend all their proceedings. The worst abuse connected with it was, that military command was so much coveted, that if we may believe Isocrates, the election of generals was often determined by the most open bribery (63).

If it were not that we have no hint of any negotiation between Athens and the confederates, before Chares had provoked the intervention of the Persian court, we might have supposed that Isocrates wrote this oration, before the threats of Persian hostility had been heard of at Athens. For he takes no notice of them, though they afforded the fairest opportunity of recommending his favourite scheme for the establishment of tranquillity and prosperity in Greece. He touches only by one slight allusion on the war, in a way which implies that in his judgement there was no more danger to be apprehended from the one quarter than the other. He conceives that there was no essential and necessary opposition between the interests of either of these princes and those of the commonwealth, and that, if they were only convinced of her pacific disposition towards them, Philip would readily resign Amphipolis, and Cersobleptes the Chersonesus, to her.* And his general conclusion is, that, notwithstanding the great loss and damage which she had suffered in the Social War, it would be her own fault, if she did not become more powerful and prosperous than ever. Let her only abstain from aggression and wrong, hold herself in readiness for self-defence, and show herself willing to protect the weak against the strong: justice would bring back an age of gold. The rich would be relieved from taxation; the poor would find employment in the arts of peace: the public revenues would be doubled; a tide of wealth would flow into Piraeus (26, 166); foreign princes would pay their court to her, and would gladly purchase her favour by the cession of a part of their territories: in Thrace alone she would be able to find ample and undisputed space for any colonies she might wish to send out: and the Greeks would look up to her with reverence and attachment, as to the guardian of their liberty and rights. A picture unhappily not more sharply contrasted with the past and the present, than with the reality of the future.

Demosthenes and Greece after the Social War

We have been used to see the Athenians making the most vigorous exertions in the midst of their greatest calamities: we might otherwise have been disposed to question the accuracy of the descriptions we have received of the disastrous consequences of the Social War. For that war was scarcely at an end, before we find them again acting on the offensive, and even ready to enter into a new contest, appar-

---

* His language (28) might lead anyone to infer that the Chersonesus was still in the hands of Cersobleptes, if it did not as strongly imply that Amphipolis was still in the possession of Athens, which, at least, was certainly not the case.

ently still more arduous and hazardous than that from which they had just retired with such heavy loss. There is reason to believe that in the course of the same summer in which they made peace with the allies, they sent an expedition against Olynthus, as to which we are informed that it was the second occasion that called forth the services of voluntary trierarchs, and that a body of Athenian cavalry was employed in it;* facts which imply a considerable effort, though we have no account of the results; nor is the precise date well ascertained. Notwithstanding the peace the public mind continued to be agitated by rumours of the Persian preparations; and it appears that there were orators—politicians, we may suppose, of the school of Isocrates—who endeavoured to instigate the people to declare war against Persia. The deliberation of the assembly on this subject is chiefly known to us as the occasion on which Demosthenes began his career as statesman, with an oration which is still extant. Our attention is thus turned toward this extraordinary man, who will henceforth occupy it more and more throughout the period comprised in this portion of our history.

There follows an account of the personal life of Demosthenes.

The account which he obtained from his guardian, when he came of age, must have convinced him that he had no hope of redress but through litigation: and their abilities, wealth, and influence, rendered them formidable adversaries. The very institution of legal proceedings against persons so closely connected with his family by blood or friendship, wore an ungracious appearance; and the parties interested did not fail to represent it as the effect of unnatural malignity, which they seem to have expressed by another opprobrious epithet.†

A hard contest lay before him, in which he must have been aware that the justice of his cause would avail him little without the aid of forensic skill: and it was one on which his after fortunes mainly depended. It was therefore for immediate use, on the most

---

* Demosthenes *Medias* 161, 197; the date of this expedition depends on that of the date of Demosthenes. See Boeckh *Public Economy of Athens* iv, 13.
† Argas, a viper: Aesch. *De F. L.* 99.

pressing occasion, that he sharpened the weapon with which he was to achieve so many memorable victories. This however was not the only motive which urged him to the study of eloquence. About the same time that he became his own master, he had been present at the trial in which Callistratus defended his conduct in the affair of Oropus. The impression made upon the youth by that masterly pleading, and by the admiration it excited, was like that which the hearing of Herodotus is commonly believed to have wrought on Thucydides: it was perhaps then first that Demosthenes felt that he too was an orator. There was however a wide interval, not to be surmounted without many years of laborious application, between the point which he had attained, and the ideal mark which he proposed to himself. He placed himself under the direction of Isaeus, an advocate of high reputation, a scholar of Isocrates, though in style much more nearly resembling Lysias. To him he may have been in some degree indebted for the grace, simplicity, and vigour, which are the most conspicuous qualities of his forensic pleadings. For this purpose he could not have found a better model: nor for any practical end any much worse than Isocrates. Yet he may have wished to obtain the instructions of so celebrated a master, and we can easily believe that, when deterred by the price which the rhetorician asked, he still diligently studied his works.* There was also a tradition, resting indeed on nameless authority, that he was for a time one of Plato's hearers: and the difference of style would not induce us to reject it: but his acquaintance, which may safely be presumed, with the philosopher's writings would sufficiently explain, if any such explanation were needed, that lofty strain of morality which pervades his great works, and which, as may be inferred from the observation of Panaetius (Plut. *Dem.* 13), he first ventured to introduce into speeches addressed to Athenian courts and assemblies, audiences, which Plato himself would scarcely have deemed worthy or capable of receiving such sublime truths.

There follows an account of Demosthenes' pleas on behalf of his own inheritance.

---

*   Callibius, in Plutarch *Dem.* 5. Compare [Plutarch] *Vit. X Orat.* 844c.

The success with which he pleaded his own cause was encouraging, but not decisive as to his higher prospects. The speeches which he delivered on that occasion were deemed worthy of his master Isaeus, and certainly give proof of no ordinary talents. But a different kind of eloquence was requisite for the debates of the assembly; and defects of utterance and gesticulation which might be overlooked by a court of justice in a youth claiming redress, appeared intolerably offensive, in one who presented himself as a public counsellor. The reception he met with on his first appearance before the assembled people, was such as might have stifled the hopes of one less conscious of his own powers. His articulation was imperfect, his action disagreeable, his voice, naturally strong, was ill managed; and even his style startled his hearers by its novelty and was thought harsh, strained and confused (Plut. *Dem.* 6). Though not silenced, he descended from the bema in the midst of murmurs and laughter. There were however among his audience persons able to discern the merit of the attempt, and friendly enough to encourage and aid him with useful advice. Old men were still living who had heard Pericles in their boyhood; and one of them it is said cheered Demosthenes with an assurance, that he reminded him of that great orator, whose fame appears to have been unrivalled at Athens. Satyrus also, the player, an amiable and estimable man, was believed to have directed his attention to the principal faults of his elocution. He saw all that he wanted, and with unconquerable resolution set himself to the task of overcoming his natural impediments, correcting his unsightly habits, and perfecting every organ and faculty which he had to employ as a public speaker. He is reported to have withdrawn for a time from society, to pursue his work without interruption; and we know that he resorted to new and very irksome methods of mastering his personal disadvantages (Pl. *Dem.* 11). These exercises he continued until he had acquired a manner of delivery, as to which it is sufficient to say, that it was thought by his contemporaries worthy of his eloquence, and that it distinguished him no less above all his rivals (Dionysius, *De Adm.* vi. dic. in Dem. 22).

It was not however merely to enable himself to satisfy the eye and ear of the public, that he entered on this course of training. He felt that the equally fastidious taste and judgement of an Athenian assembly demanded more than it had found in his first essay, which probably fell short by a much greater distance of his own idea. He applied himself to an assiduous study of all the theoretical works he could procure, which could furnish him with rules and hints for the cultivation of his art; and still more diligently consulted the great models of eloquence in which he recognized a kindred genius. In Thucydides he appears to have found, as we do, the richest mine of thought and language; and the value which he set on his history is attested by the tradition, that he copied it out eight times, and could almost recite it by heart,* and by the evidence of his own style, notwithstanding the difference required by two kinds of composition so completely distinct. In the meanwhile his pen was constantly employed in rhetorical exercises. Every question suggested to him by passing events served him for a topic of discussion, which called forth the application of his attainments to the real business of life. It was perhaps as much for the sake of such practice, as with a view to reputation or the increase of his fortune, that he accepted employment, as an advocate, which until he began to take an active part in public affairs, was offered to him in abundance. If he viewed these occasions in this light, we might believe the story that he once furnished each of the adverse parties in a cause with a speech, and yet might not consider it as a very deep stain upon his honour. His main occupation however was not with forms, or words, or sentences. The profession of an advocate itself required an extensive range of information. Causes especially which related to contested laws or decrees generally involved a number of questions, that called for a large share of legal and political knowledge. Demosthenes, who from the first was always looking forward to the widest field of action, undoubtedly did not content himself with the indispensable study of the Athenians laws and constitution, but bestowed no less earnest attention on the domestic affairs, the financial resources, and the foreign relations of the commonwealth, and on the political divisions, powers and interests of the rest of Greece. The state of the

---

* See on these reports Krueger *Leben des Thukydides*, p. 81, 82. Cicero indeed, *Orat.* 9, when he asks: '*Quis unquam Graecorum rhetorum a Thucydide quidquam duxit?*' seems never to have heard of them. But at least Demosthenes might have learnt as much for the purpose of his art from Thucydides as from Isocrates.

finances, and of the naval and military establishments of Athens, the defects of the existing system, and the means of correcting them, appear more particularly to have occupied his thoughts.

Such was the process by which he became confessedly the greatest orator among the people by whom eloquence was cultivated as it never has been since by any other nation upon earth. He brought it to its highest stage of perfection, as Sophocles the tragic drama, by the harmonious union of excellencies which before had only existed apart. The quality in his writings which excited the highest admiration of the most intelligent critics among his countrymen the later critical age was the Protean versatility with which he adapted his style to every theme, so as to furnish the most perfect examples of every order and kind of eloquence. They, who understood and felt the beauty of his compositions in a degree beyond the reach of the most learned foreigner, were aware that, with all their enthusiasm of delight, they could but faintly conceive the impression which that which they read must have produced on those who heard it animated by the voice and action of the orator, when he was addressing himself to real interests and passions (Dionys *De Adm.* vi dic, in Dem. 22). This however is a subject on which it would be foreign to our present purpose to enlarge. We will observe only that Demosthenes, like Pericles, never willingly appeared before his audience with any but the ripest fruits of his private studies; though he was quite capable of speaking on the impulse of the moment in a manner worthy of his reputation; that he continued to the end of his career to cultivate his art with unabated diligence, and that even in the midst of public business his habits were known to be those of a severe student.

With so many claims to admiration on this side, he has left, we will not say an ambiguous but a disputed character.* It would indeed have been surprising had the case been otherwise with a man whose whole life was passed in the midst of the most violent political storms and the most furious party-strife. His efforts to

---

* We need hardly observe that Quintilian's '*atqui malum virum accepimus*' (xii 1.14), as appears from the writer's annexed remark, implies no more than this: though it shows that, as usual, the scandal which Quintilian disbelieved was most eagerly read, and of course most frequently repeated.

defend the liberties of Athens and of Greece against a foreign king, have earned him still more virulent attacks in modern times, than he experienced from the sycophants of his own day, or from his personal enemies. The extreme scantiness of our information as to his private history, and indeed as to the public events of his times, must render it impossible distinctly to refute the imputations which had been thrown upon his moral worth: all that can be said on his defence is, that so far as can be now ascertained, not one of them rests upon any better foundation, than partial statements or doubtful surmises: while whatever we know with certainty of his public life is good, and often great. That he was free from faults, no one can suppose: his character was human; it was that of a Greek, and an Athenian in a corrupt and turbulent age, and in a difficult and trying station. It must not be compared with any purer models of virtue than the most illustrious statesmen of his country. From such a comparison according to the view which he himself professed to take of his public conduct and his political aims, he had no need to shrink: for many of them had been more successful but none in an undertaking so glorious as that in which he failed. Most of the graver charges which have been brought against him, are intimately connected with his public history: and our opinion of the man must be mainly regulated by the judgement we form of him as a statesman. If he truly represented the great object of his life to be that of preserving Greece from foreign domination, and if the means by which he strove to accomplish this purpose were, to husband the resources, to rouse the energies, and exalt that character of the Athenians, his own will stand in little need of an apology. This however is a question which it would be premature now to enter on, and which the history must decide. For the same reason we shall not here attempt to exhibit the portraits of any of the men who became celebrated either as his coadjutors or his adversaries, but shall resume the narrative from which we have been digressing.

In the course of the preceding year, Demosthenes had exhibited his powers in an oration which he delivered himself, in a public cause which excited great interest, as it was instituted for the repeal of a law lately enacted on the proposal of one Leptines, by which all exemptions from the expensive services technically termed *liturgies*, that had been granted to deserving citizens, or other benefactors of the commonwealth, were abolished, all such grants were declared illegal for the future, and even to solicit them from the people was forbidden under a most severe penalty. On this occasion Demosthenes appeared as the advocate of Ctesippus, the son of Chabrias, who was one of the principal parties to the cause, and deeply concerned in the issue, as their heir—a very unworthy one— of his father's privileges. Demosthenes undertook his part, chiefly it seems out of regard for his family, but not without a decided opinion on the inexpediency of the law which he opposed. It had been recommended by Leptines as a measure of relief to the citizens who were burdened with the charge of the public amusements; for the exemptions in question did not extend to the trierarchy, or to the war-taxes. To Demosthenes it appeared that the purpose might be more equitably, honourably, and usefully, answered by a fairer distribution of the burden; and in the room of the sweeping abolition of former grants, he proposed an inquiry into the claims of those who enjoyed them. The law was repealed. We do not know whether the proposal of Demosthenes—which would probably have disclosed many abuses—was adopted; but the speech, which is an admirable specimen of his oratory, must have raised him high in public estimation, and have inspired him with confidence to take a part in the debates of the assembly.

The oration however on the question of the Persian war shows that he was much less intent on making a display of eloquence than on offering useful advice. It is calm, simple, grave, statesman-like, indicating the outlines of the policy which he ever after continued to recommend. He points out the danger to which Athens would expose herself, if, relying on uncertain rumours, she should rush onto a war in which Persia might be able to combine with other maritime Greek states against her. But he urges the necessity that she should immediately place herself in a strong defensive posture, not more against the attack with which she had been threatened, than against those which might be made on her from other quarters which were avowedly hostile. It is a little surprising that though this is the general purpose of the speech, the name of Philip does not once occur in it, and it contains no direct allusion to the war with Macedonia. We may infer from this silence, that Philip's proceedings, though they had provoked the resentment of the Athenians, had not yet excited any alarm even in Demosthenes. It is likewise remarkable that he speaks of Thebes, though the popular prejudice had never been more violent against her at Athens than at this period, in an extremely mild, respectful, conciliating tone. But he does not confine himself, like Isocrates, to vague general advice: the contrast between the practical statesman and the wordy rhetorician is strongly illustrated in the one's speech, and the other's pamphlet, which were produced at so short an interval of time, under similar circumstances, and with views apparently not discordant. Demosthenes proposes a specific well-digested plan, which would enable the commonwealth to equip her fleets with the least possible delay, and, if necessary, to raise her naval force to 300 galleys. Into the details of this scheme we need not enter. It was an attempt to remedy one of the crying evils of the existing system which will be mentioned hereafter. We are not informed whether it was adopted; but the proposal of war with Persia was rejected.

Philip and Greece

It is peculiarly necessary in this period of Greek history to distinguish between the impression made by the events on the mind of the reader, who reviews them at a distance of many ages, and that which they produced on the chief actors and their contemporaries, as they occurred. To us the fall of Olynthus, which completed the subjugation of the Chalcidian peninsula, may seem to have decided Philip's contest with Athens and virtually to have made him master of Greece. Thessaly might be considered as already almost a province of Macedonia. The struggle between Thebes and Phocis had reached such a point, that the one party needed assistance, and the other could not hope to withstand the force with which he was able to support its antagonist. Then, if his arms terminated the conflict, the use to be made of the victory would depend on his will, and there remained no Greek state capable of resisting him. In Peloponnesus there was a similar division of strength and interests: and the side on which he threw his weight must prevail. He had already formed a considerable marine, which after the conquest of the Chalcidian towns he had means of continually augmenting, and which enabled him to threaten and molest the foreign possessions of Athens. The road to Thrace lay open to him: he had already gained a strong footing there: the rival princes were either his humble allies, or enemies who lay at his mercy. We see little prospect that the Greek cities on the Hellespont should long preserve their independence, or Athens the Chersonesus, if it should be his pleasure to expel her colonists. Even the principal channel through which she receives the means of subsistence may soon be closed against her commerce.

There was apparently only one event which could oppose any serious obstacle to his progress: this was a coalition among all the principal states of Greece, directed against him, animated by a spirit capable of vigorous efforts, and guided by a master mind. But it was not their clashing interests, and mutual jealousy, alone, that rendered such an event improbable, but still more perhaps the difficulty of awakening them to a lively sense of their danger. The rise of the Macedonian power was too recent, and had yet been too gradual, to be at once generally viewed in the true light. The Peloponnesians could scarcely see beyond the politics of their own peninsula. Whatever was passing in or out of Greece, was in their eyes important only as it affected the relative strength of Sparta and her hostile neighbours. They looked upon the Sacred War with interest, only so far as the issue might make Peloponnesus once more the theatre of war between Thebes and Sparta, or might release Sparta from all fear of her most dangerous rival. Philip too was deemed worth notice merely as he might be a useful ally, or a formidable enemy, to either of the contending Peloponnesian parties. The increased power of his kingdom was not contemplated as bringing it into any new relation to Greece, as a whole. It was not so long since his father had owed his throne to the protection of Sparta; and even after the power against which she had defended it was laid in the dust, she could not easily bring herself to think of the son of Amyntas, as a patron, or a master. The case was not very dissimilar with the parties immediately concerned in the Sacred War. The Phocians indeed, conscious of the insecure ground on

which they stood, dreaded his enmity, though it was but lately that
their forces had met on equal terms, and that each side had been by
turns victorious; but they did not wholly despair of propitiating it;
for Thebes might more reasonably excite his jealousy. On the other
hand Thebes was aware that her success depended on his aid: that
his opposition would defeat all her plans; but more than this could
scarcely enter into her calculations. Not many years had gone by,
since she had disposed of the Macedonian empire; still fewer since
he himself had been a hostage within her walls.

Beside these more evident causes of a false security, there were
others, which may have operated not the less forcibly, because they
were but indistinct feelings, scarcely ever reduced to a shape in
which they could become a subject of sober reflection. Demosthenes
has been charged with a gross want of candour because in defiance
of good historical testimony, proving the Hellenic origin of the
royal family of Macedonia he sometimes called Philip a barbarian.
The charge is childish, as well as false, and can only serve to keep
the real state of the case out of sight. Demosthenes everywhere
speaks, not of the man, but of the king, the chief of the nation, and
attributes its character to him; with perfect justice in respect of his
subject.* But the very judgement which was supposed to establish
Philip's Hellenic descent, implied that his people were considered as
barbarians. His ancestor had only been acknowledged as a Greek,
because he had been able to make it appear that he was not by
blood a Macedonian.† To our present purpose it is immaterial,
whether in Philip's age the line which parted the Macedonian from
the Greek was narrow or broad, whether there was any real affinity

---

* If in the reign of Peter the Great the power of Russia had been known to
threaten the liberty of Europe, would an English orator have been guilty of
falsehood or exaggeration, who should have spoken of the czar, as the Muscovite,
the Barbarian? Or would the ascendancy of such a power cease to be accounted
a less terrible calamity, if it were wielded by a prince of Teutonic blood, and
conversant with all the refinements of European culture?

† Niebuhr questions the truth of the story about the Argive descent of the
Macedonian kings, and thinks it arose out of the epithet *Argeadai* which is given
to them in the verses of the Sibyl, quoted by Pausanias vii 8.9. But it is surely
more probable that the epithet alludes to the received tradition. Wachsmuth,
Europäische Sittengeschichte, i p. 16, likewise treats the story as an idle tale.

of genius and character between them, or the resemblance was only produced by a slight varnish of Greek civilisation spread over the surface of a part of Macedonian society. The Greeks certainly had some reason for thinking so; so once they saw that the Macedonian princes were obliged to borrow from them the things on which they prided themselves most, the works of their fine arts, and the skill of their artists, and that though Philip might gain a victory over them, he could not celebrate it as he wished without their help. But we are here speaking only of the universal feeling, or if it was no more, the vulgar prejudice,* according to which the Macedonians were an inferior race, whose dominion would on that account indeed be the more odious, but, until it had become inevitable, was probably the less apprehended. With this price of birth there was coupled a consciousness of national unity, still subsisting notwithstanding the discord which prevented union: there was still always a possibility that whenever an adequate occasion should arise, a confederacy might be formed capable of resisting any foreign power, as their forefathers had repelled the Persian invasion. If the forces which met in hostile conflict a few years before at Mantinea, had been arrayed on one side, what Macedonian army could have faced them?

Philip himself, though fully sensible of his own advantages, certainly did not think meanly of the strength which Greece still possessed, and would have been very unwilling, from regard to his own safety, to provoke a coalition which might call it into action. It seems equally clear that his designs towards Greece were never hostile, any farther than his interests required. There can be little doubt that he valued himself upon his ancestry, through which he traced his pedigree up to Hercules, not less than upon his royal dignity. His blunt rough Macedonians, who called a spade a spade, made loyal subjects, and brave soldiers; but he liked to think of himself as a Greek: and it is not an extravagant supposition, that his respect for Athens, as the centre of Grecian art, knowledge and refinement, was constantly counteracting the resentment she provoked by her determined hostility. It is also nearly certain that

---

* Which however is not only attested, but avowed, by Isocrates, by way of compliment to Philip, *Philip*, 125.

Greece was never the ultimate end of his ambition. We cannot indeed pretend to determine the time when the great designs which he afterwards disclosed first took a definite shape in his mind; but from the beginning of his reign so many occasions were continually arising to draw his attention towards the East, that we may fairly presume these designs were in some measure blended with his earliest views of conquest and aggrandisement. But at least at the epoch which we have now reached, they must have been fully matured: for they became shortly after, as we shall see, a subject of reflection and discussion, of earnest desire and confident expectation to others, who assuredly did not either see farther than Philip, or to outstrip his wishes and hopes. But, that he might enter on the projected undertaking with safety, and a reasonable assurance of success, two things were necessary: that he should be master of the European coast of the Hellespont, and that Greece should be reduced to such a state, that he might have no hinderance or interruption to apprehend from her. Just to this point, if it could be found, he would have wished to see her sink: beyond this he cannot have thought it politic to degrade or hurt her. We cannot be surprised that, with such views, he should have preferred the way of negotiation, whenever it would serve his purpose, to that of arms; especially as he was conscious of extraordinary talents for diplomacy; or that notwithstanding his success in the war with Athens, he should have taken the first opportunity after the conquest of Olynthus, to signify his desire of peace. A closer inspection of the state of affairs of Greece at this time will perhaps enable us to understand both the motives which induced the Athenians gladly to listen to his overtures, and some of the especial temporary purposes with which he made them.

It was at Athens that the national consciousness, fostered by the inexhaustible recollections of the Persian war, and by the sight of no less glorious monuments of genius and art, which above all other trophies attested the superiority of the Greek over the barbarian was always most lively (Dem. xviii 83). It was there too that the extent of Philip's power was best understood, and the danger with which his ambition threatened Greece was most clearly perceived: for the encroachments which he had been incessantly making on the Athenian empire were at once provocations and warnings. And accordingly it was in the minds of Athenian statesmen, that, while others thought only of deprecating his hostility, or conciliating his favour, the project of a confederacy for the purpose of barring his progress seems first to have arisen. In the oration, which we supposed to be the last of the Olynthiacs, Demosthenes urged the expediency of sending embassies wherever there was prospect of success, to instigate the other Greeks against Philip. This advice appears to have been generally approved, and especially after the fall of Olynthus, to have been regarded as the last remaining resource of the state. It was warmly adopted by Eubulus and his party, opposed as they were on other questions to Demosthenes, and they even brought it forward in a more definite shape than their own. Hence we may infer that the measure was very popular: but yet we shall see reason to believe that Eubulus did not on this occasion act merely in compliance with the wishes of the people, but had an object in view which he hoped to accomplish by means of this proposition. We find that his first step was taken in concert with a party at Megalopolis, where, as might be expected, there were some who—whether honestly or from impure motives—desired the aid of Philip in their contest with Sparta, while others, probably the greater number, preferred the more congenial and safer alliance of Athens. Ischander, a son perhaps of the celebrated actor Neoptolemus,* seems to have been sent on a secret mission to Arcadia, and on his return made a report favourable to the views of Eubulus. The occasion is memorable, as the first on which Aeschines, afterward the celebrated rival of Demosthenes, is known to have taken a prominent part in public affairs.

An account of the Sacred War is followed by an analysis of its consequences.

The object which Philip had accomplished was important to him in several points of view. The honour of a seat in the Amphictyonic council, though conferred on the king, reflected upon his people;

---

*   But we do not know that he was himself a player, as Leland calls him (*L. of Ph.* ii, 29), deceived by the sarcastic title *deuteragonistes* by which Demosthenes manifestly alludes to the ancient profession of Aeschines (xix,10).

it was equivalent to an act of naturalisation, which wiped off the stain of its semi-barbarian origin: the Macedonians might henceforward be considered as Greeks. He probably also reckoned that it would afford him pretexts, occasions, facilities, for interference, as often as he might desire it, in the affairs of Greece. It was likewise a step towards a higher object, which now at least stood distinctly before his view, as the mark toward which all his future enterprises were to be directed. He had now a clear prospect that at no very distant time he should be able to begin his meditated attack on the Persian empire in the name of Greece, and with all the advantages that were to be derived from the consent, whether real or apparent of the nation. This project, which he had probably long harboured, had been recently presented to his mind by Isocrates, in a pamphlet, written during the interval between the conclusion of the peace with Athens and the end of the Sacred war, and addressed to him in the form of an oration: exhorting him first to interpose his authority to bring about a general pacification in Greece, which would follow as soon as he had healed the breaches that separated the leading states, Thebes and Athens, Sparta and Argos, from one another: and then to place himself at the head of the national confederacy for the invasion of Persia. This national war with Persia was the great thought which haunted Isocrates almost all his life; though perhaps he took it up at first merely as a theme for a rhetorical exercise.* In it he saw the only remedy for all the evils that afflicted Greece: a bond of union between the ambitious rivals whose discord had hitherto wasted her strength: a channel, by which the hosts of restless adventurers who preyed upon her resources might be drawn off to more alluring fields, and the needy citizens, whose poverty rendered them the ready tools of political intrigues, to foreign settlements, where they would find an ample and secure provision: and through which a portion of the wealth of the East might flow into Greece. He had recommended his project to public notice on various very different occasions. While Sparta was at the height of her power, and by the humiliation of Olynthus was breaking down one of the barriers

---

* It had before been treated by Gorgias, from whose declamation Isocrates is said to have borrowed [Plut.] *Vit. X Orat.* 837.

which she would afterwards gladly have seen standing between her and Macedonia, Isocrates, in an oration professedly designed to be recited before the spectators assembled at the national games, urged the expedience of a coalition between Sparta and Athens for war with Persia. Again, after Sparta had been reduced to the lowest stage of weakness, when Archidamus had mounted the throne, the rhetorician seems to have persuaded himself, and attempted to persuade the Spartan king, that the enterprise of pacifying Greece, and conquering Persia, did not exceed his means. But when Philip's successes had turned the eyes of all Greece toward him, Isocrates too could not doubt that this was the hero destined to execute his favourite plan. As long however as the war lasted between Athens and Macedonia, it would have been useless, and perhaps hardly safe, to propose it. The peace encouraged him to speak out.

The rhetorician lays great stress on Philip's pretended descent from Hercules, as a motive both for his good offices in behalf of the four states which in various ways had been so closely connected with his divine ancestor, and for an undertaking in which he would be emulating the glory of that mighty conqueror. And Philip, though he could not be touched by the argument, may not have been insensible to the flattery implied in it. But we can better understand the force of his appeal to history, when he encourages Philip by the examples of Jason, Agesilaus, and the Ten Thousand. Perhaps however the most remarkable passage in the whole is one on which he alludes to certain suspicions, which were current, he says, among the malignant or credulous, as to Philip's intentions. There were persons, it seems, lovers of trouble and confusion, who affected to believe, and others so senseless as to be persuaded by them, that the growth of Philip's power was dangerous to Greece: that his object was to set the Greek states at variance with each other, in order to make himself master of the Peloponnesus. Isocrates would hardly have deigned to notice these absurd suspicions, which Philip himself, in his consciousness of the purity of his intentions, might be inclined to despise, if they had not been so widely spread among the multitude of the arts of the designing. But the plan which he has suggested of uniting Greece, and conquering Persia, is the surest way to refute such calumnies.

It cannot be doubted that he was perfectly in earnest, and that he expressed all that he thought; though his infatuation may seem hardly credible, and it is not easy to find a parallel that would completely illustrate its extravagance. The Italian cities in the middle ages had reason to rejoice, when an emperor, who threatened their liberties, could be forced to embark on a crusade: because it was known that such an expedition was likely to weaken his power. But they would have suspected the sanity of a citizen who should have advised them to combine their forces to put the German emperor in possession of the Greek empire; as we should that of a modern politician, who should propose a confederacy among the European states, to aid Russia in the conquest of Turkey, Persia and India. Isocrates unquestionably believed that Philip was sure of success in the enterprise he recommended, and that when he had made himself master of Asia, he would still be a safe neighbour to the Greeks, and would look upon himself only as the general of their confederate army. Nor can it be said that he only erred through extensive confidence in Philip's generosity: for this could not ensure the moderation of his successors. Perhaps the best excuse that can be offered for the rhetorician is, that he could not conceive the thought of Greece subject to a foreign master.

A

HISTORY OF GREECE,

BY

THE REV.D CONNOP THIRLWALL.

Late Fellow of Trinity College, Cambridge.

VOL. VI.

H. Corbould, Del.   E. Finden, sc.

Alexander's confidence in his Physician.

London:
PRINTED FOR LONGMAN, ORME, BROWN, GREEN, & LONGMANS, PATERNOSTER ROW,
AND, JOHN TAYLOR, UPPER GOWER STREET,

Alexander the Great

Alexander is presented by Thirlwall as the leader who realized the potential of a unified Greece for expansion and conquest of the east. He was responsible for the Hellenisation of Asia, yet was guilty of treating the Greek cities as if they were his slaves. Thirlwall's portrait of him is separate from the tradition that idolized him absolutely: to a degree, Thirlwall's Alexander is moved by greed to establish an empire.[1] In some ways these passages, particularly in their approach to the Athenians, represent a reaction against Droysen's history.[2] Whereas Droysen saw leaders like Demosthenes as ill-equipped for the new age, and too attached to local independence, Thirlwall recognized that both Demosthenes and Lycurgus the orator were worthy leaders of the Greeks; resistance to the Macedonians at the time of the Lamian War was an illustration of this. Thirlwall's was the first narrative history of Greece to stress that Lycurgan era was a period of intense activity in Athens, and that some virtue lingered amid the degeneracy.

The Early Years of Alexander

From the remotest ages of Pelasgian antiquity down to the time of the Roman empire, the holy island of Samothrace, the seat of an awfully mysterious worship, accounted equal to Delphi in sanctity and an inviolable asylum, continued to be visited by pilgrims, who went to be initiated into the rites which were believed to secure the devotee against extraordinary perils by both land and sea and in the later period to fix his destiny after death in some brighter sphere. It had probably been always held in some great reverence by the Macedonian kings, as it was here that the last of them sought refuge in the wreck of his fortunes. Here it is said Philip first saw Olympias, when they partook at the same time in the Cabirian mysteries, and resolved to seek her hand (Plut. *Alex.* 2). For him such a scene may have had little other interest: but Olympias seems to have taken delight in such ceremonies and to have given herself up with fervour to the impression they produced. She loved the fanatical orgies celebrated by the Thracian and Macedonian women in honour of their Dionysus; and is even said to have introduced some of the symbols of this frantic worship, the huge tame snakes, which the Bacchanals wreathed round their necks and arms, into her husband's palace. It is a stroke which agrees well with the other features of her wild impetuous character. Who can estimate the degree in which this irritable, uncontrollable, nature may have contributed one element toward that combination of ardent enthusiasm with the soberest forethought, which distinguishes Alexander, perhaps above every man that ever filled a like station?

The anecdotes related of Alexander's boyhood are chiefly remarkable as indicating what may be fitly called a kingly spirit, which not only felt conscious that it was born to command, and was impatient of all opposition to its will, but also studied how it might subject all things and persons around it to its own higher purposes. This inborn royalty of soul could hardly have failed to find its way to fame, had it even been originally lodged in an obscure corner. But Alexander grew up with the full consciousness of his high rank and also his great destiny.

There follows description of the effect of philosophical training on the development of Alexander.

If we inquire what were the peculiar advantages which Alexander was likely to derive from such a teacher as Aristotle, and which could not have been expected from any other of that day, we are led to remark, that, as none of his contemporaries had taken in so wide a compass of knowledge, none, like him, had ranged over every intellectual field thrown open to human curiosity, with as lively an interest in each as if it had been the object of his undivided attention, there was none who was less likely to give any partial bias to his pupil's studies. And again, as there was no man who better understood what belonged to every station of life, none less inclined to exaggerate the importance of his own occupations, it may safely be concluded that all the instruction he gave was adapted with the most judicious regard to Alexander's station and prospects. The boy came into his hands already formed by the attainments which were deemed indispensable for every ingenious youth of his years. It was not certainly from Aristotle that he learnt to love Homer, though the copy of the Iliad which he used to place under his pillow, and which he deposited in the precious casket which he found amid the spoils of Darius, had been corrected by Aristotle's hand. Yet his strong taste for reading, which made him feel the want of a library in the midst of his conquests (Plut. *Alex.* 8), may have been both cherished and directed by the man who, so many centuries after, gave laws to the poets and critics of some of the most polished nations of Europe, as his talent for speaking was, no doubt, carefully cultivated by this great master of scientific rhetoric.* If Aristotle himself had any scientific bias, it was perhaps a hereditary one for the studies connected with medicine: and accordingly we find it expressly stated, and indeed proved by the facts, that the prince caught some measure of this predilection from him, so that he afterwards thought himself qualified to give his opinion to physicians on matters belonging to their art (Plut. *Alex.* 41). So he seconded Aristotle's researches in natural history with an expenditure for the purpose of collections, which is remarkable even among the examples of his munificence (Athenaeus ix 398e; Pliny *NH* 8.17). These facts suggest an interesting question, which however we can but propose; whether a passion for discovery, an eagerness to explore the limits of the world, was not combined as a distinct motive with his thirst for conquest and dominion, and

---

* Though the treatise on the subject addressed to Alexander, among Aristotle's works, is probably by a different hand.

whether for this he may not have been largely indebted to Aristotle's conversation. If we might depend on the genuineness of two letters which appear at least to have been early current under the names of Alexander and Aristotle (Plut. *Alex.* 7; Aul. Gell. 20.5), we should conclude that Aristotle admitted his pupil even to a knowledge of his more abstruse speculations, which related to subjects that lay the farthest of all from any practical application to human affairs. Alexander complains, that Aristotle had published some of his works which before had been reserved for the use of his hearers, and had thus deprived him of a distinction which he had before enjoyed. The reply is at least not unworthy of a philosopher: he remarks that the books he had published were still in one sense unpublished; inasmuch as they were intelligible to none but his hearers. It is perhaps difficult to believe that Aristotle wished to turn his pupil's attention so early to the highest and most subtle results of investigations, which had no doubt occupied the greater part of his life. But it would not be incredible that the ambitious youth should have desired to be initiated in these philosophical mysteries, and have listened with eager curiosity to his master's solutions of some of the difficulties which he found in the nature of things. It would then still be doubtful whether these questions led to any inquiries concerning the objects of religious belief: whether Aristotle thought it expedient to give his pupil any hints of his own theory as to the divine nature, or taught him to reconcile a devout adherence to the traditional forms of worship with the notion of a single eternal fountain of life.* We may more safely adopt the opinion, that the study of man and of society was that which the royal youth was led most assiduously to cultivate. We may indeed smile at Plutarch's rhetoric, when he enumerates Aristotle's divisions of virtue, as if they were so many qualities which Alexander acquired from his instructions (*De Alex Fort.* 1.4): but still we need not deny that the striking contrasts through which Aristotle endeavours to unfold the nature of moral excellence might not only enlarge his pupil's knowledge of

---

* The philosopher's observation on the pre-eminence of theology over mathematical and physical science (*Metaph.* 5 (6).1) bears on this question, though, on account of the unhappy parenthesis, not decisively. Compare, in the same work I 2 x (xi) 7 and xi (xii) 7.

mankind, but might aid him in the regulation of his passions. And who shall pretend to estimate the value of the theories and precepts of government which fell into such deaf ears from the author of the Politics, illustrated by such a stock of examples as he held at his command in the history and constitution of 158 states, which he had described in their minutest details? It is pleasing to find it recorded that still he wrote a book on the office of a king expressly for Alexander. Nevertheless we have unquestionable proof that even on this head the force of nature was stronger than that of education. Aristotle's national prejudices led him into extravagant notions as to the superiority of the Hellenic race over the rest of mankind: as if the distinction between Greek and barbarian was nearly the same as between man and brute, person and thing: hence slavery appeared to him not a result of injustice and cruelty, but an unalterable law of nature, a relation necessary to the welfare of society. Hence he too deduced a practical maxim, which he endeavoured to inculcate upon the future conqueror of Asia, that he should treat the Greeks as his subjects, the barbarians as his slaves (*De Alex. Fort.* 1.6). The advice was contrary to Alexander's views and sentiments: it did not suit the position which his consciousness of his own destiny led him to assume. He acted as we know on a directly opposite principle.

Alexander's Policy

The further Alexander advanced into the heart of Asia, the more clearly must he have perceived the disproportion between the forces with which he had achieved his conquests, and the extent of the territory which he had subjected to his sway. For the purpose indeed of victory, his army seemed sufficiently strong: and he had reason to believe that into whatever new regions he might penetrate, he should meet with no obstacles in nature which he could not surmount, and no enemy that he could not overpower. But his object was not merely to gain battles, and to traverse vast countries, but to found a durable empire in the East: and for this end it was necessary that his authority should be cheerfully acknowledged by the inhabitants of his new dominions: that they should be led as soon as possible to forget that they had been reduced under the yoke of a foreigner:

that his government should appear to them a continuation of that to which they had been accustomed under their native princes. It was henceforth not as the conqueror but as the successor, of the Great King, that he wished to be regarded by his Eastern subjects. The death of Darius—brought about as it had been so as to leave him without reproach—was an event of inestimable importance in this point of view. The vacancy of the throne did not indeed establish his title to the succession: but too many revolutions had happened in Persia, especially of late years, for much offence is to be taken at a change of dynasty, if in other respects national prejudices were spared. The voluntary submission of Artabanus, while it might have great weight as an example, showed that Persians the most devoted to the royal house might now acknowledge Alexander as their legitimate sovereign. The Persian kings themselves, though in the course of two centuries their authority had spread its roots far and wide in the habits and feelings of the people, derived their power—except in the small province which was the cradle of their dynasty—from conquest, and in many parts of the dominions had always looked upon as foreign masters. Alexander therefore might well step into the place of Darius.

The title under which he ascended the throne, was of much less importance than the manner in which he filled it. The policy dictated by his situation required that he should keep two objects constantly in view: the one to conciliate his subjects, the other to impress them with reverence for their new ruler. The first end was attained with little difficulty, and without any extraordinary sacrifices. It was only necessary, that all who submitted to him should find as much security for their persons and property as had been afforded by the preceding government: and with a little vigilance and activity it was easy to give more. The tribute was left on its ancient footing: all branches of the administration were conducted in the same manner as before: but tyranny and arbitrary exactions were likely to be repressed in a greater degree both by the character of the sovereign, and by the system of mutual control which he established for his own security. The provinces which bordered on the predatory tribes, which had so long been permitted to retain their independence in the heart of the empire, must have had reason to rejoice in the revolution which had transferred the sceptre to the hand that could wield the sword. It was probably at least as much with a view to conciliate the people, as to gain the support of the great families—though it would be difficult nicely to distinguish between the two kinds—that, as he left Greece at a greater distance behind him, he more and more frequently filled the vacant governments with Persians or allowed those who submitted to retain their satrapies: so that this became at last a rule from which he seldom deviated. It operated certainly as a strong lure to incline those who were still wavering to his side. But this can scarcely have been his principal motive: for after the death of Darius he had less and less reason to apprehend resistance to his arms, but might well grow more and more anxious about the means of securing his conquests: and he might think with good ground that the sight of the Macedonians filling the highest stations, even if they did not abuse their power, was likely to excite general discontent.

It was however still more necessary for an Asiatic ruler that he should be feared and reverenced than that he should be loved. It may be thought that Alexander's wonderful fortune and extraordinary endowments of body and mind, could not fail to strike the conquered nations with admiration, and that no artifices could be necessary to exalt him, in their eyes. But Alexander must soon have discovered, that it was not by such means Eastern royalty ever attracted the veneration of its subjects. No intrinsic merit could in their estimation supply the place of pomp and splendour which they always associated with the idea of greatness. The Great King, although the feeblest and worst of men, was viewed as a superior being, so long as the luxuries and ceremonies of the court were interposed between him and the rest of mankind: but no measure of wisdom and virtue could have obtained the same reverence for him, if in his dress and manner of living he had descended to a level with other men. It was therefore absolutely necessary for the security of Alexander's throne that he should adopt the principal at least of the outward distinctions, which had been always deemed essential to the majesty of his Persian predecessors: that he should assume the Eastern garb in which alone some of these distinctions could appear: that he should be surrounded by a numerous train of state attendants, and that the simple forms of the Macedonian court should be exchanged for the strict rules of Persian etiquette. The Great King wore his tiara erectly; he sat on a raised seat, on which it was a capital crime in a subject to place himself: he was to be served with certain ceremonies; and he was to be approached only with peculiar observances, which resembled a religious adoration, and were perhaps derived from a persuasion which they strongly needed to confirm, of a kind of divinity that resided in the royal person.*

Alexander was not of the character that would have permitted him to become the slave of such forms: but he was too prudent to discard them, even if they had been as perhaps as they were at first, repugnant to his feelings. It was his object, as far as was possible, to relieve and temper them with Grecian taste and freedom. In the camp he never allowed them to fetter his movements; but on state occasions it was his wish to observe all the leading points of the Persian ceremonial. But there was a great difficulty in the way. Was it to be expected that his Macedonian nobles, the partners of his toils, who had been used to terms of familiar intercourse with their princes, should submit to a foreign custom, which placed so wide a distance between him and them? Or on the other hand, was it consistent with his dignity to dispense in their case with the marks of respect which he exacted from his Persian subjects?

---

* Yet it would not be safe to attribute to the Persians any very distinct conceptions on this point. Flathe observes, that the modern Persians revere their kings as divinities: which, whatever travellers may say, it is clear no Mahometans can do. He adds, that Chardin relates, that the modern Persians ascribe powers of healing to their kings. Kings of England too, who were not looked upon either as gods or heroes, touched for the evil. The state of the case may be illustrated by a passage in the life of Timur. After having mentioned some instances of the veneration with which the Tartar conqueror was regarded by his emirs, Chereffeddin proceeds to observe (tom. ii, p. 273), 'Toutes ces démonstrations de respect et d'amour des officiers de Timur, sont non seulement des preuves de son grand mérite; mais elles marquent outre cela *quelque chose de divin, qui lui avoit été accordé d'en haut par dessus les autres hommes.*' We see that the propensity of mankind to idolise power and greatness, is common to all ages and countries, and may be indulged even where it is utterly inconsistent with the letter of a received creed.

It was a question turning indeed upon a mere form, but involving the most important consequences. The compliance of the Macedonians would reduce them, outwardly at least, to a level with the conquered people, from whom it was no doubt their wish to be distinguished as a superior race. It is probable that they viewed all the favours conferred on the Persians with jealousy, as rights withheld from themselves, and at the utmost reluctantly admitted the expediency of such concessions. Still the honours bestowed on others could not lower them. But if they submitted to the ceremony now required from them, the distinction on which they prided themselves was effaced: nor would they be able to retain any of their national privileges but at the king's pleasure: every trace of freedom might soon be lost.

There can be little doubt that it was the same reason which led Alexander to attach so much value to the ceremony. It was his intention to reduce all his subjects to the same level beneath himself: to recognise no distinction between Europeans and Asiatics, Greeks and barbarians: to admit no claims founded on any other title than personal merit, and this to be measured by the zeal shown in his service, and subject to his own judgment. In him this was perhaps not the simple effect of ordinary ambitions: it was a natural result of the view which he took of the relation in which he stood to his own people. The distance which might seem to separate him from them was so great, that any advantage that they might possess over the conquered nations, was on comparison too trifling to be regarded. The Macedonians were a semi-barbarian race, which had only been raised to the station it now occupied among nations by the effort of its kings. He, according to the traditions of his family, which he firmly believed, was not only sprung from the purest Hellenic blood, but from a heroic lineage, and on both sides traced his origin to the father of the gods. And he felt himself to be worthy of this illustrious descent. The victories, which enabled the Macedonians to look down upon other nations as their inferiors, had been his triumphs. It was he who still sustained the monarchy he had founded. The Macedonians had as much reason as the Persians to regard him as a being of a higher order.

Still, as these thoughts had been nourished and unfolded in

himself by the recent change in his fortunes, it was not expected that the Macedonians could be easily brought to adopt these views. Yet it was only so far as they were impressed with them, that they could willingly submit to a ceremony, which was both degrading in itself, and mortifying to their national self-complacency. It seems to have been for the purpose of overcoming their aversion that Alexander, about the same time that he assumed the tiara, and some other distinguishing ornaments of the royal attire, and ordered his court after the Persian model, encouraged the diffusion of a report, which in fact only expressed his own consciousness of his extraordinary genius in a mythical form: that his birth as well as his origin was divine like that of Hercules and Aeacus:* the secret which had been long kept to protect Olympias from dishonour had been revealed to the king himself by the oracle of Ammon. It was indeed that such a story should be believed, except perhaps in the ardour of military enthusiasm by the most ignorant of the private soldiers. But still it might serve as a colour for his claims, which might render them less revolting to the feelings of Macedonians and Greeks, than if they had rested merely on his power of enforcing them. The bitter consequences which flowed from this unhappy state of things will appear in the sequel.

The Last Years and Legacy of Alexander

At Susa he began a series of measures, tending, in their remote consequences, to unite the conquerors with the conquered, so as to form a new people out of both, and, in their immediate effects, to raise a new force, independent alike of Macedonian and of Persian prejudices, and entirely subservient to his ends. The first of these measures was a great festival, in which he at the same time celebrated his own nuptials with Statira, the eldest daughter

---

* Plutarch, *Alex.* 27, reports a remarkable conversation which Alexander had in Egypt with a philosopher called Psammon (Pe-Amoun?) who taught that all men are governed by God: for the ruling principle in each is divine: but Alexander was of opinion that the deity is indeed the common father of all men, but adopts the best as peculiarly his own.

of Darius (who now, it seems, took the name of Arsinoe*) and those of his principal officers with Persian and Median ladies of the noblest families. We find an intimation, that some address was needed, before the preliminaries could be arranged (Diodorus xvii 107; cf. Arrian vii 6); and this, from the known temper and views of the Macedonian generals we can easily believe. The king's example had no doubt the greatest weight in overcoming the aversion which they must have felt to such an alliance. The liberality with which he portioned their brides out of his treasure, also had its effect: and their pride was flattered by the level with himself in the ceremony. Hephaestion received the hand of Drypetis, Statira's sister: it was Alexander's express wish that his friend's children should be related to his own. Craterus was wedded to Amastris, a niece of Darius; Perdiccas to a daughter of the satrap Atropates, Ptolemy and Eumenes, to two daughters of Artabazus. For Nearchus Alexander chose the daughter of Mentor by Barsine, a mark of distinguished favour, since he himself had admitted the mother to his bed, and already had a son by her, on whom he had bestowed the name of Hercules, and who afterwards became a competitor for the throne. To Seleucus he gave a daughter of the Bactrian chief Spitamenes. These are the only names recorded by Arrian, but the whole number of the officers who followed the king's example amounted to nearly a hundred. It was not less important for his object that above 10,000 of the private Macedonians had either formed a connection, or were now induced to enter into one, with Asiatic women. To render it solemn and binding, a list was taken of their names, and a marriage portion was granted to each.

The wealth of Asia and the arts of Greece were combined to adorn the spectacle with a splendour and beauty worthy of the occasion. A gorgeous pavilion was erected, probably on a plain near the city, capable of containing not only the bridal party, but the

---

*   This is Droysen's conjecture, which seems happily to explain the variations in the name, which we find in Arrian vii 4 (compared with Photius 686, 687) and other authors. Aristoboulus related, that Alexander also married Parysatis, daughter of Ochus. There was probably some foundation for this statement: but we hear nothing more of Parysatis, and Alexander certainly never placed her on a level with Statira.

guests whom the king had invited to the banquet.* It was supported by pillars sixty feet high, glittering with gold, silver, and precious stones, and was hung and spread with the richest tissues. Ninety-two chambers, magnificently furnished, were annexed to the building: and an outer court appears to have been enclosed by a partition, likewise hung with costly tapestry, for the reception of the 10,000 newly-married soldiers, each of whom received a golden vessel for his libation, and of the strangers who had been drawn by business or curiosity to the court. In the fore-ground without, tables were spread for the rest of the immense multitude. The nuptials were solemnised according to Persian usage. A separate seat was assigned to each pair: all were ranged in a semicircle, to the right and left of the royal throne. When the last libation had been announced by a flourish of trumpets to the multitude without, the brides entered the banquet-hall, and took their places. The king first gave his hand to Statira, and saluted her as his consort; and his example was followed by the rest. This, it seems, completed the nuptial ceremony. The festivities lasted five days, which were filled up with a variety of entertainments; among the rest, musical and dramatic performances of Greek artists, and feats of Indian jugglers (*thaumatopoioi*: Athen. xii 54). Alexander's subjects from all parts of the empire vied with each other in the magnificence of their offerings to the king: and the value of the crowns which he received on this occasion is said to have amounted to 15,000 talents.

---

* That the tent described by Chares (Athenaeus, xii 54; Aelian *VH* vii 7) as erected for the marriage-feast, is the same with that described as the king's ordinary tent for solemn audiences by Phylarchus (Athen. xii 55; Aelian *VH* ix 3) may be considered as nearly certain. Droysen (p. 496) concludes, that the royal tent was fitted up for the wedding feast. It seems more probable, that one was built for the occasion. Chares distinguished the *oikos*, or inner tent, in which the tables were laid for the bridegrooms and the king's guests, from the *aule*, in which, according to him, the whole army, with the crowd of strangers, was entertained. But that an enclosure was made to contain so vast a multitude, seems highly improbable. The *aule* appears to have been destined for the Macedonian bridegrooms of lower rank. Droysen takes no notice of the outer court, but supposes that tables were laid in the tent for 9000 persons, all of distinguished rank.

Thirlwall accounts for Alexander's death before evaluating his career.

So passed from earth one of the greatest of her sons: great above most, for what he was in himself, and not as many who have borne the title for what was given to him to effect. Great, not merely in the vast compass, and the persevering ardour, of his ambition: nor in the qualities by which he was enabled to gratify it, and to crowd so many memorable actions within so short a period: but in the course which his ambition took, in the collateral aims which ennobled and purified it, so that it almost grew into one with the highest of which man is capable, the desire of knowledge, and the love of good. In a word, great as one of the benefactors of his kind. The praise however would be empty, unless it be limited as truth requires, and his claim to it must depend on the opinion we form of his designs.

It is not to be supposed, that, in any of his undertakings he was animated by speculative curiosity, or by abstract philanthropy. If he sought to discover, as well as to conquer, it was because the limits of the known world were too narrow for his ambition. His main object undoubtedly was to found a solid and flourishing empire: but the means which he adopted for this end, were such as the highest wisdom and benevolence might have suggested to him in this situation, without any selfish motive. And as his merit is not the less, because so many of his works were swept away by the inroads of savage and fanatical hordes, so it must be remembered that his untimely death left all that he had begun unfinished, and probably most of what he meditated unknown: that he could hardly be said to have completed the subjugation of all the lands comprised within the limits of the Persian empire. Still it cannot be denied that the immediate operation of his conquests was highly beneficial to the conquered people. This would be true, even if the benefit had been confined to these advantages which many seem purely material: for none were really so. The mere circulation of the immense treasures accumulated by the ancient rulers, which Alexander scattered with such unexampled profusion, was doubtless attended by innumerable happy results: by a great immediate increase of the general well-being, by a salutary excitement of industry and commercial activity. The spirit of commerce however was still more directly roused, and cherished by the foundation of new cities, in situations peculiarly adapted to its ends: by the opening of new channels of communication between opposite extremities of the empire, and the removal of obstructions—arising from the feebleness and wantonness of the ancient government—which before impeded it: by the confidence inspired by the new order of things, the growing consciousness of safety and the expectation of protection and encouragement. Let any one contemplate the contrast between the state of Asia under Alexander, and the time when Egypt was either in revolt against Persia, or visited by her irritated conquerors with the punishment of repeated insurrection, when almost every part of the great mountain-chain which traverses the length of Asia, from the Mediterranean to the borders of India, was inhabited by fierce, independent predatory tribes: when the Persian kings were forced to pay tribute before they were allowed to pass from one of their capitals to another. Let any one endeavour to enter into the feelings, with which a Phoenician merchant must have viewed the change that took place in the face of the earth, when the Egyptian Alexandria had begun to revive and pour out an inexhaustible tide of wealth: when Babylon had become a great port: when a passage was opened both by sea and land between the Euphrates and the Indus: when the forests on the shores of the Caspian had begun to resound with the axe and the hammer. It will then appear that this part of the benefits which flowed from Alexander's conquest cannot be easily exaggerated.

And yet this was perhaps the smallest part of his glory: it was much indeed so to cultivate, enrich and beautify this fairest portion of the earth: it was something more, to elevate the intellectual and moral character of the people: and this was in a great degree the effect, in a still greater degree the tendency of Alexander's measures and institutions. It may be truly asserted, that his was the first of the great monarchies founded in Asia, that opened a prospect of progressive improvement, and not of continual degradation to its subjects: it was the first that contained any element of moral and intellectual progress. That it did so is certain; but it has been disputed, how far this entered into Alexander's intention. We cannot regard him as entitled to much honour on this account, unless we admit that the great thought of his life was to unite his new subjects with the old, so as to form one nation, and for this purpose he wished to raise the Asiatics to a level with the Europeans, and according to the modern expression, to Hellenise Asia. It has been contended, that such a project of amalgamation was too chimerical to have been adopted by a prince of Alexander's sagacity and judgement: that he must have been too well aware of the obstacles which must always have rendered it impossible for the new element to penetrate and assimilate so vast and heterogeneous a mass, as the population of his Asiatic dominions: and that we must therefore consider those of his measures which seem most clearly to indicate such a design, as merely temporary expedients of a conciliating policy, forced upon him by his relative weakness. It seems however a sufficient reply to this objection to observe, that we can hardly now determine what Alexander would have found practicable in the course of a long reign: that if there were limits, in extent and degree beyond which he himself could not have hoped to have realised such an idea, it was an object still worthy of all his efforts: and that when we see him adopting a series of measures clearly tending to this end, it is reasonable to infer that he had the end in view. It may be said, that he planted Greek cities in Asia, merely as either commercial or military posts, to fill his treasury, or secure his possessions; that he educated the barbarian youth in Greek schools, merely to recruit his army; that he promoted intermarriage between the Europeans and Asiatics, merely to soothe the conquered nations. But he cannot have been blind or indifferent to the ultimate tendency of all these steps: he must have forseen that from each of his new colonies the language, arts and manners, the whole genius of Greece would radiate through the adjacent regions and would gradually enlighten, civilise and transform, their population: he must have known that by the domestic ties which he formed, and by the education of the young, he was raising up a generation which would be more open to receive his influence. The extent to which the interfusion took place and the Asiatics became Greeks in every thing but blood was by no means small: if Alexander had lived to become the founder of a peaceful dynasty, which might have prosecuted his plans, the changes wrought would have been incalculably greater.

It is another question whether this change of nationality was in all respects an unmixed good: whether, in the old frame of society, in the literature, the arts, the manners and even perhaps in the speculative systems of the conquered races, much was not lost and destroyed through it, that was worth preserving: whether the new forms were not in most cases destitute of life and reality, an empty varnish or spiritless imitation. Still less should we venture to maintain, that the infinitely diversified combination and conclusion which ensured, between the religions and mythologies of Greece and Asia, was anything in itself desirable: or that the new rites and creeds, which were the progeny of this unnatural mixture, were not often as odious and baneful, as they were wild and fantastic. They at least did not enter into Alexander's plans, who merely extended his politic protection alike to all modes of worship and belief: and it would be as unjust to charge him with their mischievous conse-quences, as it seems false to represent him on this account as the Precursor of a better Light, which, on the contrary, they contributed more than any other cause to refract and obscure. But it became Alexander, as a Greek, to believe, that the change was on the whole highly beneficial: and we, who owe so much of what is best among us to the same culture, can hardly charge him with blind parti-ality. We must rather admire the greatness of mind by which he rose above the prejudices of his Macedonians, who, themselves foreigners, indebted for all that made them worthy or even capable of their fortune to their Greek education, were loth to share it with others, whom they wished to trample as barbarians.

Still there is one side in which Alexander's administration appears in a much less favourable light. We must speak with caution on this subject, because we are very imperfectly acquainted with his measures, and he had scarcely time to unfold his views. Yet it must be owned that we cannot perceive even the first lines, that we catch no hint of any political institutions framed to secure the future welfare of his subjects. We do not find that in any case he had begun to assume the character of a lawgiver: though Arrian thought him as well entitled to divine honours as Minos or Theseus. It is probable indeed that he intended his new colonies at least should enjoy all the municipal freedom consistent with the maintenance of an absolute government. But we do not know what security he had provided for their privileges; and he seems to have left the mass of the people in this respect nearly as it had been under its former masters. The only improvement which he appears to have introduced into the old system, was to restore, perhaps to multiply, the checks by which, according to the earlier policy of the Persian kings themselves, their great officers in every province were enabled to control one another. These checks, as he discovered on his return from India, proved utterly ineffectual for the protection of life and property; and though he punished the offenders with the utmost rigour, we hear of no other precautions that he took against the recurrence of such abuses. When he seated himself in the throne of Darius, he assumed, as perhaps was necessary, the fullness of despotic sovereignty that had been exercised by his Persian predecessors: and he was too was represented by his satraps. Though he might be able to restrain them, it was to be expected, that a successor of inferior energy would be forced to connive at their license: from the highest station to the lowest, there was no permanent safeguard against misrule. The condition of the people was better; but it remained precarious. It must even be admitted that if he raised the Asiatics he brought down the Macedonians and the Greeks to meet them on the same level.

What has been said, relates only to the effect which his conquests produced in Asia: it is another question how far they were beneficial to Greece. Some advantages she no doubt derived from them. A boundless field, with brilliant prospects, was thrown open for Greek adventurers. A part of the new commerce of the East found its way into Greek ports. But we should seek in vain for any benefits of a higher order which resulted to Greece from Alexander's expedition; while, in many respects much more important, her condition was changed for the worse. She was treated no longer as a humble and useful ally of Macedonia, but as a province of the Persian empire, and made to feel her subjection by despotic, and apparently wanton and arrogant commands. And yet she had scarcely begun to taste the bitter fruits, which she was to reap from the fulfilment of those splendid visions, with which Isocrates would have consoled her for the loss of freedom.

The Spirit of Greece in the Age of Alexander

Unless the nature of the Greeks could have been changed, or their judgment blinded, by the success of the Macedonian arms, it would have been impossible that they could generally have viewed the progress of Alexander's conquests with complacency. Even if it had been acknowledged, that the supremacy acquired by Philip, might in itself—at least as it was exercised by him and his son—be a wholesome restraint on the spirit of discord which had caused so many calamities to Greece, it did not follow that any Greek patriot could look forward without alarm to the period when this supremacy should belong to a king of Macedonia, who was also master of Asia. It was at such a time not infatuation but dishonest sacrifice, to treat the Persian king as the enemy of Greece,* and to blame Demosthenes for the secret negotiations into which he entered the Persian court. The change which had taken place in the relations between Greece and Persia after the battle of Salamis was as great as that which Europe has experienced in its relation to the Turks since the battle of Lepanto. The power of Persia had become one of the chief securities of Greek liberty. Already, under a government which professed to derive its authority from the Amphictyonic council, and the assembled representatives of the nation, and to be the guardian of national institutions, the people had been made to feel the value of the political independence it had lost. The bondage of Thebes, when it was placed at the mercy of a lawless garrison, the destruction which followed its attempt to release itself, the demand for the surrender of the Athenian orators, and other acts which will be mentioned hereafter, were warnings, which showed what might be expected from the future, if the power which had thus exercised should become absolutely irresistible, if it should fall into the hands of princes, strangers to Greece, and educated in the maxims of Oriental despotism. It was not through a paltry jealousy, but from a well-rounded anxiety that the Athenians willingly listened to Demosthenes, when he encouraged them to believe that the invader

---

* As we find Aeschines (*Ctes.* 132) dexterously confounding the past with the present, as if Xerxes and the last Darius had been one person.

would be overwhelmed by the collected forces of the Persian empire. They may notwithstanding have regarded Alexander's exploits with admiration, not the less sincere because it was reluctantly yielded, and seldom openly expressed. The marks of favour they received from the conqueror were more likely to bias their judgment, but still never induced them for a moment to consider his cause as having anything in common with their interests. Her citizens entered into the service of his enemy with the feeling that they were engaging in the defence of their country.

It is rather surprising that when Agis, encouraged by the great distance which separated Alexander from Europe, by perhaps exaggerated rumours of the dangers that threatened him in Asia, and by the disasters which had befallen the Macedonians at home, ventured on his ill-fated struggle, Athens remained neutral. It was afterward made a ground of accusation against Demosthenes, that he had taken no advantage of this occasion to display the hostility which he always professed toward Alexander. The event proves that he took the most prudent course; but his motives must remain doubtful. He was perhaps restrained, not by his opinion of the hopelessness of the attempt, but by the disposition to peace, which he found prevailing at home, whether the effect of fear or of jealousy, or of any other cause.* Had the people been ready to embark in the contest, an orator probably would not have been wanting to animate them to it. But Demosthenes may still have given secret encouragement and assistance to the Peloponnesian confederates, and may have alluded to this, when, according to his adversary's report, he boasted that the league was his work (Aesch. *Ctes.* 167). The issue of that struggle and the news which arrived soon after, of the great victory by which Alexander had decided the fate of the Persian monarchy at Gaugamela, must have crushed all hope at Athens, except one, which might have been suggested by domestic experience, that the conqueror's boundless ambition might still lead him into some enterprise beyond his strength.

There was however a party there, which did not dissemble the

---

* If Plutarch's anecdote about Demades (*Reip. Ger. Pr.* 25) had contained the real cause, it at least required extraordinary impudence in Aeschines and Dinarchus (*Ctes.* 165; *Demosth.* 36) to lay blame on Demosthenes.

interest it felt in the success of the Macedonian arms. Before the battle of Issus, when Alexander was commonly believed to be in great danger and Demosthenes was assured by his correspondents, that he could not escape destruction, Aeschines says, that he was himself continually taunted by his rival, who exultingly displayed the letters that conveyed the joyful tidings, with the dejection he betrayed at the prospect of the disaster which threatened his friends. Aeschines was the active leader of the Macedonising party: all his hopes of a final triumph over his political adversaries were grounded on the Macedonian ascendancy. But Phocion, though his motives were very different, added all the weight of his influence to the same side. His sentiments were so well known, that Alexander himself treated him as a highly honoured friend; addressed letters to him from Asia, with a salutation which he used to no one else except Antipater, and repeatedly pressed him to accept magnificent presents. Phocion indeed constantly rejected them; and when Alexander wrote that their friendship must cease if he persisted to decline all his offers (Plut *Alex.* 39; *Phoc.* 18), was only moved to intercede in behalf of some prisoners, whose liberty he immediately obtained. Even among the instructions which Craterus took with him, one is said to have been, to put Phocion in possession of an Asiatic city, which he should select from four that were to be offered to him. All this may be considered as a pure tribute of disinherited reverence for extraordinary virtue, but it was not the less likely to produce a powerful effect on minds not formed to prize virtue as its own reward, or to believe that it could be so esteemed by others.

The disaster of Chaironea had held out a signal to the enemies of Demosthenes at Athens, to unite their efforts against him. He had been assailed in the period following that event until Philip's death, by every kind of legal engine that could be brought to bear upon him; by prosecutions of the most various form and colour. All these experiments had failed; the people had honoured him with more signal proofs of its confidence than he had ever before received: he had never taken a more active part, or exercised a more powerful sway, in public affairs. Yet it seems that after the Macedonian arms had completely triumphed, both in Asia and in Greece, Aeschines thought the opportunity so favourable for another attempt of the same nature, that he resolved to collect all the force of his eloquence, and all the strength of his party, for a last attack on his great rival. He endeavours indeed to shield himself from this reproach, and from the charge which he was conscious might be brought against him, that his main object was to display his zeal in Alexander's service, under the flimsy pretext, that the indictment had been laid before Philip's death. This was true; but it was no less evident, that the cause had been dropped for seven or eight years, and the state of political affairs had now induced him to revive it. This trial, the most celebrated of ancient pleadings, the most memorable event in the history of eloquence throughout all past ages, deserves mention here, chiefly for the light it throws on the character and temper of the Athenian tribunals, at a time when the people is supposed to have been verging toward utter degeneracy, so as to be hardly any longer an object of historical interest: a time it must be remembered when the rest of Greece was quailing beneath the yoke of the stranger, and his will, dictated to the so called national congress at Corinth, was sovereign and irresistible.

There follows a description of the subject of the *de Corona* dispute.

The preceding history will perhaps enable the reader, even if he should not have read that speech, to form a general conception of the principles on which the orator vindicated his public conduct. Suffice it here to observe, that his boast is, that throughout his political career he had kept one object steadily in view: to strengthen Athens within and without, and to preserve her independence, particularly against the power and the arts of Philip. He owned that he had failed; but it was after he had done all that one man in his situation—a citizen of a commonwealth—could do. He had failed in a cause in which defeat was more glorious than victory in any other, in a struggle not less worthy of Athens than those in which her heroic citizens in past ages had earned their fame. In a word, the whole oration breathes the spirit of that high philosophy, which, whether learnt in the schools or from life, has consoled the noblest of our kind in prisons, and on scaffolds and under every persecution of adverse fortune, but in the tone necessary to impress a mixed multitude with like feeling, and to elevate it for a while into a sphere above its own. The effect it produced on that most susceptible audience can be but faintly conceived by the finest critics in their closets. Yet there have certainly been few readers—perhaps none but those whose judgement has been perverted by prejudices—in whom it has not left a strong conviction of the speaker's patriotism, if not of his general integrity and political virtue. The result was that the prosecutor not only lost his cause, but did not even obtain a fifth part of the votes and consequently, according to the law incurred a small penalty (Plut. Dem. 24; X Orat. Vit. 840c). But he seems to have felt it insupportable to remain at the scene of his defeat, where he must have lived silent and obscure. He quitted Athens, and crossed over to Asia with the view it is said of seeking protection from Alexander (X Vit. Orat. 840d), through whose aid alone he could now hope to triumph over his adversaries. When this prospect vanished, he retired to Rhodes, where he opened a school of oratory, which produced a long series of voluble sophists, and is considered as the origin of a new style of eloquence, technically called the Asiatic, which stood in a relation to the Attic not unlike that of the composite capital to the Ionic volute, and was destined to prevail in the East wherever the Greek language was spoken, down to the fall of the Roman empire. He died at Samos, about nine years after Alexander, having survived both his great antagonist, and his friend Phocion, and probably was preserved from his exile from a similar fate.

The spirit displayed by the tribunal which decided in favour of Demosthenes on such grounds as he alleged, is at least as noble as that of the Roman senate and people, when they went out to meet and thank the consul on his return from Cannae. But the case may seem to exhibit the Athenian administration of justice in a much less favourable light. On one point at least it is clear that Ctesiphon's decree was contrary to the law. The attempt made by Demosthenes to prove that the law, which forbade an accountable magistrate to be crowned, did not apply to his case, only shows the extreme looseness of legal reasoning which was tolerated in Athenian courts. It seems indeed to have been admitted, that there had been numerous precedents for whatever was illegal in the decree, as to the circumstances of time and place. But this only proves the laxity which prevailed in the observance of the laws. It appears that according to that theory of the constitution which had been universally approved and acted on in the purest times, immediately after the expulsion of the thirty tyrants, the court which tried the author of a decree denounced as illegal, was bound to compare it with the letter of the law, and to give judgement on the simple question of their strict agreement. But it is evidence that the courts had afterwards assumed greater freedom; and it is not at all certain that this was repugnant either to the spirit of the institution, or to the practice of preceding ages, with the single exception of the short period in which the restoration of the democracy awakened extraordinary jealousy for the maintenance of the laws. The will of the people declared in a decree, had been subjected to the revision of a tribunal which might be expected to possess superior means of information, to secure the people itself against the pernicious consequences of temporary measures into which it might be surprised. This seems to have been the general object, to which all others were subordinate; and for this purpose it might be necessary that in such cases the courts should be invested with an ample discretion, and should not be required to adhere to the letter of the laws, so as themselves to commit wrong to injure the commonwealth. The form of the proceedings was such, that a verdict against Ctesiphon must have been interpreted as a condemnation of Demosthenes: and it was the deliberate will and the highest interest of the people, to show that it still honoured the man who had not despaired of the commonwealth. It would have been better that the prosecutor should not have been able so to embroil the question: but where he did so, it was desirable that the court should have the power to decide on what it deemed the most important point.

In the course of the same year was tried another cause, which is interesting in the same point of view. The occasion has already been mentioned. In the eighth year after the battle of Chaironea, the fugitive Leocrates returned to Athens, which he had deserted in her hour of danger, and resumed the functions of a citizen. He was impeached by Lycurgus, under the law which had been passed immediately after the battle forbidding emigration under pain of death. He pleaded that he had set out in the course of his business as a merchant, without any intention of changing his abode: but his subsequent conduct belied his professions. He was convicted, and probably suffered the penalty of the offence.

Lycurgus, the prosecutor, was one of the few men then living at Athens who could undertake such a task with dignity, as conscious of a life irreproachably spent in the service of his country. There are few Athenian statesmen of any age who can bear a comparison with him: Phocion equalled him in honesty and disinterestedness; but in his general character, and in his political conduct, seems to fall far below him. It is pleasing and instructive to contemplate the image of such a man; and it is a peculiar happiness that his biography is less meagre than that of most of his celebrated contemporaries: the principal features of his character stand out before us with sufficient distinctness.

Demosthenes was often reproached with a mixture of barbarian blood in his veins. Lycurgus was a genuine Athenian, and his family was one of the oldest and most illustrious in Athens. He traced the origin of his house, which was distinguished by the honourable appellation of the Eteoboutads,* to the royal hero Erechtheus, and thus to a divine stock. By virtue of this descent his family possessed a hereditary priesthood of Poseidon, whose worship, as probably his nature, was intimately connected with that of Erechtheus. In the Erechtheum, the temple dedicated in common to the hero and the god, the portraits of the ancestors of Lycurgus who had held office were painted on the walls. He could also boast of some, more truly noble, whose memory was endeared to the people by real services. Lycophron, his grandfather, had been put to death by the Thirty, and both he and Lycomedes, another of the orator's progenitors, had been honoured with a public funeral. Lycurgus had studied in the schools both of Plato and Isocrates; but had not learnt from the one to withdraw from active life into a visionary world, nor from the other to cultivate empty rhetoric at the expense of truth and of his country. His manly eloquence breathes a deep love and

---

* Importing, the genuine Butads or descendants of Butes, [Plutarch] *X Or. Vit.* 841 b where most of the materials of the following sketch will be found.

reverence for what was truly venerable in antiquity—his speech against Leocrates, which is still extant, shows that he dwelt with a fondness becoming his birth and station on the stirring legends of elder times—but his admiration for them had not made him indifferent or unjust toward those on which he lived. He possessed an ample hereditary fortune; but he lived, like Phocion, with Spartan simplicity. In an age of growing luxury he wore the same garments through summer and winter, and, like Socrates, was only seen with sandals on extraordinary occasions. Yet he had to struggle against the aristocratical habits and prejudices of his family. He was the author of a law, to restrain the wealthier women from shaming their poorer neighbours by the costliness of their equipages in the festive procession to Eleusis; but his own wife was the first to break it.* His frugality however did not arise from parsimony, and was confined to his personal wants. He was reproached with the liberality which he displayed toward the various masters of learning whom he employed and declared that if he could find any that would make his sons better men, he would gladly pay them with half his fortune. He devoted himself to public life in a career of quiet, unostentatious but useful activity. He was a powerful but not a ready speaker; like Pericles and Demosthenes he never willingly mounted the bema without elaborate preparation; and his writing-instruments were constantly placed by the side of the simple couch on which he rested, and from which he frequently rose in the night to pursue his labours. But to shine in the popular assembly was not the object of his studies; he seems only to have appeared there on necessary or important occasions. His genius was peculiarly formed for the management of financial affairs; and the economy of the state was the business of a large portion of his public life.

There follows an account of the financial administration of Lycurgus.

The administration of Lycurgus was distinguished above every other since Pericles by the number of public buildings which he

---

* According to *Vit*. X *Or*. he paid a talent to the sycophants to avert a prosecution, and afterwards defended himself on the plea that he had given, not taken. Aelian however (*VH* xiii 24) represents her as legally condemned.

erected or completed. Among his monuments were an arsenal, an armoury, a theatre, a gymnasium, a palaestra, a stadium. After the example of Pericles he laid up a considerable treasure in the citadel, in images, vessels, and ornaments of gold and silver, which at the same time served to heighten the splendour of the sacred festivals. It was in a different capacity, under a special commission, that he also built 400 galleys, and formed a great magazine of arms. He seems likewise to have taken Pericles for his model, so far as the difference between their times permitted, in a continual endeavour to raise the character, and to refine the taste of the people. That he instituted a choral contest in honour of his family god Poseidon, may be ascribed to a personal motive. But we find his attention entirely directed to more important branches of art and literature. He was the author of a regulation—the precise nature of which is not sufficiently ascertained to be stated here—for the better management of the comic drama. But he conferred a more lasting benefit on his country, and on all posterity, by another measure designed to honour and preserve the memory and the works of the three great tragic poets to whom Athens was indebted for so large a part of her literary fame. The dramas of Sophocles and Euripides, if not of Aeschylus, were still frequently exhibited: they were acknowledged as the most perfect models of dramatic poetry: but this did not prevent them from undergoing a fate similar to that which has so often befallen the works of our early dramatists: they were frequently interpolated and mutilated by the actors. Before the invention of the press, this was a serious evil, as it endangered the very existence of the original works. To remedy it, Lycurgus caused a new transcript or edition to be made of them by public authority, in many cases probably from the manuscripts of the authors, and to be deposited in the state-archives.* The value of this edition was proved by its fate. It was afterwards borrowed by one of the Ptolemies to be copied for the Alexandrian library, and fifteen talents were left at Athens as a pledge for its restitution. The king however sent back the copy instead of the original, and forfeited his pledge. By the decree of Lycurgus it was directed that the players should conform in their

* See Grysar, *De Graecorum Tragoedia*, 7.

representations to this authentic edition. The bronze statues of the
three poets, which he also caused to be erected, were less durable
monuments, and had become a more trivial distinction.

All these works attest the influence of Lycurgus, while they show
the spirit in which it was exerted. That influence was founded, not
on his birth, or wealth or eloquence or ability, but simply on the
confidence which a jealous people reposed in his integrity and
probity. As the state entrusted him with its revenues so private
persons deposited their property in his custody. When a piece of
ground was required for his new stadium, Dinias, its owner, made
a present of it to the people, with the extraordinary declaration,
that he gave it for the sake of Lycurgus. His testimony was sought
as the most efficacious aid in the courts of justice. He was once
summoned by an adversary of Demosthenes. Demosthenes said he
should only ask whether Lycurgus would consent to be thought
like the man whom he befriended (Rutilius Lupus ii 4). In his own
judicial contests, whether he appeared as prosecutor or defendant,
he always gained his cause. He could venture sharply to rebuke the
assembled people, when he was interrupted in a speech by clamours
of disapprobation. When the philosopher Xenocrates was seized in
the street, as liable to the alien-tax, by one of the farmers of the
customs, Lycurgus struck the man with his staff, and committed
him to prison; and his conduct on this occasion was universally
praised. We hear but of one case in which he may seem to have
courted popular favour by a deviation from his principles in the
management of the public funds. He had convicted a wealthy man
named Diphilus* of a gross and very pernicious fraud on the state
in the working of the mines at Laurium. The offender was put to
death, and his whole estate confiscated, and Lycurgus consented
at least to distribute the sum which it brought into the treasury
among the people, as the whole produce of the mines had been
distributed before the time of Themistocles. The general tendency
of his measures, and the impression produced by his character, were
rather of an opposite kind. He inspired a feeling approaching to

---

* Perhaps the same person for whom Demosthenes had obtained the public
hours mentioned by Dinarchus, *Demosthenes* 44.

awe by his antique, Spartan-like austerity, as he publicly avowed his admiration of the old Spartan manners. When he was appointed to superintend the police of the city, the measures by which he cleared it of rogues and vagrants were deemed so rigorous, as to be compared with the laws of Draco. On the other hand, one of his celebrated enactments was a provision against one of the grosser abuses of the slave trade, by which it sometimes happened that free persons were sold under false pretexts in the Athenian market.

The accountability and public approbation of Lycurgus is described before an evaluation of his career.

The fragments here collected from the biography of a truly illustrious man, who has not generally attracted all the notice he deserves, will perhaps not be thought to occupy too much room, when it is considered over a period during which the history of Athens is almost a blank. They lead us to believe that the life of the people at this period cannot have been so worthless and insignificant as we often find it described: a people in which the midst of a swarm of profligate political adventurers, sycophants, and parasites, bestowed its esteem, its confidence, its highest honours, on two such men, so widely at variance with each other as Phocion and Lycurgus: a people, it may be added which could even be misled by such a speech as that of Demosthenes in his defence,* was not hopelessly corrupt, not dead to all right and noble feelings, nor ready to sink into ruin through its own internal feebleness and levity. Notwithstanding the vast extent of the Macedonian conquests, and the magnificence of the new dynasties which arose out of Alexander's empire, we need not be ashamed to regard the struggle which this people made for liberty as not less interesting than the contests of some ambitious soldiers of fortune for their shares of that rich spoil.

---

*   At the same time I am aware how cautiously such arguments should be used, and into what grievous mistakes we are likely to fall when we attempt to infer the character of an age from the sentiments contained in its books.

A

HISTORY OF GREECE.

BY

THE REV.ᴰ CONNOP THIRLWALL.

Late Fellow of Trinity College, Cambridge.

VOL. VII.

Death of Demosthenes.

Hellenistic Greece

Thirlwall clearly believed that there was much of political importance in the history of Greece after Alexander. Greece's hope lay in the prospects for resistance to the Macedonians offered by the unity of federal government: the institution of this by the Aetolian and the Achaian confederacies was, alongside the resistance to the invasion of the Gauls, the major Greek political achievement of the Hellenistic period. Thirlwall's enthusiasm for federal government can be traced as early as his interest in Amphictyonies and the 'Effects of the Olympic Festival as an Instrument of National Union' in volume i, pp.373–92, and in his approval of the Panhellenic rhetoric of Isocrates (vol.v, p.376). His interest attracted the praise of Edward Freeman, author of *A History of Federal Government*. By concentrating on the history of the landmass of Greece in the Hellenistic period, Thirlwall's work is distinguished from that of Droysen on Hellenismus. Droysen's interest was not in the history of Greece but rather in the impact of Hellenic culture on the areas of the world conquered by Alexander and engulfed in the Hellenistic kingdoms.[1] The excerpts that follow aim to represent the aspects of Hellenistic Greece which most excited Thirlwall.

Demetrius the Phalerian

It was now more than ten years that Athens had remained under the government of Demetrius the Phalerian, who, under the modest title of Guardian, with the Macedonian garrison, and the fear of Cassander to support him, in fact exercised unlimited authority. The accounts which remain of his administration would be perplexing from the appearance of the contradiction they present, if the length of the period during which his rule lasted did not enable us to reconcile them. Demetrius was of very low, if not servile origin (Aelian *VH* 12.83): yet he was liberally educated, was a hearer of Aristotle's scholar, Theophrastus, and diligently cultivated rhetoric, criticism, historical learning, and political philosophy. He was an agreeable speaker, an elegant and voluminous writer. It was perhaps by his literary pursuits, that he first recommended himself to the patronage of Cassander, who was so warm a lover of Homer, that he copied out the Iliad and Odyssey with his own hand and could repeat almost every verse: and one of the measures of Demetrius was to revive the public recitation of the Homeric poems in a new form (Athenaeus, xiv 12).* For some time after his elevation to power, he appears to have wielded it moderately and wisely. It seems as if he aspired to emulate Solon and Pisistratus. He introduced indeed no fundamental changes into the constitution, but preserved its forms, while he enacted many laws, of which Cicero and other impartial judges speak with great approbation. He adorned the city with useful, if not magnificent buildings:† he raised the public revenue to the same amount (1200 Talents) as it had reached during the administration of Lycurgus. A very surprising proof of the general prosperity which Athens enjoyed under his sway,‡ is afforded by the census which he took of the population, probably in the year of his archonship 309, from which it appeared that Attica contained 21,000 freemen, 10,000 resident aliens, and the prodigious number of 400,000 slaves. The 21,000 must have included all the citizens who were debarred from the exercise of their franchise by the want of the requisite qualification; their proportion to the rest is not

---

*   See Bode, *Geschichte der Hellenischen Dichtkunst* i, 272.

†   Diogenes Laertius v 75. We are informed indeed by Cicero (*de Off.* ii 15) that Demetrius censured Pericles, for having laid out so large a sum on the Propylaea. But Schlosser, (ii. i. p. 118), and Droysen, who subscribes to his opinion, have pressed this passage too much: it is not clear that Demetrius condemned temples, porticoes, and theatres, or in general every kind of expenditure, which was not to produce some immediate profit. That he was averse to the theatrical exhibitions, Cicero does not in the remotest degree hint; and his institution of the Homeric recitations in a dramatic form need not be imputed to parsimony. His patronage of Menander also bears on this question.

‡   Which was acknowledged even by his enemy Demochares (Polybius xii 13).

stated: but, since 12,000 were excluded by Antipater's regulation, the number of slaves possessed by the remaining 9000 citizens, and by the aliens, must have been enormous: not much less, it would seem, than twenty to each. It is remarkable that sumptuary laws were among the laws of Demetrius, which we find mentioned. He limited the number of guests at feasts,* and, to check the excessive magnificence which was displayed by the wealthy at funerals, ordered them to be celebrated before daylight. He himself appears to have retained the early simplicity of his habits, and the philosophical frugality of his meals, even after he had risen to his high stallion: but probably not for any long time.

A very different picture is drawn of the man and his administration by other hands (Duris in Athenaeus xii 60), but apparently with equal fidelity. The time came when he began to devote but a small part of the public revenue, which passed through his hands, to public purposes, and squandered the rest in extravagant luxury. In the costliness of his ordinary banquets he surpassed the Macedonian grandees: in their exquisite elegance the effeminate princes of Cyprus and Phoenicia. It was remarked that even the floors of his rooms were adorned by skilful artists: that his guests were sprinkled with precious ointments, that the superfluity of his table enabled his cook—the most celebrated of his day—to purchase three large houses. He betrayed a ridiculous vanity by the attention which he paid to his personal appearance. The disciple of Theophrastus was not ashamed to colour his hair, to paint his cheeks, to wear an artificial smile. And unhappily this weakness was connected with sensual passions, which he indulged without reserve, at the expense not only of his own dignity but of the peace and honour of his subjects. He became, not only in the political but in the moral sense, tyrant of Athens.

It is not difficult to account for the change. It was the natural effect of the sudden acquisition of power and wealth on a man of undecided character, who had probably fancied himself as a philosopher while he seemed destined to a humble station but found his

---

* To thirty. Athenaeus vi 45. Officers called the *gynaikonomoi* had power to enter houses and count their guests; and the members of the Areopagus were associated with them in this grave function.

desires swell with the growth of his fortune. There was however another cause which contributed to stifle his better dispositions, and to make him more and more indifferent to the esteem of the wise and good. The forbearance and discretion which he showed at the outset probably won the hearts of the Athenians notwithstanding any prejudice they may have felt against him as Cassander's creature. They repaid him with extravagant tokens of admiration and gratitude. Honours of all kinds had become so common that only very gross exaggeration could render them significant. Some parasite of the assembly desired a new distinction for the benefactor of Athens: he proposed to erect as many statues as there were days in the year: and in less than 300 days, 360 bronze statues, mostly equestrian, or representing him in a chariot attested the popular enthusiasm. That it soon cooled, and in time was followed by opposite senti-ments, may be easily conceived: as easily, that while this change was taking place, the voice of flattery grew louder than ever, and that his vanity and vices were humoured with more studied obsequiousness. So in the year when he filled the office of archon—the ninth of his government—as he headed the Dionysiac procession, the poet who furnished the hymn of the chorus, celebrated his illustrious birth, and the dazzling radiance of his aspect. When this kind of intoxication was added to that of pleasure, it is no wonder than he forgot himself more and more, and wallowed in the foulest depths of sensuality. Yet in one very important point he continued to the last to deserve praise; his administration seems to have been quite free from the stain of cruelty: he continued, it seems, to exercise his authority mildly even after he had become conscious that the people were weary of it.*

The Gaulish invasions

Ceraunus did not enjoy the fruit of all these crimes much longer than a year and a half, during which he had to defend his dominions

---

* The fable (Phaedrus v. 1) is alleged by Grauert and Droysen as a proof of the contrary; but surely need not be construed so strictly: and Cassander's hatred of the Athenians, mentioned by Pausanias (i 25.7) appears to have been provoked by their expulsion of his governor.

against the Dardanian king, who had given shelter to the son of Lysimachus.* He was then deprived at once of his kingdom and his life by a sudden calamity, which the ancients with a right feeling, regarded as a stroke of Divine vengeance; the rather, as he seemed to have exposed himself to his fate, with an infatuation which might well be considered as judicial, though it was a natural result of the success which had attended him in so many criminal enterprises. The irruption of the Gauls, which produced this, and other momentous changes in the affairs both of Macedonia and Greece, might indeed have been anticipated, without any uncommon reach of sagacity, by any one whose political horizon was not bounded by the limits of civilised society in the West. For it appears that Celtic tribes had been long in possession of the countries on the eastern side of the Adriatic, from which the invaders issued, and had been engaged in continual warfare with their neighbours, which kept them as averse as they had ever been from habits of peaceful industry, and as impatient of any fixed abode. Their presence in regions not very remote from Macedonia had been announced by the embassy which Alexander had received on the banks of the Danube; and their movements though scarcely heard of beyond their immediate vicinity, were probably felt as far as the shores of the Aegean, through their influence on the Thracian wars of Lysimachus. But they were too far out of sight to attract notice in the Hellenic world; and the storm burst upon it not the less suddenly because it had been long gathering. The immediate occasion of this movement, or the causes which removed the hinderances that had hitherto prevented it, lie beyond the reach of history. Ceraunus himself first received warning of his danger from the king of the Dardanians,†

---

* Prolog. Trog. Pomp. 24: 'Bellum quod Ptolemaeus Ceraunus in Macedonia cum Monio (Monumio) Illyrio, et Ptolemaeo Lysimachi filio habuit.'

† From a silver tetradrachma bearing the superscription MONOYNIOY ... ΣΙΛΕΩ, and apparently not much later than the age of Alexander, coupled with the fact, that a Mounius was king of the Dardanians in the period of the war with Perseus (Livy, xliv 30 cf. Polybius xix 5), and that the same name occurs on a coin of Dyrrhachium (ΒΑΣΙΛΕΩΣ MONOYNIOY ΔΥΡΡΑ), Droysen (*Zimmermann's Zeitschrift*, 1836, no. 104) has, with his usual sagacity, shown a degree of probability nearly amounting to certainty, that this king of the

who, though he had been but a short time before at war with him, regarded it as so pressing and threatening to his own safety, that he at the same time offered him a body of 20,000 auxiliaries. In the blindness of ignorance, or the confidence of prosperous wickedness, Ceraunus disdainfully rejected this offer, treating it as degrading to the honour of his kingdom, to suppose that Macedonia could need the protection of the Dardanians against such an enemy.* It was not long before he received more direct intimation of the approach of the Celts, from an embassy which they sent to him with proposals for peace, if he was willing to purchase it by tribute. Their object, it appears, was not so much to conquest as plunder; and they would have been content to drain the Macedonian treasury without a blow. Ceraunus attributed their overtures to fear, and replied by an arrogant message, bidding them if they wished for peace, send him their chiefs as hostages, and lay down their arms. This language would have been not unworthy of a high spirited prince, resolved to risk all for liberty and honour, if he had been better acquainted with the force which he defied, and had not so rashly neglected the means of defence which the friendship of the Dardanian king would have enabled him to command. As it was, it only served to quicken the steps of the invaders, who, threatening that he should soon learn whether their offer of peace more concerned their safety or his own, advanced without delay, and in the course of a few days began to pour into Macedonia. We have little information as to his preparations or his movements, beside the simple fact that he met them in the field. It seems that, though greatly outnumbered, he engaged prematurely, against the advice of his friends, before he had collected all his forces (Diodorus xxii). He probably relied on the strength of the phalanx, and the show of his elephants; but he found these advantages more than counterbalanced by that which the Celts derived from the impetuosity of their onset, and the strangeness of their aspect and mode of fighting. He

---

Dardanians was the Mounius of these coins, and that his name ought to be substituted for *Monio* and *Mytillo*, in the Prologues to Trogus, 24 and 25.

* Justin, xxiv 4. Droysen however thinks that the conduct of Ceraunus may be better explained by his just distrust of a prince who had so lately been his enemy.

was defeated, and having been thrown by the elephant on which he rode, fell into the enemy's hands, and was presently dispatched; according to one of the more authentic accounts, torn to pieces, as if in a contest among the captors for the ornaments of his person (Memnon, 226 b). His head was struck off, and carried about the field on the point of a lance, to heighten the consternation of his army, which is said to have been so completely routed, that almost all were slain or taken (Justin xxiv 5: 280 BC).*

An account of the Celtic occupation of Greece to the Gaulish sacking of Delphi follows.

The accounts remaining to us of the events which ensued, are as full of wonders as the description given by Herodotus of the disasters which befell the Persians on the same ground, and the prodigies said to have happened on both occasions are so similar that the later report might seem a mere repetition of the earlier one. We are informed that the oracle was consulted and declared the god would protect his sanctuary; and that the promise was fulfilled by an earthquake,† which rent the rocks, and brought down huge masses on the heads of the assailants, by a tempest, in which many of them were consumed by the lightning and by the appearance of celestial warriors who fought against them. But this is no proof that these marvellous incidents of the later story are merely fictions borrowed by the author to embellish his narrative. No doubt a great change had taken place in the heart and the mind of the nation since the Persian war. The people had become somewhat less credulous, and less disposed to expect a supernatural interposition on any occasion. The scenes of the Sacred War had also tended to weaken the ancient reverence for the oracles and the temple, which had been so openly and repeatedly profaned with impunity. But Delphi was still commonly regarded as holy ground, and as favoured at times with a Divine presence. The remembrance of local traditions would be forcibly awakened in the little band which had devoted itself to

---

* In the fifth month of Ol. 125.1 (Porphyr ap. Eus. *Ar. p.* 330).
† According to Pausanias x 23.1, exactly co-extensive with the ground occupied by the Celts.

the defence of the temple, while it awaited the enemy's approach, and might readily suggest the hope of Divine assistance; and the guardians of the oracle would not neglect any of the pious arts which had been practised on like occasions by their predecessors, to cherish and direct the enthusiasm of their champions. We may therefore easily account for the rise of a genuine popular legend in the subject.*

Be this as it may, the supernatural element of the story has not so disfigured it, as wholly to conceal the real course and connection of the events. It seems that Brennus, when he arrived in the valley of the Pleistus, was advised by his Greek guides to proceed without delay to the attack of Delphi (Justin xxiv 7). But either because he thought that his troops needed refreshment, or because he was unable to restrain them, he permitted them first to gorge themselves with the plunder of the farms and hamlets, where large stores of corn and wine had, it is said, been purposely left. In the meanwhile, the approaches of the city were fortified, and preparations made to take the utmost advantage of all the means of resistance offered by the nature of the ground. When the Celts advanced to the assault, they were perhaps stupified and bewildered by their recent excesses, so as to be more than usually susceptible of superstitious terrors. Brennus, we are told, endeavoured to stimulate their rapacity, by the assertion that the gilded statues which they saw gleaming from the terraces of Delphi, were of solid gold (Justin xxiv 7). It may be doubted whether he himself was aware of the loss which the treasury had suffered in the Phocic war. The assailants, who in general were easily deterred by slight obstacles in such operations, were repulsed and disheartened. Fragments of rock rolled down from the top of cliffs, contributed to their defeat and consternation. A sudden change of weather to frost and snow, and the effects of surfeit followed by scarcity, and by disease arising out of both began to thin their ranks, and determined Brennus to abandon the hopeless enterprise. The order for retreat was to the Greeks a signal for a series of attacks, with which they continued to harass

---

* On the tenacity of popular belief among the Greeks, one may refer with pleasure to an Essay of G. W. Nitzsch, *Die Heldensage der Griechen nach ihrer nationalen Geltung.*

the enemy as far as the camp at Thermopylae, where a division had
been left to guard the booty. The junction with Acichorius, which
seems to have taken place soon after the retreat began, only served
to increase the confusion and to retard the march of the Celts,
while the numbers and the confidence of the Greeks were growing
from day to day. Brennus, who had been wounded before Delphi,
is said to have destroyed himself to escape the resentment of his
countrymen;* and Acichorius, who succeeded to the command, to
have put his sick and wounded to death (Diodorus xxii), and to
have abandoned his baggage to secure his retreat. No estimate can
be safely formed of the amount of the loss sustained by the Celts
in their passage through Greece and Macedonia. But the assertion,
with which some of our authors round the tale, that they were
cut off to a man, is a patriotic exaggeration, almost as gross as
the fictions with which the Roman historians, to save the national
honour, disguised the issue of the Celtic expedition against Rome.
We are informed that one part of the host of Brennus, commanded
by a chief named Bathanatius,† reached the banks of the Danube,
near its confluence with the Save (Justin xxxii 3), while another,
under Comontorius, was strong enough to effect a settlement, and
to establish an independent kingdom, with a capital named Tyle, in
the maritime part of Thrace (Polybius iv 46; Steph. Byz. *Tulis*). And
it is probable that the bands of Celtic adventurers, whom we shall
find a few years later in Macedonia and Epirus, and in the pay of
Greek princes, were a remnant of the same body.‡

The most important immediate effect produced on Greece by
the Celtic invasion was perhaps that it raised the reputation and
the confidence of the Aetolians, who claimed the largest share in
the issue of the war, and cherished the recollection of their exploits
with almost as much self-complacency as the Athenians that of their
victories over the Persians. They dedicated a trophy, and a statue

---

* Pausanias x 23.12; Justin xxiv 8, cum dolores vulnerum ferre non posset.

† Athenaeus vi 25. Zeuss however (*Die Deutschen*), p. 175, thinks it more
probable that Bathanatius was the chief who first led the Celts into Illyria.

‡ Diefenbach (*Celtica*, ii 1, 243) would draw a like inference from a passage
of Pausanias (x 19.1), the meaning of which he has strangely mistaken, as if
epithentes diken referred to a pecuniary mulct.

representing Aetolia, as an armed heroine at Delphi, for a perpetual memorial of the vengeance they had inflicted on the destroyers of Callium (Paus. x 19.1) But the consequence which most deeply and permanently affected the whole state of Greece and of the ancient world, was the restoration of Antigonus to the throne of Macedonia, which took place within a few months after the retreat of Brennus, though he was destined yet to experience many vicissitudes of fortune before the final establishment of his dynasty.

The Aetolian League

The death of Antigonus produced no immediate visible change in the state of affairs; but yet it may be considered as the main cause of the movements which ensued, and which soon after involved Greece in another wasteful and calamitous war. The occasion of this new struggle arose indeed at a great distance from Macedonia, without any intervention of the Macedonian government, and seemingly more through accident than design; yet it could hardly have taken place, and certainly would not have been attended with such consequences, if the restraint hitherto imposed on those who were desirous of change by the ability and success of Antigonus, had not been withdrawn. When his sceptre passed into the hands of a boy of seventeen, the Aetolians believed that they had nothing to apprehend on the side of Macedonia, and readily followed the first impulse which they had received from turbulent and ambitious leaders, who wished for private ends to disturb the quiet of Greece.

As the internal state of Aetolia throws some light on the origin of these movements and is illustrated by them, this may be a convenient place for a general survey of its political constitution and social relations. The main points which have been preserved to us by incidental notices of the ancient writers lie within a narrow compass. We are not able to trace the steps by which the primitive monarchical form of government was exchanged for that which we find established in the period we have now reached. The title of king was retained in one district, that of the Agraeans, down to the Peloponnesian War. In the reign of Philip I, all were united in

a democratical confederacy or commonwealth:* and it is probable
that no other polity subsisted in any of the towns but it is not clear
what degree of independence each canton preserved in its internal
administration, nor indeed is it quite certain than it is more correct
to consider the whole body as a league than as a single republic. It
seems that the union of the Aetolians was still closer than that of the
Achaeans; that there was a deeper consciousness of national unity,
and a greater concentration of power in the national government.
The great council of the nation, called the Panaetolicon, on which
it is probable all freemen who had reached the age of thirty had
a voice, was assembled once a year at the autumnal equinox at
Thermus for the election of magistrates, general legislation, and
the general decision of all great national questions, more especially
those which related to transactions with foreign states. We find
no indication of any other ordinary general assembly. But there
was another deliberative body called the Apocletes,—a name which
appears to have been permanent, though we do not know whether
it held regular sittings, or was only convoked as occasion required.
It was so numerous that a committee of thirty might be drawn
from it for the transaction of special business.† The chief magistrate,

---

* Schorn (p. 25) infers from Arrian's account of the Aetolian embassy to
Alexander, as *kata ethne* (i 10), that the league was not then formed; but that it
existed at least as early as the reign of Philip, not only appears (as is observed
by Nitzsch, *Polybius* p. 119) from an inscription on the statue of Aetolus at
Therma, quoted by Ephorus (in Strabo x 463; cf. Strabo ix 427 and Boeckh
CIG i p. 857).

† Schorn (p. 27) considers it as an aristocratical council, which represented the
noble families, probably relying on Livy's description (xxxv 45), where *triginta
principes* answers to *triakonta ton apokleton* in Polyb. xx 1. But it seems that no
reliance can be safely placed on Livy's expression, as it is clear that he mistook
these thirty for the entire council, and supposed that they were appointed on
extraordinary occasions by the national assembly. Tittman (p. 727) regards
them as a standing committee for foreign affairs; and so Pastoret (*Hist de le Leg.*
viii p. 378): 'C'étoit une sorte de commission intermédiaire des états nationaux;'
adding, without the slightest evidence, that the assembly delegated to it 'la
decision des objets d'un ordre inférieur.' but this view likewise seems to rest
on Livy's misconception. Another question is, whether the *synedroi* mentioned
in the inscriptions (Boeckh *CIG* 2350, 3046 *synedrous aei tous enarchous*) are
connected with the *apokletoi*—or were an entirely distinct body. Boeckh's

who bore the title of *strategus*, was annually elected, presided in the assemblies, represented the sovereignty of the people, and disposed of its military force. His office, among such a people, conferred great power; and there is an indication that it was viewed with some degree of jealousy, for it seems that he was not allowed to speak in the assembly on a question of war or peace. A commander of the cavalry (*Hipparchus*) served under him in the field, and perhaps filled his place, when necessary, at home. A chief secretary (*grammateus*) was also elected annually.

The Aetolians still retained their predatory habits, which Thucydides had pointed out to his contemporaries as an illustration of the primitive semibarbarous manners of Greece. The ruggedness of their land, the strength of their mountain fastnesses, the vicinity of still wilder tribes in the north, concurred with the hardy, reckless, self-confident character of the people, to prevent any change in this part of their hereditary usages. They were still a nation of freebooters and pirates. Plunder was to them what eloquence or music was to other Grecian races,—their study, their business, their pleasure, their pride.* In their marauding excursions they spared nothing. They paid as little regard to the sanctity of the things and the places which were most revered in Greece as if they had professed a different religion; yet we have no reason to believe that they were freer from superstition than their more civilised neighbours. One of the consequences of this appetite for plunder was that the democratical character of the Aetolian institutions was in no small degree tempered by the influence which the chiefs who took the lead in such expeditions naturally acquired over their followers, and the weight which they thus gained in the councils of the nation. But it seems that they found it necessary to sustain the popularity which they earned in the foray by the exercise of liberality and hospitality at home, on which they frequently spent more than their share of the booty, and thus were often induced

---

opinion about them is not quite clearly expressed (*CIG* ii p. 633: 'synedri *sunt concilii Aetolici magistratus ordinarii*, senatus *quippe*).

* Maximus Tyrius, *Diss.* 23.2. Flathe (ii p.139) endeavours to rescue them from this reproach, but only damages his own reputation for impartiality by his attacks on Polybius.

to look to predatory excursions, as the readiest means of repairing their damaged fortunes. Many of the leading men possessed houses at Thermus which they had adorned with great magnificence, and at the time of the annual elections they appeared to have vied with one another in the splendour of their entertainments. For though they had made so little progress in civilisation, the Aetolians were not at all behind the other Greeks in luxury. An ancient author expressly connects their eager pursuit of pleasure with their contempt of death (Agatharchides ap. Athen. xii 33). They were willing, it seems, to crowd the enjoyments for which alone they valued life, by profuse expenditure, into a narrow compass. The sanctuary of Apollo at Thermus was adorned with a multitude of statues, works indeed of foreign schools, but not the less gratifying to the national vanity as a display of wealth and refinement: and those yearly meetings were probably not inferior in exhibitions of art, particularly dramatic and musical entertainments, to any of the kind which were celebrated in the rest of Greece.*

It seems that nearly as soon as the national union was firmly cemented, the Aetolians began to aim at extending their power and enlarging their territory. One of the earliest occasions on which they appear acting as one body is that on which they acquired Naupactus from the Achaeans; and they never afterwards omitted any opportunity of gaining ground upon their neighbours, until, elated by the success with which they had defended themselves against the Macedonian and Celtic invaders, and encouraged by the weakness of the other states, they aspired to take the lead in Grecian politics. Their conquests, as we have already seen, were not confined to northern Greece, where in process of time they made themselves masters of Locris, Phocis, Boeotia, and parts of Acarnania, Epirus, and Thessaly, and assumed the entire control of the Delphic oracle and Amphictyony.† They also annexed some Peloponnesian cities to their dominions; and we afterwards find not only the island of Cephallenia, but places at a great distance from their frontier,— cities of Thrace and Asia Minor—in a similar relation to them.

---

* A law is specially providing for the security of the artists (*hoi Dionysiakoi technitai*) is referred to in the inscription, *CIG* 3046.
† Plut. *Demetrius* 40; Polyb. iv 25.8; *CIG* 1694.

Hence a question of some importance arises as to the origin and the precise nature of this relation. That in most cases it was the effect of compulsion, as is expressly related with regard to the Trachinian Heraclea (Paus. x 20.9), can hardly be doubted, but rather whether there is sufficient reason to believe that it was in any instance purely voluntary, so that it may be attributed to a peaceful attraction which the Aetolian League exercised upon foreign states. We are informed indeed by Polybius that Mantinea of its own accord abandoned its connection with the Achaeans to attach itself to the Aetolian League;* and this was no doubt true in the limited sense which the historian's argument required. But whether this accession took place, as appears most probable at least with regard to Tegea and Orchomenus, in the course of the expedition in which the Aetolians swept Laconia, or after Megalopolis had become a member of the Achaean confederacy, on either supposition motives may be suggested for it quite distinct from a preference grounded on the character of the Aetolian League.† In the more distant dependencies, such as Lysimachia on the Hellespont, and Cios on the eastern coast of the Propontis (Polyb. xvii 3.11, 12), the object was either protection from more dreaded neighbours or security against the piratical excursions of the Aetolians themselves, who were not least formidable to those who had never injured them. We know that the people of Cios were glad to plead their mythical connection with Naupactus, after it had fallen into the hands of the Aetolians, to obtain exemption from the attacks of Aetolian privateers (*CIG* 2350). And we may collect from the inscription which records this transaction, that the Aetolians not unfrequently abused the power they had usurped over the temple at Delphi, and the name of the Amphictyonic council which they had appropriated to themselves, to give a legal and even a religious colour to their aggressions. Even Teos thought it worth while to send an embassy to Thermus to conclude a treaty of the

---

*   2.57.1. Brückner (in *Zimmermann's Zeitschrift*, 1837, p.1226, n. 7) expresses a doubt as to the fact, but only refers to Plut. *Arat.* 31, 32, 35, where I can find nothing even inconsistent with the assertion of Polybius, much less capable of overthrowing his authority.

†   Brückner justly remarks that Mantinea seems to have been from the time of Epaminondas in constant opposition to Megalopolis.

closest amity, which provided against the violation of its city and
territory (*CIG* 3046). These examples illustrate the mode in which
the Aetolians gained adherents into their League on the continent
of Greece. On the whole, notwithstanding their impetuous courage
and love of freedom, it seems that they were never either liked or
respected by the other Greeks: they were regarded, as they were, as
a half-civilised race; and even if the Achaean League had not been
in their way, would probably never have been able to extend their
own so as to embrace the whole nation.

Another interesting question relates to the terms on which they
admitted new members into their body. So little information has
been afforded to us by the ancient authors on this point, that room
has been left for directly opposite opinions on the subject among
modern writers, some of whom represent the relation as one of
subordination and dependence,* while others suppose the newly
incorporated members to have been received on a footing of perfect
equality,† and to have enjoyed every privilege of Aetolian citizens,
with the single exception, that none but native Aetolians were
eligible to the supreme dignity. The truth seems to lie midway. It is
nearly certain that the term *sympolity*, which is most frequently used
to describe the condition of newly admitted states, was applied to a
great variety of very different relations. That the general assemblies
were sometimes held beyond the borders of Aetolia, as at Naupactus,
Heraclea, and Hypata, undoubtedly raises a strong presumption,
that the citizens of those towns shared all the political franchises of
Aetolians: but it would be rash to conclude that this was the case
with all, even if there were not evidence that in some instances at
least the relation was one of simple subjection,‡ and the payment of

---

*   Niebuhr, *History of Rome*, 2.51, English translation.

†   Flathe, ii, 151.

‡   Schorn (p. 29) infers this with regard to Cephallenia from the article by
which it was excluded from the treaty (Polyb. xxii 13, 15; Livy xxxviii 9.11).
He argues that if it had been in sympoly with the Aetolians it would have
been expressly ceded; if it had been a free ally, like Elis, it would not have been
necessary to mention it at all. But it seems that the same thing may be inferred
as to places which were said to 'partake in the *sympoliteia* of the Aetolians'
(Polyb. iv 25.7).

tribute enforced by the constant presence of an Aetolian garrison.

Such appears to have been the case with the Arcadian town of Phigalea, which was situated near the right bank of the Neda, close to the borders of Triphylia and Messenia, and not many miles from the coast. As it was thus easily accessible to the Aetolians, it lay very commodiously for the prosecution of any designs which they might form against the southern part of Peloponnesus, and might serve as a starting-point for their inroads, and a place of refuge where they might deposit their booty. We can only conjecture when the connection began: but at the death of Antigonus Doson, we find it under the protection of the Aetolians, and furnishing them with a pretext for enterprises which involved Greece in a fresh war, one of those which received the name of the Social.

A
HISTORY OF GREECE,
BY
THE RIGHT REVD CONNOP THIRLWALL.

Lord Bishop of St Davids.

VOL. VIII.

CHAPTER TEN

Greece under the Romans and Beyond

From the Embassy of Callicrates to Rome to the Reduction
of Greece into a Roman Province (vol. viii, chapter lxvi,
pp. 457–73)   221

Thirlwall's explanation of the eclipse of Greece as the political epicentre of the
Mediterranean was 'a want of reverence for the order of nature, for the natural
revelation of the will of God' (vol.viii, p.465), which was manifested in the progress
of luxury and the practice of infanticide. But Thirlwall's investigation into Greece
at the time of the Roman invasion was perfunctory; contemporary with Thirlwall's
History was George Finlay's specialist work on the subject, *Greece under the Romans*
(Edinburgh, 1844).[1] Thirlwall's *History* closes with a commentary on the controversial
work of Fallmerayer,[2] who argued that the Slavic conquests wiped out the original
population of northern Greece by the end of the eighth century.

Polybius rendered other services to his country which were clearly
more solid and important, though we are not sufficiently informed
as to their precise nature fully to appreciate them. We learn from
Pausanias, that he framed political institutions and laws for the
cities of the Achaean confederacy (viii 30.9), and he himself relates,
that he was directed by the commissioners, when they were on the
point of departing homeward, in the spring after the fall of Corinth,
to make a circuit round the cities, for the purpose of determining
doubtful points, until the people should have become familiar with
the constitution and the laws (xl 10). It would seem therefore that
he drew up the laws and forms of municipal government, of which
Pausanias speaks, in the course of the preceding winter. We do not
know what cities shared the benefit of his legislation, for which

the Macedonian code of Aemilius Paullus might perhaps serve as a model. The political institutions were of course, according to the senate's decree, strictly oligarchical. And in this respect no alteration seems ever to have been granted by the Roman government. But in some other points the rigour of its original regulations was a few years afterward greatly relaxed. The fines imposed on the Achaeans, and on the Boeotians and Euboeans, were remitted; the restraints on intercourse and commerce were withdrawn; and the federal unions which had been abolished were revived (Paus. vii 16.10). There can be no doubt but that this indulgence was obtained through the intercession of Polybius, and the influence of his friend Aemilianus (Plut. *Reip. Gr. Praec.* 18). An inscription on the base of a statue erected to Polybius by his grateful countrymen at Megalopolis, recorded his extensive travels, the services he had rendered to the Romans in their wars, and the success of his mediation, by which he had appeased their resentment against the Greeks. An inscription on another statue declared, that Greece would not have fallen if she had always followed the advice of Polybius, and that after her fall she had found succour through him alone (Paus. viii 30.37). The Romans in their official language seem to have described this renewal of the old forms as a restoration of liberty to Greece.* But even if the monument in which this sounding phrase appears to be applied to it, did not itself illustrate the vigilance with which the exercise of political freedom was checked by the provincial government, we might be sure that these revived confederations answered no other purpose than that of affording an occasion for some periodical festivals and some empty titles, soothing perhaps to the feelings of the people but without the slightest effect on

---

* *CIG* 1543, Rose p. 405. An inscription found among the ruins of Dyme by Mr. Hawkins, and presented by him to the library of Trinity College, Cambridge: a letter from the proconsul, Q. Fabius Maximus, Q. F., to the magistrates and council of Dyme, in which he alludes to an attempt made by one Sosus, who had written laws contrary to the constitution which had been restored to the Achaeans by the Romans, and had given rise to a sedition in which the public archives of Dyme had been burnt—proceedings which appeared to the proconsul to tend to the subversion of social order and of the liberty which had been restored to the Greeks.

their welfare. The end of the Achaean war was the last stage of the lingering process by which Rome enclosed her victim in the coils of her insidious diplomacy, covered it with the slime of her sycophants and hirelings, crushed it when it began to struggle and then calmly preyed upon its vitals.

We have brought the political history of ancient Greece down to a point which may be fitly regarded as its close; since in the changes which afterwards befell the country the people remained nearly passive. The events of the Mithridatic war, in which the Achaeans and Lacedaimonians, and all Boeotia, except Thespiae, are said to have declared themselves against Rome, and the royal army in Greece received a reinforcement of Lacedaemonian and Achaean troops (Appian *Mithrid.* 29), might serve to indicate that the national spirit was not wholly extinct, or that the Roman dominion was felt to be intolerably oppressive. But Athens certainly no more deserved Sylla's bloody vengeance for the resistance into which she was forced by the tyranny of Athenio, than for the credulity with which she had listened to his lying promises. In another point of view however, it will not be foreign to the plan of this work to take a brief survey of the fortunes of Greece after its incorporation into the Roman empire.

No historical fact is more clearly ascertained than that from this epoch the nation was continually wasting away. Strabo, who visited Greece but a little more than a century later (x 485: 29 BC) found desolation everywhere prevailing. Beside his special enumeration of ruined towns and deserted sites, and his emphatic silence as to the present, while he explores the faint vestiges or doubtful traditions of the past, the description of almost every region furnishes occasion for some general remark illustrating the melancholy truth. Messenia was for the most part deserted; and the population of Laconia very scanty in comparison with its ancient condition; for beside Sparta it contained but thirty small towns in the room of the 100 for which it had been celebrated (viii 362). Of Arcadia it was not worthwhile to say much, on account of its utter decay (viii 388). There was scarcely any part of the land in tillage, but vast sheep-walks, and abundant pasture for herds of cattle, especially horses; and so the solitude of

Aetolia and Acarnania had become no less favourable to the rearing of horses than Thessaly. Both Acarnania and Aetolia—he repeats elsewhere—are now utterly worn out and exhausted; as are many of the other nations (x 460). Of the towns of Doris scarcely a trace was left; the case was the same with the Aenianes (ix 427). Thebes had sunk to an insignificant village; and the other Boeotian cities in proportion, that is, as he elsewhere explains himself, they were reduced to ruins and names, all but Tanagra and Thespiae, which, compared with the others, were tolerably well preserved (ix 402). Thessaly would furnish a long list of celebrated names, but few of its towns retained their early importance; Larissa more than any other (ix 430).

It has been usual in modern times to attribute this decline of population to the loss of independence, to the withering influence of a foreign yoke, in a word to Roman misrule. And it would be bold and probably an error, to assert, that it was wholly interconnected with the nature of the government to which Greece was subject as a Roman province. It is too well known what that government was; how seldom it was uprightly administered (Cicero *Manilius* 22), how easily, even in the purest hands, it became the instrument of oppression (Cicero *Epist. ad Q. Fratrem*). The ordinary burdens were heavy. The fisherman of Gyarus, who was sent ambassador to Augustus, to complain that a tax of 150 drachmas was laid upon this island which could hardly pay two thirds of that sum (Strabo x 485; Tacitus *Annals* x 76), afforded but a specimen of a common grievance. Greece was not exempt from those abuses which provoked the massacre of the Romans in Asia at the outbreak of the Mithridatic war (Plut. *Lucull.* 20). And even if we had no express information on the subject, we might have concluded that it did not escape the still more oppressive arbitrary exactions of corrupt magistrates, and their greedy officers. 'Who does not know,' Cicero asks, 'that the Achaeans pay a large sum yearly to L. Piso?' (*De Prov. Cons.* 3). It was notorious that he had received 100 Talents from them, beside plunder and extortion of other kinds (*Piso* 37). The picture which Cicero draws of the evils inflicted by him upon Greece is no doubt rhetorically overcharged; but it is one of utter impoverishment, exhaustion, and ruin (*Piso* 40). And here we may remark that the privileges of the free cities included in the province afforded no security against the rapacity and oppression of a Piso or a Verres. The Lacedaimonians, Strabo observes, were peculiarly favoured, and remained free, paying nothing but voluntary offerings (viii 365). But these were among the most burdensome imposts; and so Athens, which enjoyed the like immunity, was nevertheless, according to Cicero's phrase, torn to pieces by Piso. To this it must be added that the oligarchical institutions everywhere established— and even Athens was forced to so qualify her democracy, that little more than the name seems to have been left (Strabo ix 398 cf. Appian *Mithrid.* 39)—tended to promote the accumulation of property in a few hands: as we read that the whole island of Cephallenia was subject to C. Antonius as his private estate (Strabo x 455).

Nevertheless it seems certain that when these are represented as the main causes of the decline of population in Greece, which followed the loss of her independence, their importance has been greatly exaggerated, while others much more efficacious have been overlooked or disparaged. For on the one hand it is clear that this decline did not begin at that epoch, but had been going on for many generations before. A comparison of the forces brought into the field to meet the Celtic invasion by the states of northern Greece with those which they furnished in the Persian war, would be sufficient to prove the fact with regard to them: while as to Peloponnesus, it is expressly attested by Polybius, who does not scruple to declare that in the period of the Cleomenic war, it had been utterly wasted (ii 62.3). Polybius is indeed in this passage speaking of the financial resources of the Peloponnesians; but the cause which he assigns for the decay, is manifestly one by which the population must have been affected in proportion. He attributes it to foreign invasion, and intestine warfare. The long continuance of destructive wars is also the cause assigned by Strabo for the desolation which he beheld. Yet in his time Peloponnesus and the greater part of northern Greece had enjoyed a century of uninterrupted peace and tranquility. This shows that the evil lay deeper than the ravages of war. And we have now the evidence of Polybius, that in the period either immediately preceding, or immediately subsequent to the establishment of the Roman government—a period which he describes as one of concord and comparative prosperity (ii 62.4), when the wounds which had been inflicted on the peninsula were beginning to heal—even then the population was rapidly shrinking, through causes quite independent of any external agency, and intimately connected with the moral character and habits of the society itself. He is giving an example of a case in which it was unnecessary to consult an oracle. 'For instance,' he observes, 'in our times all Greece has been afflicted with a failure of offspring, in a word with a scarcity of men; so that the cities have been left desolate and the land waste; though we have not been visited either with a series of wars, or with epidemic diseases. Would it not,' he asks, 'be absurd, to send to inquire of the oracles by what means our numbers may be increased, and our cities become more flourishing, when the cause is manifest, and the remedy rests with ourselves? For when men gave themselves up to ease and comfort, and indolence, and would neither marry nor rear children born out of marriage, or at most only one or two, in order to leave these rich, and to bring them up in luxury, the evil soon spread, imperceptibly, but with rapid growth; for when there was only a child or two in a family for war or disease to carry off, the inevitable consequence was that houses were left desolate, and cities by degrees became like deserted hives. And there is no need to consult the gods about the mode of deliverance from this evil: for any man would tell us, that the first thing we have to do is to change our habits, or at all events to enact laws compelling parents to rear their children.'

We see then the evil was not that the stream of population was violently absorbed, but that it flowed feebly, because there was an influence at work which tended to dry up the fountain-head. Marriages were rare and unfruitful through the prevalence of indifference or aversion toward the duties and enjoyments of domestic life. The historian traces this unhealthy state of feeling to a taste for luxury and ostentation. But this explanation, which could only apply to the wealthy, seems by no means adequate to the result. The real cause struck deeper, and was much more widely spread. Described in general terms it was a want of reverence for the order of nature, for the natural revelation of the will of God: and the sanction of infanticide was by no means the most destructive or the most loathsome form in which it manifested itself.* This was the cancer which had been for many generations eating into the life of Greece. The progress of luxury which followed Alexander's conquests, no doubt quickened and extended its ravages and the subsequent political chances probably contributed to heighten its effects, though no others could have remedied or materially checked the mischief. The despondency produced by a single overthrow drove the Boeotians, as Polybius informs us (xx 4.6), into a round of sensual dissipation, in which all duties, both public and private, were utterly neglected, and we cannot doubt that the far heavier despair which weighed upon the spirit of the entire nation when at length it felt its chains and saw itself bestridden by the Roman Colossus, was everywhere in some degree attended with like consequences. The more active and hopeful migrated to seek employment, wealth, and reputation, in Italy or the East.

How little the vices of the Roman government had to do with the decrease of population in Greece, becomes still more apparent as we follow its course through the history of Empire. The change from republican to monarchical institutions was in general beneficial to the provinces, and especially to Greece, which was not only exempt from the danger of arbitrary oppression, but was distinguished by many marks of Imperial favour. Within the space of a few years, about the beginning of this period, three new colonies animated the south coast of the Corinthian gulf. Pompey planted a settlement of pirates in the solitude of Dyme (Strabo viii 387; Plut. *Pompey* 28). His great rival restored Corinth, and, if he had lived longer, would perhaps have opened a canal through the Isthmus. Though the commerce, which at the fall of Corinth had been diverted to Delos (Strabo x 486), and afterwards dispersed by the Mithridatic war, may not have wholly returned into its ancient channel, still there can be no question that the advantages of this restoration were very largely felt throughout Greece. Augustus founded another populous

---

*   All that F. Jacobs has said (*Vermischte Schriften, Akademische Reden* i, 212–54) on the subject here alluded to is one side of the truth, but no more. The other is exhibited by Zumpt, in an instructive essay on the Transactions of the Berlin Academy, 1841, *Ueber den Stand der Bevölkerung und die Volksvermehrung in Alterthum*, 14–16.

Roman colony at Patrae, which enjoyed the privileges of a free city
(Paus. vii 18.7). Nicopolis indeed was rather designed as a monument
of his victory, than to promote the prosperity of Greece; for it was
peopled from the decayed towns of the adjacent regions, and the
effect was to turn Acarnania and Aetolia into a wilderness (Strabo
vii 325; Paus. v 23.3, viii 24.11, vii 18.8; x 38.4). Athens too had soon
repaired the loss it suffered through Sylla's massacre, though Piraeus
did not rise out of its ruins (Serv. Sulpicius, *Ep. ad Div* 4.5; Strabo ix
395). But the Athenian population was recruited, as it had long been,
by the lavish grant or cheap sale of the franchise. It was like the
galley of Theseus, retaining nothing but the name and semblance
of the old Athenian people, without any real natural identity of
race: so that it was no exaggeration, when Piso called it a jumble of
diverse nations.* The poverty indeed of the city, which had been a
main cause of its unfortunate accession to the side of Mithridates
(Posidonius in Athen. iv 48), still continued and was but slightly
relieved by the bounty of benefactors like Pomponius and Herodes
Atticus, or even by the growing influx of wealthy strangers who
came to pursue rhetorical or philosophical studies there. While its
splendour was increased by the magnificent structures added to it
by Hadrian and Herodes, perhaps the larger part of the freemen was
never quite secure of their daily meal. Still the good-will of the early
emperors was unequivocally manifested. They seem always to have
lent a favourable ear to the complaints and petitions of the province
(Tacit. *Annals* i 76; Strabo viii 366): and Nero went so far as to
reward the Greeks for their skilful flattery of his musical talents by
an entire and general exemption from provincial government, which
may have compensated for the presents he exacted from them.†
The Greeks, it is said, abused their new privileges by discord and
tumults, and Vespasian restored the proconsular administration,
and above all the tribute—which was perhaps his real motive—

---

*   Tacitus *Annals* ii 55: Non Athenienses, tot claudibus extinctos, sed colluviem
illam nationum. And with this may be combined what is said in Philostratus
(*V. S.* 2.7) on the decay of the purity of the language at Athens—though there
attributed to the influx of the sojourners.

†   Paus. vii 17.3; Plut. *Flam.* 12; Tacit. *Annals* xv 45. His spoliation of the works
of art did not impoverish the country.

with the remark, that they had forgotten the use of liberty (Paus. viii 17.14). But it is evident that on the whole, from the reign of Augustus to that of Trajan, the increase of the population was not checked by oppression or by calamity. Yet at the end of this period we find Plutarch declaring, that Greece had shared more largely than any other country in the general failure of population which had been caused by the wars and civil conflicts of former times over almost all the world (*De Def. Or.* 8): so that it could then hardly furnish 3000 heavy-armed soldiers—the number raised by Megara alone for the Persian war; and his assertion is confirmed by another contemporary witness of the desolation which had overspread some of its most fertile regions.*

In times when the present was so void and cheerless, the future so dark and hopeless, it was natural that men should seek consolation in the past, even though it had been less full, than was the case among the Greeks of power and beauty, prosperity and glory. Nor was it necessary then to evoke its images by learned toil out of the dust of libraries or archives. The whole land was covered with its monuments in the most faultless productions of human genius and art. There was no region so desolate, no corner so secluded, as to be destitute of them. Even the rapacity of the Romans could not exhaust these treasures. Though Mummius was said to have filled Italy with the sculptures which he carried away, it is probable that in the immense multitude which remained, their absence, in point of number, might be scarcely perceived. If Nero robbed Delphi of 500 statues (Paus. x 7.1), there might still be more than 2000 left there.† The expressive silence of these memorials was interpreted by legends which lived in the mind and the heart of the people; and so long as any inhabitants remained in a place, a guide was to be found thoroughly versed in this traditional lore. The town of Panopeus at the northern foot of Parnassus, though celebrated by Homer as a royal residence (*Il.* xvii 307), had been reduced, when it was visited by

---

*   Dio Chrys. Venator, see especially T i 233 Reisk and ii 11.

†   Plin. *Nat. Hist.* xxxiv 17: Rhodi etiamnum tria millia signorum esse Mutianus ter consul prodidit: nec pauciora Athenis, Olympiae, Delphis, superesse creduntur. The identity of the number in these four places rather lessens the authority of the statement.

Pausanias, to a miserable assemblage of huts, in which the traveller could find nothing to deserve the name of a city, as it contained neither a market-place, nor a fountain; but the people remembered that they were not of Phocian, but of Phlegyan origin: they could show the grave which covered the vast bulk of the great Titus, and remnants of the clay out of which Prometheus had moulded the human race (x 4). Relics of like antiquity were at the same period treasured in most parts of Greece.* The memory of the past was still more effectually preserved by a great variety of festivals, games, public sacrifices, and other religious solemnities. After the extinction of the national independence, the battle of Plataea did not cease to be commemorated by the Feast of Liberty (Plut. *Aristides* 21); as notwithstanding the absence of all political interests, the forms of deliberation were kept up in the Amphictyonic (Paus. 7.24.4), the Achaean, Phocian, and Boeotian councils (ix 34.1). The heroes both of the mythical and the historical age were still honoured with anniversary rites: Aratus (Plut. *Aratus.* 53) and Demosthenes (Paus. ii 33.5), and the slain at Marathon (i 32.4), no less than Ajax (i 35.3) and Achilles (ii 1.8), Temenus, Phoroneus, and Melampus.

The religion of the Greeks, which was so intimately associated with almost all their social pleasures and their most important affairs, had never lost its hold on the great body of the nation. We hear much of the change wrought in the state of religious feeling by the speculations of the sophists, and the later kindred philosophical schools, by the frequent examples of sacrilegious violence by the progress of luxury, and the growing corruption of manners. But the effect seems to have been confined to a not very large circle of the higher classes. With the common people Paganism continued, probably as long as it subsisted at all, to be not a mere hereditary usage, but a personal, living, breathing, and active faith. In the age of the Antonines the Attic husbandmen still believed in the potent agency of their hero Marathon (Philostrat. *V. S.* 2.7), as the

---

* So, the bones of Pelops (Paus. vii 22.1), of Arcas (viii 9.3 and 36.8), and Linus (ix 29.8), the head of Medusa (ii 21.5), and her hair (viii 47.5), the skin of the Calydonian boar (viii 47.2), the dice of Palamedes (ii 20.3), the wood of the plane-tree at Aulis (ix 19.7), the trophy of Polydeuces (iii 14.7), the staff of Agamemnon (ix 40.11).

Arcadian herdsmen fancied that they could hear the piping of Pan on the top of Maenalus (viii 36.8). The national misfortunes, as they led the Greeks to cling the more fondly to their recollections of the past tended to strengthen the influence of the old religion, and rendered them the less disposed to admit a new faith which shocked their patriotic pride, and dispelled many pleasing illusions, while it ran counter to all their tastes and habits, and deprived them of their principal enjoyments. Accordingly it seems that Christianity, notwithstanding the consolations it offered for all that it took away made very slow progress beyond the cities in which it was first planted; and its ascendancy was not formally established long before the beginning of a period in which a series of new calamities threatened the very existence of the nation.

The result of the Persian invasion in the mind of the victorious people was a feeling of exulting self-confidence, which fostered the development of all its powers and resources. The terror of the Celtic inroad was followed by a sense of security earned in a great measure by an honourable struggle. Far different was the impression left by the irruption of Alaric, when Greece was at length delivered from his presence. The progress of the barbarians had been topped by no resistance before they reached the utmost limits of the land. They retreated indeed before Stilicho, but not broken or discomfited, carrying off all their booty to take undisturbed possession of another, not a distant province. It was long indeed before the Greeks experienced a repetition of this calamity, but henceforth they lived in the consciousness that they were continually exposed to it. They neither had strength to defend themselves, nor could rely on their rulers for protection. The safety of Greece was one of the last objects which occupied the attention of the court of Constantinople. In the utter uncertainty how soon a fresh invader might tread in the steps of Alaric, every rumour of the movements of the hordes which successively crossed the Danube, might well spread alarm, even in the remotest corners of Peloponnesus. The direction which they might take could be as little calculated as the course of lightning. Who could have forseen that Attila and Theodoric would be diverted from their career to fall upon other prey? that Genseric after his repulse before Taenarus would not renew his invasion? that the Bulgarians would be so long detained by the plunder of the northern provinces? In the reign of Justinian the advances of barbarians became more and more threatening, and in the year 540 northern Greece was again devastated by a mixed swarm of Huns and other equally ferocious spoilers, chiefly of the Slavonic race. The strengthened fortifications of the Isthmus indeed withstood this flood, though they could not shelter the Peloponnesians from the earthquakes and the pestilence, which during this unhappy period were constantly wasting the scanty remains of the Hellenic population which had escaped or survived the inroads of the barbarians. Justinian's enormous line of fortresses revealed the imminence of the danger, but could not long avert it. In the course of the seventh and eighth centuries the worst forbodings were realized: after many transient incursions the country was permanently occupied by Slavonic settlers. The extent of the transformation which ensued is most clearly proved by the number of new names which succeeded to those of the ancient geography. But it is also described by historians in terms which have suggested the belief that the native population was utterly swept away, and that the modern Greeks are the descendants of barbarous tribes which subsequently became subject to the empire, and received the language and religion which they have since retained form Byzantine missionaries and Anatolian colonists: and such is the obscurity which hands over the final destiny of the most renowned nation of the earth, that it is much easier to show the weakness of the grounds on which this hypothesis has been reared, than to prove that it is very wide of the truth.*

---

* The texts on which the author of this hypothesis (Fallmerayer, *Geschichte der Morea*) mainly builds, are a passage of Evagrius (*Hist. Eccles.* 6.10 in which the Avars are said to have stormed and enslaved Singidon, Anchialus and the whole of Greece); a letter of a patriarch of Constantinople in the year 1081 (in Leunclavius, *Jus Graeco-Romanorum*, 279, in which the Avars are said to have occupied the Peloponnesus for 218 years before the deliverance of Patras in 807); and an expression of Constantine Porphyrogenitus (de Them, 2.6). But Fallmerayer himself proves by his own example how unsafe it would be to rely on such phrases in writers from whom accuracy is so little to be expected. In his preface (p. 141) he asserts that not a drop of pure and unmixed Hellenic blood flows in the veins of the Christian population of modern Greece. But in the work itself we find this statement gradually qualified, so that at vol. i,

The discussion of this subject would be altogether beyond the limits of this work, and the question has been alluded to only for the sake of one concluding remark.

We have lived to witness a memorable and happy coincidence. The prostration of Greece under the Turkish yoke was intimately connected with the revival of the study of Greek literature in the rest of Europe. The opening of a new era for philology even more important than that of the fifteenth century, one which has already added more to our knowledge of the old Grecian world than had been gained in the three preceding centuries, has been followed by the emancipation of the Greeks from their bondage, and was certainly not without its share in the preparation of that

---

p. 239 it appears that at the end of the Slavonic immigration the Hellenic portion of the Peloponnesian population formed one-eighth of the whole: a proportion of course merely arbitrary. The inferences which Fallmerayer draws from the geographical names are, as Zinkeisen and others have shown, no less precarious. But still, when his strong phrases are reduced to their precise value, the difference between him and his opponents as to the extent of the change which took place in this period does not seem to be very material. But then the effect of the subsequent wars and of the Albanian immigration remain to be taken into the account. Fallmerayer also insists on the disappearance of the old dialects of the language as an argument in favour of this hypothesis. Thiersch however is believed to have shown that the Tzakonian dialect contains old Greek roots, which are peculiar to it. But a solitary exception rather confirms than invalidates the rule. On the other hand a very candid and philosophical observer (Brandis, *Mittheilungen ueber Griechenland* iii p.9)—who however admits that the great majority of the ancient population was extirpated in the seventh and eighth centuries—conceives that the modern Greek language exhibits a character irreconcilable with Fallmerayer's hypothesis of its origin. Another impartial and intelligent traveller, whose judgment carries with it all the weight that can be derived from an accurate knowledge of Greece, both as it was and as it is (Brønsted, *Reisen in Griechenland*, Vorrede, xvi), observes, 'that the modern Greeks resemble their forefathers, the Hellenes, in their natural endowments, their failings, their form and physiognomy, much more closely than could have been expected.' It should not be forgotten that the primitive Hellenes are represented as bearing a very small proportion in point of numbers to the earlier population: though on the other hand there is reason to believe that the great mass of the Pelasgian tribes was much more nearly akin to them than any portion of the Slavonic race.

glorious event.* The better the free Greeks become acquainted with the people from which they believe themselves sprung, the more unwilling they must be to part with the persuasion of such an illustrious origin. But still it is well that they should remember that their title to the sympathy of civilised Europe and to the rich inheritance of their land and their language, does not rest on their descent but has been earned by struggles and sacrifices of their own equal to any recorded in history: struggles and sacrifices however, in which their Albanian brethen who make no pretensions to such a descent, bore their full share. And it might perhaps be a less burdensome and yet equally animating consciousness of their relation to their great predecessors, if they were content to regard them, not as ancestors, whom they represent and whom they may therefore be expected to resemble and emulate, but simply as departed benefactors, whose memory they are bound to cherish, while they enjoy their bequests, but not so as either to overlook their errors and faults, or to strain after the excellence of a mould, which the power that formed it appears to have broken.

---

*   See Jacobs, *Verm. Schr.*, 120–50.

APPENDIX

On the Trial of Socrates

Appendix viii to volume iv (2nd edition), pp. 526–41

Thirlwall's second edition of volume iv, published in 1847, included an appendix consisting of a critique of Hegel's writings on Socrates, enunciated in his *Lectures on the History of Philosophy*. Hegel argued that both Socrates and the Sophists marked a fundamental turning point in the development of Greek thought. He saw their age as one of enlightenment, when the main current came to be the division of the world into categories determined by analysis and subjective reason as opposed to collective religion. The Sophists nurtured a reflective and critical culture which in turn led to religious scepticism. Hegel interpreted the thought of Socrates as a further progression in this line of thinking: Socrates fostered a new kind of reflective morality (*Moralität*) that was to be distinguished from unreflective custom and religion (*Sittlichkeit*). This explained the execution of Socrates and also the decline of the city-state in the fourth century: the Socratic principle undermined the spirit of the city-state community. Thirlwall sprang to the defence of what Turner called the 'Liberal Anglican' Socrates, an ancient moralist who had embraced reason without spurning every aspect of religious belief (see F. Turner, *The Greek Heritage in Victorian Britain*, Yale University Press, 1981, 274–83). Thirlwall's critique of Hegel betrays his moral standpoint. For him, there existed good and bad uses of reason. His Socrates used the faculties of critical reason for good ends and to establish certain principles of moral conduct, while the Sophists used it for self-seeking ends and for undermining morality. He had stood up for traditional morality, religion and obedience to the law, while the Sophists had undermined morality and existing institutions. This Liberal Anglican interpretation of Socrates and the Sophists was soon forgotten after George Grote's re-evaluation of the Sophists' contribution to Greek philosophy.

Until of late years the prevailing, almost universal opinion among men of letters had been, that if any ethical question could arise on the Trial of Socrates, it was only whether his judges were more justly chargeable with flagrant injustice, or with gross credulity. It was a great step beyond the circle of traditional declamation, when it was shown that we might retain all the reverence which had been so long inspired by the name of Socrates, and yet might acquit his countrymen who condemned him, of atrocious guilt, without thinking very meanly of their understandings. Even according to the accounts transmitted to us by his disciples and admirers, causes were assigned which might prevent the great mass of his contemporaries from forming so correct an estimate of his character, as we can do at this day. But this observation had not long been made public, before it suggested another view of the subject, less favourable to the reputation of Socrates, though still not inconsistent with a high respect for the qualities of his mind and heart. It was contended that, notwithstanding his virtues, abilities, and good intentions, he was probably a dangerous and mischievous person, who, by his injudicious endeavours to uphold religion and morality, really contributed to undermine them; so that the better the Athenians are supposed to have understood the tendency of his habits and pursuits, the more they must have been disposed to concur with his prosecutors.

At this point the inquiry appears to have stopped among ourselves, and this last view of the subject has been adopted as perfectly satisfactory, by no less an authority than Schlosser. But it was not of a nature to gain an extensive or permanent ascendancy in Germany; and it seems to have been there very widely superseded by one, perhaps more attractive in itself, and recommended by a more celebrated name. From the summit of his philosophy Hegel had looked down with serene impartiality on this question, and had resolved to set it at rest by a decision equally honourable to the Athenians and to Socrates. Socrates was rightly accused, and justly condemned; and yet he was not only an innocent and admirably virtuous man, but an eminent benefactor of mankind. This it is that renders his fate truly tragical. It was not merely a mournful occurrence—a good man perishing by the death of a criminal—it was the result of a necessary collision between two antagonist principles, each of which had an equal right to maintain itself against the other. Hegel's discussion on this subject, which is contained in his *Lectures on the History of Ancient Philosophy*, in the posthumous edition of his Works (Vol. xiv p. 42–122), has been much admired even out of his own school: as by Droysen, who speaks of it as if it left little more to be said. Of the ability shown by the author no specimen, of course, is meant to be given in these pages; but it may not be uninteresting to the English reader, to see by what considerations this renowned master of logic and metaphysics has been led to the paradoxical result just stated, and at the same time how far it is confirmed by historical evidence.

As Hegel's main business with Socrates in those Lectures, was to assign the place which properly belonged to him in the history of Greek philosophy, he has first to determine the relation in which he stood to the Sophists; and this is the point on which all his conclusions principally depend. To illustrate and establish this fundamental position is the chief object with which, after an able portraiture of the personal character of the man, he proceeds to exhibit the leading features of his philosophical method; and the concluding observations on the Trial of Socrates are likewise brought into connection with the same starting-point. Our present inquiry, on the other hand, is chiefly concerned with the Trial, and is designed to discover how far his philosophical character was, either in reason or in fact, connected with his condemnation.

Hegel, while he admits that Socrates was constantly at war with the Sophists, maintains that he and they stood on a common ground, and were in fact alike opposed to the ancient principle of simple faith, of instinctive, unreflective, unreasoning obedience and conformity to law, custom and tradition, which had always been regarded as the only firm basis of social order in every Greek state. This was the great contrast which marked this period as a momentous stage in the development of the human mind; in comparison with this, the difference between Socrates and the Sophists was immaterial. They had taught, with Protagoras, that the human mind was the measure of all truth; that is, according to the interpretation which, as a class, they put upon the doctrine, the judgement of each individual, however modified by his intellectual and moral peculiarities, which might perhaps deprive it of all claims to the assent or respect of others, was still for that individual the rightful supreme arbiter of every question, religious, moral, and political, that could be brought under its cognizance.

Now this, as Hegel asserts, was just the principle of Socrates, only with one qualification, which amounted to nothing more than this: Socrates, instead of admitting such a right of private judgement, or, in other words setting up a rule of action which varied with every man's passions and prejudices, and therefore was liable to continual changes even in the same individual, conceived that there was a law of conduct, independent of the agent's personal inclinations, which any man might discover, in a measure sufficient in most cases for his practical guidance, and which all men, in proportion as their intellectual faculties were more diligently exercised, and their judgements were less warped by their particular interests and affections, would be more ready to own it was good for them to obey. Whether any such law exists, or is discoverable by human reason, is not the question. The question is, whether Hegel is right in his estimate of the difference between Socrates and the Sophists, supposing it to be such as has been just described, and in what sense it may be said that he stood on the same ground with them. Hegel observes that the opposition of Socrates and Plato to the Sophists was not that of adherents of the ancient faith to a new school—not in the spirit in which Anaxagoras and Protagoras were condemned, in the interest of Greek religion, manners, and ancient usage. On the contrary, reflection and an appeal in the last resort to the consciousness (purified and enlightened in the one case, blind and turbid in the other), of the individual, was common to them and the Sophists. The principle of Socrates is that man has to find out the truths of practical morality by his own thinking powers. But the language of simple faith and conformity to established usage is that which Sophocles puts into the mouth of Antigone (454): '*The eternal laws of the gods are here, and no one knows whence they came*'.

Now it must be admitted that there was an affinity between Socrates and the Sophists to this extent: that he and they alike addressed themselves to the reasoning faculties of their hearers, and aimed at producing a certain conviction or persuasion in their minds, by an intellectual process; neither he nor they laid claim to the authority of a lawgiver or an oracle, and required implicit faith, or passive submission to their dogmas or precepts. Socrates fought the Sophists with their own weapons, not with those which Anytus wielded against him. But if in this respect it may be allowable to say that they stood on a common ground, totally distinct from that of law and prescription, it is no less evident, that in another sense the relation in which Socrates stood to antiquity, to established order, to law and tradition, was not that of the Sophists, but diametrically opposite to theirs. To instructions which tended to put a wholesome restraint on the selfish appetites and passions of the citizens, and to regulate their conduct with a view to the public good—to such institutions Socrates was an ally, the Sophists were enemies, in fact, if not avowedly. If therefore Socrates, of his own mere motion, without any urgent occasion, had stepped forward to add the strength of reason to the authority of the laws, however he might have been open to censure for undertaking a superfluous task, it would surely be an abuse of language to say that he came into collision with that authority, and, though with a laudable aim, provoked the tragical destiny by which he perished, and that the Athenians, even with a full knowledge of his character and purposes, were justified in condemning him as a representative of the sophistical principle. But the paradox becomes more extravagant, when we consider that Socrates was morally forced into the position which he occupied, and that the common ground on which he stood with the Sophists was no other than a field of battle, where he posted himself on the side of law and justice, to repel their attacks. If the Athenians, with a knowledge of these facts, had condemned Socrates on the ground assigned by Hegel, it would certainly have been no easy matter to vindicate them from the charge either of odious ingratitude or of pitiable folly.

But this is not all. Hegel's notion of the principle of simple faith, and unreflecting obedience, with which he supposes the philosophy of Socrates to have come into collision, appears to me, if not wholly false, at least so vague and exaggerated, as to be quite inapplicable to this or any other question; and if Hegel could have been induced to qualify it so as to make it more consistent with the truth, he would probably have found it useless for his argument. It is true that at Athens—as every where else in the world—in the time of Socrates—as at all times—with the bulk of the people, motives not derived from reflection, and operating instinctively, reverence and fear of the laws, religious awe, usage, and authority, supplied the place of rational moral principles; and experience has shown that when those motives lose their force, the most logical system of morality will, with the great mass of mankind, be a very ineffectual substitute for them. But they are motives endued with a considerable share of vitality and tenacity, and they are in little danger of being impaired by an attempt—whether successful or unsuccessful—to show that they are, as to the practical result, in unconscious accordance with the conclusions of a sound philosophy. It seems certain at least that at Athens the principle of implicit obedience was not of so delicate a texture. If it subsisted until it was assailed by Socrates, it had stood a long series of much harder trails. It was not Socrates, nor the Sophists, who first opened a discussion on questions of right and wrong, with reference not only to the conduct of individuals and of states, but to the merits or demerits of the laws themselves. Such questions had been freely agitated in the hearing of all Athens ever since there had been public assemblies and popular tribunals. The laws were so far from being the objects of passive, unreflecting obedience, that they were continually, from time to time, called to account, and obliged to defend themselves, and when the defence proved unsatisfactory, as had often been the case, were subject to repeal or alteration. Solon, without pretending to follow any other light but that of his own reason, had introduced most important and extensive changes into them, and he had provided legal means of effecting farther reformations, whenever the people should be convinced that they were desirable. Many years before his death, Socrates has presided in an assembly in which an appeal to the law was drowned by a general exclamation: *that it was strange if the people were not allowed to do as they would.* Socrates alone refused to put the illegal question. *He, for his part*—this is Xenophon's statement—*said that he would only act according to the law.* Hegel wishes us to believe that the same people who on this occasion threatened him with death for his resistance to their arbitrary will, afterwards actually condemned him, on the ground that the majesty of the law was in their eyes a thing too sacred to be touched by philosophical argument, even for the purpose of supporting it when it seemed to totter.

I might also observe that Hegel throughout tacitly assumes that the range of subjects to which Socrates directed his inquiries was the same as that which had been previously occupied by the authority of law and usage; so that whenever he mooted an ethical question, he virtually denied the validity or sufficiency of the previous decision. But this assumption, though essential to Hegel's view, is wide of the truth. Neither law nor public opinion did in fact cover the whole of the field over which Socrates pursued his investigation, but left a very large space for the exercise of private judgement on a vast variety of debatable topics, affecting all the relations of public and private life: and these appear to have been precisely the subjects to which the attention of Socrates was most frequently turned.

Thus then, generally considered, Hegel's theory, though unjust toward Socrates, altogether fails to exculpate the Athenians, or to assign a rational motive for their conduct. It supposes them to have laid an extravagant stress on a superficial resemblance, while they wilfully neglected a broad and essential distinction. It represents them as seized with a sudden dread of a principle, which, under various forms, had been for many generations the soul of their institutions, the condition of their greatness; and then as, in their blind jealousy, confounding friends and foes, and striking at the man whose efforts had been exerted in defence of the interests which they imagined to be in danger. Still it may easily be conceived that, though Hegel's general description of the relation in which Socrates stood to the Sophists is liable to these objections, the mode in which he carried on the contest with them, may have been such as not only to lend a plausible colour to misrepresentation, but to be justly chargeable with a tendency similar to that of their teaching. And Hegel enters into many details on the philosophy, and more particularly on the philosophical method and manner of Socrates, with a view to show that this was really the case. Many of his observations on this head are just enough, though they are less original in proportion as they contain less of paradox, and bring the question back to the footing on which it had been placed by others, who had thought it sufficient to point out how Socrates might easily have been misunderstood by his contemporaries. I must not omit to own that, though these Lectures are probably a specimen of

Hegel's most popular and perspicuous style, there are passages, in this portion of them, in which I have not been able to divine his meaning; though, to judge from the context, the obscurity does not appear to arise from the abstruseness of the ideas. A French writer, who has taken great pains to enable his countrymen to appreciate the merits of the Hegelian philosophy (Ott. *Hegel et la Philosophie Allemande*), observes on these Lectures (p. 497), *C'est ici surtout que notre auteur fait usage de ces artifices de langage qui lui sont familiers, et qui ont pour réultat de changer complétement le sens d'une pensée en l'exprimant d'une certain façon.* Whoever has only followed this writer in his exposure of the jugglery with words which is the main arm employed by Hegel in his series of assaults on the human understanding—the title perhaps that might most properly be inscribed on his works—will know that this is saying a great deal. But, happily, enough is intelligible to leave no doubt as to the general train of the reasoning, so far at least as it bears on our present subject.

It cannot be disputed, that the philosophy of Socrates presented two aspects, one positive, the other negative, and that on the negative side it must have seemed to come very close to the doctrine of the sophistical school, as Pascal often argues so much like Bayle, that Victor Cousin suspected him of a universal scepticism, from which he could only find refuge in a voluntary abnegation of his reason. The question as to Socrates is, which of these qualities is predominant, so as to stamp the character of the whole.

Now it cannot be denied that to a superficial observation the tendency of a conversation with Socrates might often appear to be purely negative. This was the impression which would be most naturally produced by the irony of Socrates, as to which Hegel found it necessary to enter into an explanation, which would not have been required for any but German readers, to guard them against confounding the Socratic irony with one of a totally different nature, which has made a great figure in the philosophical and esthetical literature of Germany. That which Socrates employed was, as he observes, no more than a mode of behaviour. It might perhaps be considered as only a peculiar form of Attic urbanity; though it was no doubt the most appropriate that could have been selected for the purpose. Socrates expressly disclaimed the possession of superior knowledge and the functions of a teacher. At the outset he placed himself no higher than on a level with his interlocutor, and professed to be taking part in an inquiry interesting to both, without being able to forsee the issue. At the utmost he was only qualified, by his larger experience, to lend some help by guiding the investigation in a right direction, so as to prevent it from being utterly fruitless. But still he himself was only seeking, and whatever might be discovered had been elicited by their joint researches out of the mind of his fellow-inquirer. Often the irony was carried farther, and Socrates assumed the tone of a learner who came for instruction to the person whom he was about to convict of utter ignorance on the subject of their discourse. But in almost every case the progress of the inquiry in its earlier stage must have exhibited a negative character. It tended to detect some error, to bring to light some difficulty or ambiguity which the other speaker had not at first perceived, to convince him that the view of the matter with which he had hitherto been satisfied was either totally wrong, or at least very imperfect or confused. But further, there can be little doubt that in a great many instances the final result of the whole discussion was negative: that the conversation terminated in a confession of ignorance and perplexity on both sides. *This perplexity*, Hegel observes, *has the effect of leading men to reflexion; and this is the object of Socrates. This merely negative side is the main thing. Perplexity is the beginning and the first product of philosophy. It is necessary that every thing should be subjected to doubt, and all suppositions given up, in order that they may be recovered as the result of the philosophical process (als durch der Begriff Erzeugtes).* Only it must be observed, that we could never know as to a conversation of this kind, however faithfully it might be reported, that it was really the end of the discussion between the parties, and that Socrates did not intend to take up the threat he had dropped on some fresh occasion.

Hegel does not deny that the philosophy of Socrates had a positive side in respect to which he was opposed to the Sophists. Their general proposition, *that man is the measure of all things*, was indeed adopted by Socrates, but with a limitation which guarded it

against abuse, and rendered it capable of serving as the foundation
of a system of moral philosophy. The Sophists, Hegel observes,
ought not to be condemned because they did not themselves so
limit their proposition. Every invention has its own time; and the
honour of this happened to be reserved for Socrates. The nature
of this important limitation Hegel only hints at, very briefly and
rather obscurely; but it deserves to be more distinctly stated. The
sophistical dogma, in its generality, lent itself to the interpretation,
which seems to have been commonly put upon it in the school
from which it proceeded: that no individual has any surer criterion
of truth than his own judgement, however formed; and again, that
no individual can propose to himself any better end than his own
interest, according to any view which he may happen to take of
it. Socrates also might have said *man is the measure of all things*;
but man as a rational being—capable of distinguishing truth from
error, and of giving an intelligent preference to that good which
most properly belongs to his nature over every other end. It is the
difference between a confused, distorted image of things, and one
received through an untroubled medium, and with a rightly adjusted
instrument: between one which did not, and one which did answer
to the reality. Such an instrument Socrates presented in his dialectic
art, which however required a certain state of the moral atmosphere
for the due performance of its functions.

But, though willing to allow Socrates this degree of superiority
over the Sophists, Hegel is led by the progress of his inquiry to a
very unfavourable estimate of the immediate, practical and positive
value of the Socratic philosophy. In the first place the principle
of Socrates, *that man*—in the same sense just explained—*is the
measure of all things*, is still directly opposed to that which had
hitherto prevailed in Greece—the principle of unconscious morality,
of habitual, unreflecting conformity to old rules and ways. Not that
this novelty was a fault in Socrates; it was his merit, and his glory; it
was an important stage in the development of the human mind; and
in Socrates the spirit of his age first became fully conscious of its own
tendency; but, as the representative of a new epoch, he came into
an unavoidable conflict with the spirit of the past, which, without
any fault of the Athenians, proved fatal to him. Relatively to the

previous state of things, his principle was a dangerous innovation, a corruption of the simple faith and practice of antiquity. It established the supremacy of reason and reflection over laws and usages which had hitherto claimed absolute unhesitating submission. Socrates felt that the old authority no longer sufficed: that the time had come when, as Hegel expresses it, every man must provide himself with his own principles of morality; and he endeavoured to awaken in others the consciousness of this want, and to put them in the way of supplying it. And this Hegel supposes to have been the meaning of the Platonic doctrine, that *virtue cannot be learnt*, that is, it cannot be received passively from without, but, so far as it implies knowledge and conviction, must be drawn by every man for himself out of his own intelligence. Whether Socrates taught that doctrine in this sense, may be doubtful. But we are informed by Aristotle that one of his tenets was, that *all the virtues are sciences* (*Eth. Nic.* vi 13). Aristotle objects to this description, that it omits own essential elements in the nature of virtue; namely, the feeling (*pathos*) and the habit (*ethos*). Socrates would have been in the right if he had said that there could be no virtue without knowledge, or intelligent consciousness. Hegel applauds this criticism, and observes that what Socrates overlooked in his definition of virtue, was the very thing which had begun to disappear in society, that is, the moral disposition, the will to realize that which was seen to be true and good. One may however be permitted, without questioning the authority of Aristotle, to doubt whether Socrates was really guilty of so strange an oversight; and whether in his view the knowledge he spoke of did not imply a corresponding bent of the will: whether he did not conceive that such a good could not be clearly perceived without exciting an earnest desire for it, and so impelling to action. Socrates might be completely mistaken in this opinion, which is unhappily at variance with the largest observation of human nature; but it was an error into which he might easily be led by his own experience.

But, if on closer inspection the theory of Socrates might have been vindicated from this censure, it can hardly be denied that his notion of Good, or the moral End, was so indeterminate or undeveloped as to be of little practical use. It appears indeed that he inculcated obedience to the laws both by example and precept, as in the dialogue with Hippias (*Mem.* iv 4); but we do not find that he attempted to deduce the obligation to this obedience from his philosophical theory of Good; and therefore Hegel considers such a defence of the laws as an abandonment of this principle, which would have required that the enactments of law should first have been tried by the test of reason. But perhaps it rather indicates that Hegel's view of the principle he attributes to Socrates is exaggerated and erroneous. There can be no real inconsistency— as Hegel himself seems to admit—between a rational morality and submission to the laws. And we do not know whether Socrates distinctly saw and pointed out the connection between these two things, or simply abstained from interfering with the legitimate province of law. But at least it would seem that if his dialectics were in this respect faulty, his inconsistency, in proportion as it detracted from his merit as a philosopher, should have excepted him from prosecution as a dangerous innovator. Hegel however contends that Socrates exhibited the negative side of his philosophy when, as in the conversation with Euthydemus reported by Xenophon (*Mem.* iv 2) he showed that many general rules of conduct which to an ordinary person at first sight might appear of the most unquestionable certainty, were not absolutely and invariably right, but admitted and required many exceptions or modifications, according to the circumstances in which they are applied. Thus Euthydemus, after he has laid it down that it is a manifest breach of justice to lie, cheat, steal or enthral by force, is brought to acknowledge that there may be occasions in which all these acts are allowable and just: as when they are performed toward a public enemy in time of war, or toward a friend, to save him from harm. Whether the casuistry ascribed to Socrates in this instance was good or bad, is of course immaterial; but to talk of such a very simple remark as a specimen of the Negative in his philosophy, seems to me a piece of wretched trifling, which would have shocked the common sense even of an Athenian court of justice, if it had been suggested as a charge against Socrates; for everybody would have known that the merits of half the causes brought before the tribunals depended on such distinctions. Hegel himself was fully aware—as appears in a subsequent page—that the process of discrimination through which Socrates conducted Euthydemus was one which every Athenian, however deficient in intellectual culture, was continually performing for himself, only unconsciously. The same man, he observed, who knew that he was commanded to do no murder, would not have scrupled to kill his enemy in the field of battle, but would never have thought of treating a private adversary, however odious to him, in like manner. But Hegel imagines that if this man's attention had been drawn, as that of Euthydemus by Socrates, to these variations of the general rule, the effect would have been to unsettle all his notions of right and wrong. I can only repeat that to me this seems a most arbitrary and improbable supposition; but as it can be no more refuted than proved, it must be left to the reader's judgement. And it would be to as little purpose to dispute with Hegel about his opinion that the negative character of the Socratic philosophy is faithfully and justly represented by Aristophanes in the *Clouds*. Even the measurement of the flea's leap, though not historically true, was, as Hegel thinks, a fair illustration of that one side of that philosophy; for it was meant to ridicule the searching minuteness of the philosopher's investigations, and proves how correctly the poet had seized their character. And after a short sketch of the plot of the play, he proceeds to observe that Aristophanes cannot be said to have done injustice to Socrates, though he may have pressed the method which he attacks into its extreme consequences with an excess of bitterness. 'But Aristophanes is not unjust; indeed one cannot but admire the penetration with which he discerned the negative side of the dialectic method of Socrates, and exhibited it (in his own way) with so sure a pencil. For in the method of Socrates the decision is always referred to the *subject*, the conscience of the individual; but where that is bad, the history of Strepsiades must be repeated.' The simple answer to this naked assertion is, that if this had been the case there could have been no such difference as that which Hegel had indicated between the sense in which the proposition, *man is the measure of all things*, was understood by Socrates, and that in which it was understood by the Sophists. Everybody before Hegel had seen that to them—according to that view which Hegel himself takes of them—the satire of the *Clouds* was fairly applicable;

and all that Hegel has done to earn the credit of originality in this respect is first to contrast them with Socrates, and then to slip Socrates into their place. Considering the solemnity of the process, and the irrelevancy and injustice of the pretended result, one might be tempted to say that this stroke of Hegelian legerdemian was not inaptly foreshadowed in the feat, by which Socrates in the play, having sprinkled the table with fine dust, and bent a spit into a pair of compasses—filched a cloak from the palaestra.

The amount of good or harm which Socrates did in his generation can manifestly be no more than matter of very uncertain conjecture to us; and the question is complicated by the difficulty of distinguishing between the effect of his teaching and that of his character. My belief is that both the good and the harm have been greatly exaggerated. It has been thought that such a method as his must have tended to unsettle the practical convictions, more especially of uneducated persons; and it may be asked whether he was not at least guilty of a culpable imprudence when he awakened doubts in their minds on matters such as those which were the subjects of his ordinary discourse. So Schlosser observes: *it seems to be not without reason that Critias in Xenophon (Mem. i 2.37) tells Socrates, that the cobblers and tailors would do better to keep their work than engage in a talk about morality, which could never lead them to any fixed ultimate principle, and must confuse their natural feelings.* And then, after having quoted the passage more literally in a note, he adds a remark: that he must not be understood to deny that there was much in what Socrates says in the contest that is excellent and useful; only he thinks that it could never *in that form* keep men's passions under, an end for which mere morality, particularly in a southern climate, is too feeble an instrument. The reader who consults the original passage of Xenophon will be very much at a loss to understand what the sayings of Socrates are on which Schlosser bestows his praise; but he will see that Schlosser has totally mistaken the meaning of the words of Critias which he quotes. It is quite plain, as Ruhnken had observed, that Critias is not speaking of the conversations held by Socrates with various classes of artisans, but of the illustrations which he was fond of borrowing from their callings in his reasoning with others. But the justice of the remark might be questioned, even if the passage had been correctly interpreted. For it may be doubted whether it is justified by the difference which really existed at Athens between the higher and lower classes of citizens, in education and intellectual culture. The great schools of moral and political instruction, the assemblies, the courts of justice, the theatres were open to all, and frequented by all alike. The dialectical subtleties of Socrates were probably disagreeable to those who were either unable to follow them, or took no interest in the subject; and such persons were no doubt to be found in every class. But there is no reason to think that any Athenian was more disqualified for such inquiries, or more liable to receive injury from them, than others, on account of his station. On the other hand, the society of Socrates could rarely produce a beneficial effect on the character of any but those who sought it from a love of truth and of goodness; not on a Critias or an Alcibiades; and the number of those who were attracted to him by better motives may have been small. But whatever influence he exerted was probably in every case more or less, morally as well as intellectually, wholesome. But we must return to Hegel.

One of the most singular parts of his disquisition is the view he gives of what he calls the *Genius* of Socrates. He attaches the highest importance to this mysterious phenomenon, as characteristic of the relation in which Socrates stood to his age. It was not, according to his view, an effect of an accidental, constitutional peculiarity of the individual Socrates, but was intimately connected with his philosophical principles, by which the decision of all practical questions was submitted to private judgement. 'The *Genius* was the peculiar form in which this private judgement appeared in Socrates himself. It was that which, in his own case, supplied the defect of a positive, real element in his system, but which at the same time most strikingly indicated the contrast between the spirit of this system, and that which until then had prevailed in Grecian society.' 'The Greek,' Hegel repeats, 'had never been used to determine his actions by a process of reflection; *still less was there then in existence the thing we call conscience*. Its place was supplied—as we have already heard—by habitual conformity to law and usage. For the path of duty was so accurately marked, as seldom to leave room for hesitation. And even in the cases which were not expressly determined by the legitimate authority, neither individuals, nor even the state itself, had ever presumed to decide for themselves on rational grounds. *The general or even the people*—these are Hegel's words literally rendered—*did not take upon themselves to decide what was best for the state; and so neither did the individual in his private concerns.* They sought the guidance of the gods by consulting an oracle, or by some mode of divination. And with Socrates, as we are distinctly informed by Xenophon, his genius supplied the place of an oracle.'

It can hardly be necessary to point out to the reader, that these statements about the Greek divination are mere empty paradoxes. A Greek general or statesman did not the less actively exert his faculties in military or political affairs, he did not the less confidently make up his mind on the measures to be adopted, because, when the event was uncertain, he wished to learn whether the gods were favourable to his plan. It was not as a substitute for forethought and deliberation, that oracles or sacrifices were ordinarily resorted to; though a supposed discovery of the will of the gods might suspend or even prevent the execution of a design. When the aspect of the entrails was adverse, it was not conferred that the plan of the campaign was ill concerted; only a fresh element, which no human sagacity could have detected, was introduced into the calculation. Hegel's remark is perfectly useless for this purpose, unless it applies to the Greek divination in general; whereas it is only true with regard to that very small number of cases, in which oracles or soothsayers were consulted for *advice.* And after all, the occasions, either public or private, on which the aid of divination was called in at all, were infinitely rare, in comparison with those on which men followed the suggestions of their own judgement. We do not find for instance that in the debate on the massacre of the Mytilenaeans, or the Melians, it was proposed to suspend the execution until the pleasure of the gods had been ascertained. The assembly, in such cases, decided for itself on the arguments which it heard, according to the prevailing notion of right and wrong. Nor does it appear that private persons scrupled to exercise their own discretion, and to let themselves be governed by the view they took of their own interest in their pecuniary contracts, their matrimonial alliances, and other transactions most deeply affecting their welfare. Sacrifices for the purpose of divination—which were unknown to the Homeric age, and perhaps did not come into use before the sixth century BC (see Boettiger, *Ideen z. Kunstmythologie* i p. 76)—were always confined by usage to a few extraordinary occasions. Hegel makes the exception the rule, and builds his theory on its supposed universality.

But what was the thing which Hegel—more conveniently for his own hypothesis than consistently with the proper meaning of the Greek word, which signifies nothing more than *the supernatural sign*—chooses to call the *Genius* of Socrates? Its general import he states to be this: *that man has now begun to decide according to his own discernment (er enthaelt das, dass jetzt der Mensch nach seiner Einsicht aus sich entscheidet)*. Considering the importance of the position which is thus assigned to it, one might suppose that it regulated all the actions of Socrates. But we know, and Hegel admits, that its operation was limited to a much narrower compass. Before he explains what it was, he thinks it necessary to warn his hearers against two erroneous views of its nature. It must not, he says, be conceived as a kind of guardian spirit or angel, nor again as the conscience. Nobody probably would have been in much danger of forming the first of these notions about it, unless it had been suggested by the ill-chosen word with which Hegel has described it; but whether it would be equally improper to consider it was connected with the conscience, remains to be seen when we have heard Hegel's own explanation, which, as far as I can understand, is this. Socrates was led by a psychological process, which however is not clearly traced, to contemplate the decisions of his own mind, on practical questions, as objects distinct from himself. 'The Genius is not Socrates himself; not his opinion, or conviction, but something unconscious: Socrates is impelled. At the same time the oracle is not anything external: it is *his* oracle. It has the form of knowledge combined with the absence of consciousness.' Lest this should seem hard to understand, it is illustrated by the example of persons under the influence of mesmerism. But this is not a mere illustration; for a few pages after Hegel distinctly expresses his opinion, that the state in which Socrates received the intimations of his Genius, was one approaching to somnambulism, or as he farther explains it, duplicity of consciousness (*Gedoppelheit des Bewusstseins*), a view which he thinks is confirmed by the description of his long musings in the camp before Potidaea, which appear to have been something like a magnetic trance. This state in Socrates is not to be considered as a morbid one; far from it; it was the form which the Socratic principle of reflection and self-decision, at its first appearance, could not fail to assume. This, he concludes, is the central point of the great revolution effected by the principle of Socrates, that the witness of the individual mind has taken the place of the oracle, and that the *subject* has undertaken to decide for himself.

Whether these analogies throw any light on the origin and nature of the phenomenon in question may be left to the reader's judgement; at all events it would not be a more fanciful and arbitrary conjecture, if any one should think it possible, that Socrates might be led to strong convictions by processes of association which passed so rapidly as to escape his observation and recollection, and to leave the final result as a simple impression on his mind. But the futility of Hegel's attempt to connect this inward sign with the principle of the Socratic philosophy will perhaps be sufficiently proved by two considerations. In the first place, the sign was perfectly consistent with all the branches of the ordinary divination; and as we find that Socrates sometimes was guided by it in the advice he gave to his friends, though he encouraged them to inquire by the ordinary methods after the will of the gods, so we have no reason to doubt that he complied with established usage, wherever it prescribed the use of divinatory experiments, or attention to certain outward signs. The other objection, which seems still more decisive, and which could hardly have escaped Hegel's attention, if it had not been absorbed by his theory, is: that the cases in which Socrates is related to have been thus inwardly warned, were not cases in which it was usual, even for a pious Greek, either to consult an oracle, or to seek divine direction in any other way.

Thirlwall then goes on to criticise Hegel's approach to the trial of Socrates, dismissing as fanciful his notion that Socrates' Genius was contrary to the system of oracles and divination (542). He also challenged Hegel's idea that Socrates had corrupted youth by interfering with those parental relationships which were so sacred to the Greeks

(545). **Thirlwall goes on to attack other German followers of Hegel, in particular Forchhammer's *Die Athener und Sokrates, Die Gesetzlichen und der Revolutionär* (*The Athenians and Socrates, the Men of the Laws and the Man of the Revolution*), which argued that there existed a discrepancy between the religious sentiments of Socrates and state religion. Thirlwall's reply (pp. 552–3) is as follows:**

It should be remembered that the laws of every Greek state necessarily, from the nature of the case, allowed a very great latitude of religious opinion; because there was no authentic standard of religious truth. There was no canon, no book, by which a doctrine could be tried; no living authority to which appeal could be made for the decision of religious controversies. Beyond the bare fact of the existence of the beings who were objects of public worship, there was hardly a circumstance in their history which had not been related in many different ways; and there was no form of the legend which had more or less claim to be received than another. So that if Socrates rejected every version of the fable which appeared to him to have an immoral tendency, he was only exercising a right which could not be legally disputed, and was taking no greater liberty than had been used by many others without and scandal, as for instance by Pindar with the story of Pelops (*Ol.* i 59).

Finally, the attack on Hegel is revealed as not only a matter of interpretation but as one of territory: Thirlwall appears to have been disturbed by the encroachment of a philosopher into what he sees as the exclusive territory of the scholar of the ancient world (p. 557):

Here is a German scholar, of some note in the literary world; of unquestionable learning and showy talents; one of a class which has exercised and is likely more and more to exert a powerful influence on the political destinies of his country, living in a period of great political excitement and in the midst of a general expectation of organic changes in the national institutions; and he betrays such gross ignorance of the first principles of law, justice, and rational freedom, as proves that he is not only incompetent to have a voice on any great political question, but that he would be utterly unqualified to serve on a common jury.

Editor's Notes

Notes to Chapter 1. Introduction

1. On the British travellers, with reference to Thirlwall, see E. Glasgow, 'Some British Travellers in Greece', 62–92, in J. Hogg (ed.), *Salzburg Studies in English Literature*, 1975; see also the comprehensive bibliography in G. Tolias, *British Travellers in Greece*, 1750–1820: exhibition catalogue with introduction by C. Koumarianou, London, 1995.
2. Thirlwall, 'On Kruse's Hellas', 305ff. in *Philological Museum* i.
3. Boeckh had a category of *Inscriptiones Fourmonti Spuriae*, *Corpus Inscriptionum Graecarum* vol. i, pp. 61–104 with A. Spawforth, 'Fourmontiana. *IG* V(1) 515: Another Forgery "From Amyklai"', *ABSA* 20, 1976 pp. 139–46. See further O. Augustinos, *French Odysseys: Greece in French Travel Literature from the Renaissance to the Roman Era*, Baltimore/London, 1994, pp. 87–91.
4. D. Constantine, *Early Greek Travellers*, 1984, p. 9.

Notes to Chapter 2. The Inhabitants of Early Greece

1. See C. Sourvinou-Inwood, 'Herodotus (and others) on Pelasgians: Some Perceptions of Ethnicity', 103–44 in P. S. Derow and R. C. T. Parker (edd.), *Herodotus and his World*, Oxford, 2003.
2. M. Bernal, *Black Athena: the Afroasiatic roots of Classical Civilization*, London, 1987, 2 vols; for a restatement of Bernal's views, see D. C. Moore (ed.), *Black Athena Writes Back: Martin Bernal responds to is critics*, London, 2001.
3. Bernal, n. 5 above, 326.
4. For a critique of Bernal's historiographical acumen, see J. H. Blok, 'Proof and Persuasion in Black Athena I: the case of K. O. Müller', 173–208 in J. P. Stronk and M. D. Weerd (edd.), Black Athena: Ten Years After, *Talanta* 28–29, 1996–7; more generally, see M. Lefkowitz (ed.), *Black Athena Revisited*, Chapel Hill and London, 1996.

Notes to Chapter 3. History and Mythology

1. For a modern political reading of epic, see ch. 1 in E. Robinson (ed.), *Ancient Greek Democracy: Readings and Sources*, Oxford, 1998.
2. See Mark Salber Philips, 'Reconsiderations on History and Antiquarianism: Arnaldo Momigliano and the Historiography of Eighteenth-Century Britain, *The Journal of the History of Ideas* 57, 1996, 196–316.

Notes to Chapter 5. Periclean Athens

1. K. Demetriou, 'Bishop Connop Thirlwall: Historian of Ancient Greece', *Quaderni di Storia* 56, 2002, pp. 67–74 and *George Grote on Plato and Athenian Democracy*, Koinon 2, Frankfurt-am-Main, 1999, pp. 51–7.
2. C. Thirlwall, *Remains literary and theological*, J. Perowne (ed.), London, 1877, vol. ii, p. 216.

Notes to Chapter 6. The Decline of Athens

1. For deconstruction of the idea of crisis in fourth-century Greece, see Davies, J. K., 'The fourth century crisis: what crisis?', 29–39 in W. Eder (ed.) *Die athenische Demokratie im 4. Jahrhundert v. Chr.*, Stuttgart, 1995.
2. G. F. Schoemann, *De Comitiis Atheniensium Libri Tres*, Greifswald, 1819.
3. Macaulay, 'On the Athenian Orators', first published in August 1824, *Knight's Quarterly Magazine*; reprinted in Lady Trevelyan (ed.), *The Works of Lord Macaulay*, London, 1866, vol. vii, pp. 660–72.
4. J. Gillies, *The orations of Lysias and Isocrates translated from the Greek with some account of their lives; and a discourse on the History, Manners, and Character of the Greeks, from the Conclusion of the Peloponnesian War to the Battle of Chaironea*, London, 1778, p. 3.

Notes to Chapter 7. Greece and Philip II

1. Gooch, G. P., *History and Historians in the Nineteenth Century*, London, 1913, 311.
2. For instance see Gillies, J., *A View of the Reign of Frederick II of Prussia; with a parallel between that Prince and Philip II of Macedon*, Dublin, 1789; generally, see Thomas, S. A., *Makedonien und Preußen: Die Geschichte einer Analogie*, Frankfurt, 1994; Knipfing, J., 'German historians and Macedon', *American Historical Review* 26, 1920–21, 657–71.
3. A. M. Adam, 'Philip Alias Hitler', *Greece and Rome* 10, 1941, 105–113; cf. S. Pomeroy, S. Burstein, W. Donlan, J. T. Roberts, *Ancient Greece: a political, social and cultural history*, Oxford University Press, 1999, 393.
4. The comparison of mercenaries in the fourth century with the fifteenth-century Condottieri was used in Macaulay's essay 'On the Athenian Orators', first published in August 1824, *Knight's Quarterly Magazine*; reprinted in Lady Trevelyan (ed.), *The Works of Lord Macaulay*, London, 1866, vol. vii, pp. 660–72.
5. Inserted in the second edition, vol. v, p. 278: 'The military profession became the habitual refuge and resource of all vagrants and outcasts of society: of men who had been forced by indigence or crime to quit their homes, or had deserted from the armies of their country (Isoc. *Peace* 168)'.

Notes to Chapter 8. Alexander the Great

1. On the image of Alexander in nineteenth-century historiography, see K. N. Demetriou, 'Historians on Macedonian Imperialism and Alexander

the Great', *Journal of Modern Greek Studies* 19, 2001, pp. 23–60.

2. J. G. Droysen, *Geschichte Alexanders des Grossen*, Hamburg, 1833.

Note to Chapter 9. Hellenistic Greece

1. J. G. Droysen, *Geschichte des Hellenismus*, 2 vols, Hamburg, 1836–43.

Notes to Chapter 10. Greece under the Romans and beyond

1. The copy of the first edition of Thirlwall's *History* in the library of the British School at Athens has been annotated probably by Finlay; it gives some indication of Finlay's objections to Thirlwall's explanation the decline of Greece under Roman rule.

2. J. P. Fallmerayer, *Geschichte der Halbinsel Morea während des Mittelalters*, Stuttgart, 1830–36.

Index